Mentoring in Religious Education

Mentoring in Religious Education

Leona M. English

Religious Education Press
Birmingham, Alabama

The paper in this book meets the guidelines for permanence and durability of the Committee on Production Guidelines of the Council for Library Resources.

Library of Congress Cataloguing-in-Publication Data

English, Leona M., 1963–
    Mentoring in religious education / Leona M. English.
      p. cm.
    Includes bibliographical references and indexes.
    ISBN 0-89135-107-8 (pbk. : alk. paper)
    1. Mentoring in Christian education. I. Title.
    BV1533.5.E54 1998
    268′.3—dc21
                                            98-20191
                                           CIP

Religious Education Press
5316 Meadow Brook Road
Birmingham, Alabama 35242-3315
10 9 8 7 6 5 4 3 2

Religious Education Press publishes books exclusively in religious education and in areas closely related to religious education. It is committed to enhancing and professionalizing religious education through the publication of serious, significant, and scholarly works.

PUBLISHER TO THE PROFESSION

DEDICATION

To the memory of my father, Ambrose Leo English
(1918–1989)

CONTENTS

FIGURES

PREFACE

Thou wert my guide, philosopher, and friend.

—Alexander Pope[1]

The possibility of providing guides, philosophers, and friends for religious educators intrigued me long before I became familiar with the
word "mentor." I knew intuitively that many fine religious educators
required more opportunities for professional support and continuous
learning than they typically received from either church or educational administrators. My own professional experiences in religious
education challenged me to think often about the all-too-many individuals who have served our profession well but have been inade-
quately supported in their work. Though the examples I use in this
book are fictitious, many religious educators will identify with them,
especially with those related to isolation in our field.

In this book I propose that religious education leaders think seriously about how they can facilitate the initiation of new professionals
in the field. Specifically, I suggest the implementation of a formalized
mentoring process which will assist religious educators in continuing
the educational preparation process which they began in their university or seminary degree programs. Wholehearted commitment to professionalizing religious education is urgently needed, and I believe
that the mentoring process can be a key activity in providing this assistance. Educational research supports mentorship as a cost-effective
means of providing vital learning for new professionals. Mentorship
honors the commitment and skills of the mentee as well as the practice

---

1. Alexander Pope, "Essay on Man IV," in *Alexander Pope: Selected Poetry and
Prose*, ed. and intro. William K. Wimsatt (New York: Holt, Rinehart & Winston,
1962), p. 167, line 390.

of religious education. It also contributes to the renewal of the more experienced religious educators who serve as mentors. In short, mentorship is a strategic and time-tested means of furthering the religious education profession.

My firm commitment is to the ongoing professional education of all religious educators. Although I concern myself here mainly with informal learning at the initiation stage of the profession, I believe the mentoring process can readily be adapted and implemented for mid- and late-career religious educators. I have scoured the literature on mentorship, and I present a summary of research findings in this book so that all religious education administrators will have a useful resource from which to develop their own mentorship programs.

The first step in initiating a successful mentoring program is believing that religious education mentorship can be effectively designed and implemented in a local church environment. Concomitant with this belief are commitment and dedication to ensuring that dreams about mentorship become reality in a religious education setting. In this book I proceed on the assumption that not only can religious education mentorship be implemented but that it is a necessary means of providing ongoing education for professionals.[2] Though the mentoring process likely will contain some glitches, wholehearted engagement in it can be beneficial not only for the mentor but also for the mentee and for the overall church environment. I concur completely with Timothy Arthur Lines, who maintains that if religious educators desire to grow professionally they can expect "to experience the excitement, the confusion, the upset, and the enthusiasm that is inherent in the process."[3] In this book I offer my own vision for the type of interrelationships that are necessary for the improvement and growth of the religious education profession and its constituent members.

---

2. Adult educator Ronald M. Cervero is an adherent of the role of the "critical viewpoint" in the continuing education of professionals. According to Cervero, the critical viewpoint encourages the use of ongoing dialogue and critical thinking in continuing education, so the professions continue to reshape and grow. Cervero's desired goal is not consensus but rather a process of continuous renegotiation and reframing of what constitutes professional practice. See "Continuing Education for the Professions," in *Handbook of Adult and Continuing Education*, ed. Sharan B. Merrian and Phyllis M. Cunningham (San Francisco: Jossey-Bass, 1989), pp. 518–19.

3. Timothy Arthur Lines, *Systemic Religious Education* (Birmingham, Ala.: Religious Education Press, 1987), p. 242.

To facilitate the actual realization of this vision in the local church I will now outline briefly the salient points developed in this volume, for the effective and efficient design, implementation, and evaluation of religious education mentorship. Chapters 1–4 establish the basis for mentorship of religious educators. These chapters show that mentorship is an integral part of the Christian tradition and that religious educators today are in need of such an induction support system. Chapters 5–10 provide concrete examples and information on how effective mentorship can be implemented in a church situation. These chapters challenge the religious educator to adapt the process I recommend to fit the local faith community's need for religious education induction.

Chapter 1, "Introduction to Mentorship," highlights the fact that mentorship can be a rewarding undertaking for a local church community. This chapter defines mentorship and identifies the primary mentor functions of teaching, counseling, befriending, sponsoring, and encouraging. Although informal mentorship serendipitously occurs in human cultures and religious traditions, the everyday professional experience of religious educators typically confirms that some of us never experience it. To ensure systematic induction for a greater number of religious educators, this chapter recommends that formalized mentoring programs be introduced in local church situations. Education research findings are offered which affirm that mentorship can be beneficial for all those who participate in it, either directly or indirectly. Finally, this chapter contends that mentorship is one of the most effective means available of revitalizing religious education and for ensuring the continuous growth of the profession.

Chapter 2, "Mentors from the Religious Tradition," demonstrates that the practice of providing a professional mentor for new religious educators is deeply grounded in religious history. Christianity, the religion with which I am most familiar, has long benefited from the consistent provision of intensive formation for neophytes through both a novitiate process and spiritual direction. This chapter examines three examples of religiously based mentorship: the desert dwellers' mentoring of each other into a monastic way of life; the Helfta mystics' intercommunity mentoring system which supported their writing and prayer life; and Teresa of Avila's mentoring of John of the Cross in his reform of the male Carmelite Order. A relatively thick, rich description of the historical cases offers considerable insight into mentorship for present-day mentoring program planners.

Chapter 3, "Educational Research Findings on Mentorship," reviews the educational literature on mentorship which highlights the fact that academic and professional interest in mentorship is very strong, especially in general education. This chapter shows that the use of mentorship to facilitate entry for new religious educators and to contribute to their personal and professional growth has a firm theoretical research base in the professional educational literature. It also points out that female mentees especially can benefit from the mentoring experience.

Chapter 4, "Basic Guidelines for Mentorship," presents a series of five guiding principles to undergird the development of a professional religious education mentorship program. These guiding principles include the following: (1) effective mentorship requires collaboration among a cross-section of the faith community; (2) positive mentor-mentee experiences are cultivated in a mentoring environment; (3) mentorship is part of a the full professionalization of religious education; (4) religious education mentorship includes a spiritual dimension; and (5) an effective mentorship program has a process orientation. This chapter emphasizes that continuous evaluation of a church's attention to these basic guidelines will assist in effective implementation of religious education mentorship.

Chapter 5, "Establishing the Basis for Mentorship," discusses the need for an extensive preprogram plan for effective mentorship. This chapter recommends a designated period of preparation, information gathering, needs assessment, goal setting, and team building before the actual mentoring program components are put in place. This chapter suggests that as part of this preprogram process, local church groups examine their commitment to mentorship, especially as articulated in existing mission statements and ministerial activity. Chapter 5 also points out that this pre-program period is the appropriate time for addressing false myths that surround mentorship. The need to pay close attention to a local church community's readiness for mentorship, as well as its openness to mentorship, is also underscored.

Chapter 6, "Recruiting, Selecting, and Matching Mentors and Mentees," outlines a series of decisions and steps involved in recruiting, selecting, and matching mentors and mentees. This chapter notes that the persons who are chosen to mentor must not only be proficient in their instructional skills but must also have adequate time to dedicate to the designated mentee. Potential mentors ought to be engaged in a vigorous self-assessment and interview process before they assume the role of mentor in the professional life of the religious education mentee. Furthermore, mentors and mentees ought to be involved in the complex selection and matching process.

Chapter 7, "Preparing Mentors and Mentees," is based on the principle that before professional religious educators assume the duties and responsibilities of mentor or mentee they need to be adequately prepared for the task. Once in the roles of mentors or mentees, they need to be provided with continuing professional educational opportunities to further prepare them for their challenging tasks. Consistent with established adult education practice, this chapter strongly recommends needs assessment of the program participants and the ongoing adjustment of content and structure of the preparation program in order to meet adequately individual and institutional needs. The entire preparation plan ought to be designed to reflect a culture of continuous learning within the religious education profession.

Chapter 8, "Compensating the Mentors," outlines a series of compensation alternatives that mentor program planners can choose. Most treatments of the topic maintain that mentors ought to be compensated for their commitment of time, resources, and professional expertise. Of the variety of compensation alternatives that currently exist, this chapter deals with eight: released time, public announcements, opportunities to share mentoring experience, recognition of knowledge and skills, provision of social activities with other religious education mentors, professional recognition, ritualized celebration of mentoring contributions, and professional development opportunities. Choosing an appropriate compensation alternative involves a careful consideration of local norms, church values, and participant requirements. Providing appropriate compensation, which honors the contributions of the religious education mentors, is a challenging but necessary part of any effective mentorship process.

Chapter 9, "Maintaining the Mentoring Relationship," contends that many supports, such as a mentoring covenant, must be put in place for the desired mentoring relationship to grow and develop successfully. In particular, it is important to note that religious education mentors and mentees pass through various phases in their relationship, and they may require assistance in negotiating difficulties such as interpersonal conflict. Religious education administrators ought to provide strong leadership, set the overall positive tone or educational climate, and be available to assist in addressing major structural problems. Furthermore, the entire church community needs to be involved in actively supporting the mentoring relationship.

Chapter 10, "Evaluating the Mentoring Program," provides an intensive evaluation process for religious education mentorship. The evaluation of a mentorship program includes assessment of the actual program components such as training and organization, as well as ongoing formative and summative assessment of the professional progress of the selected mentor and mentee. A comprehensive evaluation plan can provide useful data for revising existing religious education mentoring programs and initiating new ones. A deliberate effort to conduct systematic evaluation will assist in the ongoing improvement of religious education mentoring programs.

All the issues in religious education mentorship are not clear-cut.[4] The educational research evidence indicates that there are no definitive ways to develop an effective mentoring plan, to successfully recruit and select mentors, to provide adequate professional preparation, or to systematically evaluate the actual program. Ultimately, the ideas I offer in this book need to be examined closely by particular congregations or church-related groups and adjusted to local requirements. I challenge every religious education agency to begin the mentorship process.

This present book on religious education mentoring began a number of years ago, while I was a doctoral student at Teachers College, Columbia University. Douglas Sloan, William Bean Kennedy, Karen Zumwalt, and Victoria Marsick, advisers and mentors, supervised my fledgling research on mentorship and assisted me in completing the dissertation process. To all of these distinguished academics I am indebted. The people with whom I now work in the Department of Adult Education at St. Francis Xavier University, Marie Gillen, Allan Quigley, and Angela Stewart, have created a mentoring environment for writing this book. I am appreciative of their untiring support and ongoing encouragement when even I was uncertain of completion.

---

4. Michael Galbraith and Norman Cohen offer one of the most comprehensive discussions of the issues and challenges that remain for mentorship in their "Issues and Challenges Confronting Mentoring," *Mentoring: New Strategies and Challenges*, New Directions for Adult and Continuing Education, no. 66 (San Francisco: Jossey-Bass, 1995), pp. 89–93.

Dorothy Lander, Robert MacMillan, and John Reigle provided invaluable editorial support and critical commentary for various chapters of the book. Emilie MacIsaac gave generously of her time to edit the entire volume. For the depth of the collective insight of these individuals I am forever thankful. I would be remiss if I did not acknowledge the professional mentoring climate created by my Canadian colleagues in religious education. I thank especially Lorna Bowman of the University of St. Michael's College, Toronto; Nöel Shuell of Memorial University, Newfoundland, and Carmel Doyle of Beaconsfield High School, Newfoundland. Without the invitation of James Michael Lee this book would never have been written. I thank him and the vice president of Religious Education Press, Nancy Vickers, for their constant challenge to write a book that would serve well the religious education profession. Nothing but my best would do for either of them.

Introduction to Mentorship

Pray that the journey be long . . . . To many Egyptian cities go, to learn, and to learn from the learned.

—Constantine Kavafy[1]

Constantine Kavafy's words contain the essence of the mentoring relationship: to learn and to learn from the learned. Writing in the early part of the twentieth century, Kavafy clearly understood the basic premise that being mentored is an integral part of a full and productive life. This understanding has been a foundational one in the Christian religion, though its practice has not been fully mined and utilized for religious educators.[2] In this book, I will present insights on mentorship from Christian history and from educational literature, which I will use as a basis for the organization and the facilitation of a

---

1. Constantine Kavafy, "Ithaca," in *With Ithaca on My Mind: An Anthropologist's Journey*, by Lambros Comitas (New York: Teachers College, Columbia University, 1989), p. 6.

2. I have chosen the term "religious educator" deliberately, realizing that terms such as "catechist," "Christian religious educator," "Christian educator," and "religious instructor" could also be used. See Timothy Arthur Lines's discussion of the importance of terminology in *Functional Images of the Religious Educator* (Birmingham Ala.: Religious Education Press, 1992), pp. 10–14. Interestingly, Lines also chooses "religious educator." See also Thomas Groome's discussion of terms (he chooses "Christian religious educator" as his preferred term) in *Christian Religious Education: Sharing Our Story and Vision* (San Francisco: HarperSanFrancisco, 1980), pp. 23–26.

mentoring process that is useful for religious educators working in settings as varied as schools, hospitals, churches, and private homes.[3]

Although mentorship is a definite need for religious educators, some receive mentorship only serendipitously. Those who do experience mentorship have a greater level of support and, consequently, a greater opportunity for success in their chosen profession. The haphazard incidence of mentorship is troubling, given the complex task of religious educators: to educate others in the faith and its traditions. These same traditions, ironically enough, are rife with instances of mentors who counseled, supported, and guided others in fulfilling their vocation.

In this chapter I will provide an overview of mentorship: its foundation in the religious tradition, working definitions of mentor and mentee, functions of the mentor, and recorded benefits of mentoring relationships. In subsequent chapters I will develop these points further and present a full description of a mentoring process that can be put in place for religious educators.

TRADITION OF MENTORS IN CHRISTIANITY

Writer Yves Raguin has noted that spiritual guidance is a universal religious phenomenon.[4] Within the Christian religion mentorship

---

3. My understanding of mentorship of religious educators is grounded in the social sciences. From years of experience as a religious educator and as an internal consultant for religious education, I have become convinced that educational theory and practice provide the insight necessary to understand areas of religious education such as teaching and learning, counseling and administration, all of which influence the religious education mentoring process. My approach to religious education is consistent with that of James Michael Lee, who has delineated his macrotheory of the social science approach to religious education in a massive trilogy. See *The Shape of Religious Instruction* (Birmingham, Ala.: Religious Education Press, 1971), especially chapter 7, "Religious Instruction as Social Science." *Shape* argues that religious instruction is a social science field in its own right, not an offshoot of theology. The second book, *The Flow of Religious Instruction* (Birmingham, Ala.: Religious Education Press, 1973), deals with the pedagogical practice of religious education. The third, *The Content of Religious Instruction* (Birmingham, Ala.: Religious Education Press, 1985), focuses on the substantive content of religion teaching.

4. Yves Raguin, "The Spiritual Father: Toward Integrating Western and Eastern Spirituality," in *Abba: Guides to Wholeness and Holiness East and West*, ed. John R. Sommerfeldt, Cistercian Studies Series, no. 38 (Kalamazoo, Mich.: Cistercian Publications, 1982). See especially page 290.

surfaces in myriad places and configurations. One of the most prominent structures is mentorship in the form of spiritual direction, the systematic pairing of elders with novices for the purpose of inducting them into religious life. This early mode of mentorship provided guidance in self-understanding and daily living for the new members. Spiritual direction was the primary model at work in the Egyptian desert in the fourth century and the one that has continued to be operative among clergy and members of religious orders for centuries. Other strong examples of mentorship in the religious tradition include the wise counselor role of the women mystics at Helfta in Saxony, Germany, in the thirteenth century. Yet another model is the vigorous, prodding role of Teresa of Avila (1515–1582) in her role as a vocational mentor to John of the Cross (1542–1591) and Jerónimo Gratián (1545–1614) in Castile, Spain, in the sixteenth century. These examples are a testament to the strong tradition of support and guidance that was an acknowledged right of those involved in active church ministry. In chapter 2 of this book I will highlight all three models and discuss their relevance for religious education mentorship today.

The role of a more experienced person in guiding an apprentice is not an exclusively Christian concept. The basic premise that one should have a mentor remains constant, though the ways in which people are mentored changes with circumstances. The Hindu religion, for example, is replete with examples of gurus who serve as mentors for individuals seeking direction.[5] Likewise, the Hasidic master holds a place of privilege within the Jewish tradition.[6] Classical literature, too, has recorded many examples of effective

---

5. The guru is an integral part of the Hindu religion. Francis Acharya defines the Hindu guru as "the guide and mentor of the inward path, the bringer of light" ("The Guru: The Spiritual Father in the Hindu Tradition," in *Abba,* p. 273). See also Rosemary Jeans Antze, "Teacher, Student, Lineage," *Parabola* 17 (August 1992): 73–77; Martin Forward, "Gods, Guides, and Gurus: A South Asian Pilgrimage," pt.1, *Aeropagus* 6, no. 3 (1993): 37–41; pt. 2, *Aeropagus* 6, no. 4 (1993): 14–17; Savithri de Tourreil, "A Female Hindu Ascetic," *Ecumenism* 115 (September 1994): 10–12.

6. Elie Wiesel familiarized the non-Jewish world with the role of Hasidic master in his popular collection *Souls on Fire: Portraits and Legends of Hasidic Masters,* trans. Marion Wiesel (New York: Simon & Schuster, 1972). See especially Wiesel's portrait of the famous Hasidic master, Israel Baal Shem Tov, pp. 3–39.

mentors. In Homer's *The Odyssey*, the Greek goddess Athene, disguised as Mentor, helps Telemachus, the troubled son of Odysseus, find his father.[7] In Dante's *Inferno*, Virgil leads Dante up from the burning fires of hell,[8] and in Dostoevsky's *The Brothers Karamazov*, Father Zossima is the starets or wise elder in the boy Aloysha's life.[9]

Writer Donald Corcoran points out that the Christian guide is distinguished from classical notions of guide because of the unique Christian understanding of the director/directee relationship as a "begetting in the spirit"; as in other contexts, the Christian guide was gentle and kind and yet could correct the disciple.[10] The relationship was based neither on a parental model nor on a simple friendship model: it was focused on engendering the Spirit in the life of the disciple.[11] This specifically Christian form of mentorship is the one that is intended in this book. The assumption is that religious educators are, or ought to be, working in conditions that promote their spiritual growth as well as their professional development. Within religious circles, mentorship in the form of spiritual direction has been a constant tradition, albeit usually for clergy and members of religious orders. Now that the secular world is discovering its benefits, the church has a unique opportunity to uncover its own particular understandings of mentorship and use these to benefit everyone involved in religious education.

---

7. As Telemachus embarked on his voyage, Athene, disguised as Mentor, "led the way at a smart pace and Telemachus followed in the footsteps of the goddess." Homer, *The Odyssey,* trans. E. V. Rieu (New York: Penguin, 1982), p. 48.

8. Dante accepts Virgil's assistance in escaping from hell, saying, "Now on, for a single will is in us both; you are my leader, you are my master and my teacher." Dante Alighieri, *The Divine Comedy, vol. 1, Inferno,* trans. Charles S. Singleton, Bollingen Series, no. 80 (Princeton: Princeton University Press, 1970), p. 32, lines 139–142.

9. Fyodor Dostoevsky, *The Brothers Karamazov,* trans. Constance Garnett, Modern Library (New York: Random House, 1950). See especially Dostoevsky's description of the relationship between Aloysha and Fr. Zossima, pp. 24–33.

10. Donald Corcoran, "Spiritual Guidance," in *Christian Spirituality: Origins to the Twelfth Century*, ed. Bernard McGinn and John Meyendorff, with Jean Leclercq, vol.16 of *World Spirituality: An Encyclopedic History of the Religious Quest* (New York: Crossroad, 1985), p. 447. For another insightful discussion of the guide, see Donald Corcoran, "The Spiritual Guide: Midwife of the Higher Spiritual Self," in *Abba*, pp. 336–339.

11. Corcoran, "Spiritual Guidance," p. 450.

BASIC CONCEPTS OF MENTORSHIP

Mentorship as a form of induction is hardly a new concept, though it is known by other names in various occupations. In the trades, apprenticeship is the primary means of inducting new craftspeople and artisans into a way of working and living.[12] An apprentice in mechanics, for example, is required to complete a lengthy period of supervised work or apprenticeship until all the qualifications for journeyman status are met. In the legal profession, the new lawyer articles for a year before being admitted to the bar. Similarly, in medicine, the candidate interns in a clinical setting. The provision of an induction period is, and has been, key to the continuance and enhancement of many occupations. For religious educators the provision of mentorship is one way of demonstrating that the religious education profession not only considers itself a profession but that it acts on this understanding by showing due regard for the induction of new members.

Variety of Meanings

Frustrations abound with myriad definitions used to describe mentoring relationships.[13] The term has taken on so many meanings that adult educator Laurent Daloz observed that mentorship has

---

12. Two insightful works on the history and usefulness of craft apprentices are Ian M. G. Quimby, *Apprenticeship in Colonial Philadelphia* (New York: Garland, 1985) and William Joseph Rorabaugh, *The Craft Apprentice: From Franklyn to the Machine Age in America* (New York: Oxford University Press, 1986).

13. The variety of definitions of mentorship is considerable. Educational researcher Richard Kay, for instance, gives the mentor a very limited, functional role. Kay argues that the mentor's task is to help the mentee become self-reliant and accountable. See "A Definition for Developing Self-Reliance," in *Mentoring: Developing Successful New Teachers*, ed. Theresa M. Bey and C. Thomas Holmes (Reston, Va.: Association of Teacher Educators, 1990), p. 35. For some other definitions, see Eugene M. Anderson and Anne Lucasse Shannon, "Toward a Conceptualization of Mentoring," *Journal of Teacher Education* 39, no. 1 (1988): 39–40; Ann D. Carden, "Mentoring and Adult Career Development: The Evolution of a Theory," *The Counseling Psychologist* 18, no. 2 (1990): 278–281; Nathalie J. Gehrke, "Toward a Definition of Mentoring," *Theory into Practice* 27, no. 3 (1988): 190; N. Lunt et al.,"Understanding Mentoring," *The Vocational Aspect of Education* 44, no. 1 (1992): 138; Peeter A. Poldre, "Mentoring Programs: A Question of Design," *Interchange* 25, no. 2 (1994): 184–185.

"developed a middle-aged spread."[14] The variety of definitions and meanings indicates the difficulty of arriving at a definition that will have relevance for every situation. Fully formulated and well-thought-out definitions of both mentor and mentee are important because these definitions have implications for how individuals view the mentoring relationship and, ultimately, for how effective it becomes. An unclear definition will result in communication problems and unmet expectations for the religious education mentor and for the mentee.

Among the many educational attempts to develop a definition of mentorship, Eugene Anderson's efforts are most appropriate for a religious education context. Anderson discusses the mentoring process as one in which the "more skilled or more experienced person, serving as a role model, teaches, sponsors, encourages, counsels, and befriends a less skilled or less experienced person for the purpose of promoting the latter's professional and/or personal development."[15] Anderson is careful to point out that genuine mentorship occurs in the context of an ongoing caring relationship.

A principle strength of Anderson's definition is that it captures the spirit of the mentoring process as caring and nurturing, components that are integral to a religious education setting. The most distinctive aspect of the definition, however, is its stress on the deliberate and intentional teaching function of mentorship. Anderson recognized that effective mentors ought to provide more than a personal support system. Another benefit is that Anderson has also identified five essential mentor functions: teaching, sponsoring, encouraging, counseling, and befriending.[16]

---

14. Laurent Daloz, "Mentors: Teachers who Make a Difference," *Change* 15, no. 6 (1983): 25.

15. Eugene M. Anderson, "Definitions of Mentoring," unpublished manuscript, 1987, quoted in Anderson and Shannon, "Toward a Conceptualization of Mentoring," p. 40.

16. Mayra Bloom has identified similar roles and functions of the mentor, for women, in "Multiple Roles of the Mentor: Supporting Women's Adult Development," *Learning Environments for Women's Adult Development: Bridges Toward Change*, ed. Kathleen Taylor and Catherine Marienau, New Directions for Adult and Continuing Education, no. 65 (San Francisco: Jossey-Bass, 1995), pp. 63–72. Bloom observes that at various times the mentor is called on to stand behind the mentee; lead the mentee; listen, question, and connect with the mentee; and stand shoulder to shoulder or alongside the mentee. I prefer to use Anderson's definition because of the very clear meanings attached to each component and because he intends mentoring for males and females.

One person, however, may be called on to display select functions in particular situations.

The strong relational component, which Anderson identifies as a key for mentorship, captures the essential mutual respect and honor that should characterize a religious education mentoring relationship.[17] Similarly, educational researcher Nathalie Gehrke uses the metaphor of mentorship as gift exchange, capturing the notion of mutual self-giving in the mentor-mentee interchange.[18] Gehrke further develops this metaphor by using Martin Buber's classical "I-Thou/ I-It" distinction to show that regarding the other as "it" in a functional sense is what defines a helping relationship, not a mentoring one. An I-Thou relationship facilitates mentor and mentee personal and professional development, the "stretching to be more because someone believes in your potential."[19] The I-Thou sense is clearly the one that Anderson intends, and one that captures the meaning intended for religious education in this book.

Mentor as Role Model

Another significant aspect of Anderson's definition of mentorship is that it recognizes role-modeling as the base from which the five functions flow. To be a role model means to demonstrate your commitment to religious education with your whole life stance or attitude. In a graduate school, for instance, the religious education faculty member ought to be the epitome of guide, critic, and challenger for the master's or doctoral student. The mentee needs to be able to see the mentor as embodying the joy of teaching or having what the poet Wystan Auden has described as the "eye-on-the-object look." In Auden's words, the people who have really found their vocation

---

17. For similar approaches to mentorship, see Nathalie J. Gehrke, "On Preserving the Essence of Mentoring as One Form of Teacher Leadership," *Journal of Teacher Education* 39, no.1 (1988): 43–45; Gehrke, "Toward a Definition of Mentoring," pp. 190–94; Beverly Hardcastle, "Spiritual Connections: Protégés' Reflections on Significant Mentorships," *Theory into Practice* 27, no. 3 (1988): 201–208; Kaoru Yamamoto, "To See Life Grow: The Meaning of Mentorship," *Theory into Practice* 27, no. 3 (1988): 183–89.

18. Gehrke, "Toward a Definition of Mentoring," pp. 190–94; Gehrke, "Preserving the Essence of Mentoring," pp. 43–45.

19. Ibid., p. 44; Martin Buber, *I and Thou*, trans. Ronald Gregor Smith, 2d ed. (New York: Scribner's, 1958).

"wear the same rapt expression/forgetting themselves in a function."[20]

When teaching is obviously the person's vocation, the chances increase that he or she will want to mentor new religious educators into that same vocation. The mentor knows and loves the profession of teaching and is sufficiently committed to want to initiate a mentee. The religious education mentor is expected to be an exemplary role model of the profession in every sense of the word.

Functions of Mentorship

Teacher: The first of the five specific functions of the mentor which derive from the role model that Anderson identifies is that of teaching.[21] This function highlights the fact that there is a deliberate educational role in the mentoring process. In a classroom situation, for instance, a religious education mentor demonstrates to the new faculty member how to teach well and how to build on learners' interests during the instructional act. The effective religious education mentor leads in a step-by-step fashion until the teaching concept is grasped and the mentee has an opportunity to practice teaching and receive feedback on performance. The relationship between the religious education mentor and mentee is similar to that of master-disciple, since the deliberative teaching function is the core component of the relationship. In the optimum religious education setting, teaching is viewed as more than imparting knowledge; it is seen as using the skills appropriate to the learners, whether they be children or adults, to actually raise their level of knowledge and skills, and positively influence their lifestyle behaviors.

A practical application of the teacher-mentee relationship can be seen in the case of Carmen, newly appointed to teach in a church-related school. Carmen's mentor is Maria, another faculty member who meets with her in her classroom to discuss her difficulty with

---

20. Wystan Hugh Auden, "Horae Canonicae,"in *Collected Shorter Poems, 1927–1957* (London: Faber & Faber, 1966), p. 325.

21. The definition of teaching used here approximates Timothy Arthur Lines's use of coach in *Functional Images of the Religious Educator* (Birmingham, Ala.: Religious Education Press, 1992). See chapter 5, "The Religious Educator as Coach." The coach not only provides preservice education but also provides support during the actual job. According to Lines, the coach supervises, trains, motivates, and plans strategy with the mentee.

evaluating students. Carmen has learned the theory of evaluation in her university classes; she has been taught how to assess learner comprehension and how to grade student essays. However, when it comes to actual implementation of theory, Carmen needs Maria's mentorship to help her overcome difficulties.

Sponsor: The second function of the religious education mentor is to sponsor. In the role of sponsor, the designated mentor gives the mentee entrée into the profession and becomes a sponsor and guide on the mentee's vocational journey. In one local church situation, for example, the mentor, Enrico, ensures that his mentee, adult religious educator Simon, is recommended for congregational committees, encouraged to initiate educational activities, and introduced to congregational members who have similar interests and will be supportive of, if not involved in, the religious education programs Simon is offering. Because Enrico has a positive reputation in this community he is able to give Simon good sponsorship, thereby facilitating Simon's effectiveness in the profession.

Encourager: In the third role, encourager, the religious education mentor gives feedback on the mentee's progress and gently pushes the mentee to constructive action. The mentor is pleased with the mentee's successes, small and large, and wants the mentee to fully realize his or her potential as a religious educator. In one congregationally based ministry, the assistant pastor Sula has gradually taken on the role of encourager in the professional life of Rochelle, the new youth minister. Sula is quick to affirm Rochelle's good work habits, her effective communication skills, and the religious education programs she has initiated for youth. With Sula's encouragement Rochelle has grown in confidence and initiative in her parish duties.

Counselor. The fourth role, counselor, is one of the more challenging for the religious education mentor and one that is often resisted because of the therapeutic connotations associated with the word "counsel." Given that the optimum mentor-mentee relationship assumes that participants are in good health, counseling refers here to the interpersonal skills of listening and communicating effectively with the mentee. In a Sunday Bible study program, for example, the mentor as counselor role surfaces when a retired teacher, Mrs. Poirier, makes herself available on a confidential basis to help Jeanne, the convener of the Bible study program, sort out her communication problems with challenging learners and parents. Mrs. Poirier is most effective in having Jeanne reflect on particular conflicts and in helping her develop skills to deal with contentious situations that might arise. Both mentor and mentee understand that this discernment process is crucial to the mentee's professional development.

Befriender: The fifth function of the religious education mentor, befriender, is essential in a church context when one considers the plethora of examples of fulfilling friendships within Christianity.[22] Aelred of Rievaulx's notion of spiritual friendship and the Celtic notion of an *anamchara*, or soul friend, are just two of several that have been important in the Christian religious tradition.[23] Because friendship operates on many levels that are not always easy to distinguish, friendship may be misunderstood in a mentoring context. Since the religious education mentor and the mentee are unlikely to begin as equals, at least in terms of their professional expertise, a lasting friendship may not be a realistic or desirable expectation. Nonetheless, the mentoring friendship can be efficacious. For Nona Aglukak, an Inuit woman, being new to both an isolated northern region and to a religion curriculum development position created considerable stress in her life. However, the church education center where Nona worked provided her with colleagues who understood her dilemma and offered her their patience, their respect, and their

---

22. The notion of befriending is very strong in the Christian tradition. Educator David Shields argues that Christian religious education must enable friends to deepen their relationship and to see the working of God within it. For Shields, friendship is very clearly the arena in which God's love is active and is therefore worthy of special attention. See "Friendship: Context and Content of Christian Religious Education," *Religious Education* 91, no. 1 (1996): 116–17.

Two excellent studies of Christian friendship are Brian P. McGuire, *Friendship and Community: The Monastic Experience,* Cistercian Studies Series, no. 95 (Kalamazoo, Mich.: Cistercian Publications, 1988) and Carolinne White, *Christian Friendship in the Fourth Century* (Cambridge: Cambridge University Press, 1992).

23. Aelred of Rievaulx, *Spiritual Friendship* (Kalamazoo, Mich.: Cistercian Publications, 1974). For a discussion of the importance of the Celtic *anamchara,* see Diarmuid O'Laaoghaire, "Celtic Spirituality," in *The Study of Spirituality,* ed. Cheslyn Jones, Geoffrey Wainwright, and Edward Yarnold (New York: Oxford University Press, 1986), p. 222. See also chapter 3 of Edward Sellner, "The Irish Soul Friend," in *Mentoring: The Ministry of Spiritual Kinship* (Notre Dame, Ind.: Ave Maria, 1990). Sellner quotes St. Brigid as saying, "Anyone without a soul friend is like a body without a head." Ibid., p. 61.

friendship. Consequently, they were successful in retaining Nona and her expertise.

The roles of teacher, sponsor, encourager, counselor, and befriender point to the demanding functions of the mentor. No one person can fill all of these roles perfectly, but establishing them as desirable in a definition of mentor is crucial for the conceptualization of the mentor role. In my own life, I have experienced the mentoring influence of many strong, supportive people who have guided me in my development as a professional religious educator. I remember especially Jean, the supervisor of my parish field placement for my master's degree in religious education. Jean, herself a graduate student with many years of experience in adult religious education, was the coordinator of a parish religious education program, the Rite of Christian Initiation of Adults (RCIA). Jean affirmed my leadership in the RCIA group, supported me verbally when I encountered theological differences with a belligerent pastor, and nurtured my dream of further graduate study in religious education. Likewise, Bob, who was once my spiritual director, later became a life mentor. He challenged me to examine some of my own personal assumptions, befriended me when my workplace became chaotic, and helped me recognize the presence of God in my own teaching. Though I was not in daily contact with these religious education mentors, I did benefit from the mentoring roles they played in my life. My experience with individuals such as these confirms my belief that mentors are essential for all religious educators.

Distinctions between Mentor and Mentee

Though I have focused the discussion on religious education mentors, an understanding of the word "mentee" is equally crucial, given that mentors and mentees play complementary roles in the mentoring process. The mentee is more than the passive recipient of the largesse of the religious education mentor. The mentee sometimes chooses the mentor and is the one who has to learn, either by being instructed directly or by observing the mentor in action. The mentee has to critically discern the mentor's ways and needs to decide which teaching skills or habits can be appropriated from the mentor's repertoire. The term "mentee" is used in this book to refer to one who is guided and taught by the mentor. As it is used here, mentee is meant to capture the spirit of the promising religious educator who can benefit from the positive skills and attitudes of the mentor.[24]

MENTORSHIP IN
RELIGIOUS EDUCATION PRACTICE

There are two basic types of mentoring relationships: informal and formal. Educational research favors formalized relationships because of the present emphasis on developing organized mentoring programs for new educators. Informal relationships, although less common than formal mentoring relationships, are often quite significant in the life of the religious education mentee. In addition to being less frequent, informal mentoring relationships are also less precise and more difficult to document.

Informal Mentoring Relationships

An informal mentoring relationship is one that arises naturally between two people who are drawn to each other. The relationship is not dictated or prescribed by bureaucracy; it arises naturally and develops over a period of time. In chapter 9 I discuss the stages of development that often characterize this serendipitous relationship.

One typical case of a informal mentoring relationship involves Susan, who was hired at Beth El synagogue when the congregation needed someone to administer its day school program. The previous teacher, Jael, retired after a twenty-year tenure and was loved and missed by the congregation. Jael understood how Susan might be threatened by her continuing presence in the congregation as a worshiping member, so she decided to invite Susan to her place for friendly visits and to answer any questions she might have. She made a point of distancing herself from the synagogue to allow Susan ample leeway to complete her job independently. When Susan asked for advice on administrative matters, Jael gave her examples of how she and

---

24. Mentees are also known as inductees, neophytes, protégés, and new teachers. I chose "mentee" knowing that any term selected to represent this unique role would have caused difficulties. Though the word "mentee" may suggest the passive recipient of the knowledge of the mentor, in this book the mentee is assumed to be an active agent in the learning process. For a discussion of the variety of names for mentor, see Nancy L. Zimpher and Susan R. Rieger, "Mentoring Teachers: What are the Issues?" *Theory into Practice* 27, no. 3 (1988): 175–177.

her colleagues in other synagogues had handled similar situations. Susan mulled over these options and found some that fit her own character and educational style. When Jael felt that Susan was relying on her excessively, she pulled back and encouraged Susan to make her own decisions and learn from her mistakes. At the end of that first year, Susan realized that she had grown considerably since joining the synagogue staff. She noticed that she did not see Jael much, nor did she feel she needed to rely on her to make decisions. This informal relationship helped initiate Susan into her religious education ministry and allowed her to grow into her new role and identity without compromising her personal integrity.

Formalized Mentoring Relationships

The second type of mentorship involves formalized mentoring relationships.[25] Though I recognize that some religious educators do indeed form successful mentoring relationships informally, I want to make meaningful relationships available for everyone. Formalized relationships can contain elements of happenstance, but their true value is that they allow everyone to have an opportunity to partake in a positive mentoring relationship.

Consider the case of Bob, a pastoral care worker at All Saints Children's Hospital in an inner city. When Bob joined the pastoral care department in September, he knew that a large part of his job was to educate staff and patients on the ethical concerns that arise in difficult medical situations. Though Bob had an extensive background in pediatric pastoral care and had encountered serious illness and large hospital bureaucratic structures before, he was unsure of the new religious education focus in his present work. One of the pastoral team workers, an ordained minister, Tom, was asked by the department chair to mentor Bob through the first year. During their daily hospital routines, Tom and Bob met informally as colleagues, but their formalized relationship initiated by the department added another dimension to their professional lives. Tom discussed difficult cases with Bob, encouraged

---

25. Formalized mentorship is also known as "organizationally sponsored mentorship." See Kenneth M. Kerr, Donald R. Schulze, and Lyle E. Woodward, "Organizationally Sponsored Mentorship," in *Mentoring: New Strategies and Challenges,* ed. Michael W. Galbraith and Norman H. Cohen, New Directions for Adult and Continuing Education, no. 66 (San Francisco: Jossey-Bass, 1995), pp. 33–41.

him to continue when the job seemed overwhelming, and gave him information when needed on hospital policy and structure. Tom was most helpful on advising Bob on how best to assist patients and their families with the task of sorting out the crucial issues to consider when making medical decisions. Bob doubted that he could have survived the year without Tom's help. This formalized mentorship provided both Tom and Bob with an opportunity to mentor and be mentored, and it enriched their lives.

Both informal and formal mentoring relationships are possible, and both can be beneficial. Because informal relationships are sporadic in nature, in this book I concentrate on developing and fostering formalized mentoring relationships for those new to the religious education profession.

RELIGIOUS EDUCATORS REQUIRE MENTORS

Religious educators I have known, studied, and worked with fall into the following categories: (1) those who had mentoring relationships and benefitted from them and (2) those who did not have them but felt they needed them. The literature confirms the experience of both groups of people. Religious educators from higher education have provided the best documented instances of informal mentoring relationships. In a collection of autobiographical essays of significant religious education, researchers such as Campbell Wyckoff, Johannes Hofinger, and Randolph Crump Miller acknowledge their debts to mentors who made significant contributions to their scholarly and personal achievements.[26] It is likely that if some religious educators working in other settings had the opportunity to tell their stories, similar mentor connections would become obvious.

Among religious educators the need for a mentor is particularly acute.[27] A survey of all first year teachers (94 percent response rate) in

26. Marlene Mayr, ed., *Modern Masters of Religious Education* (Birmingham, Ala.: Religious Education Press, 1983), especially chapter 4, "From Practice to Theory—And Back Again," in which religious educator Campbell Wyckoff recounts the many mentors who influenced his distinguished career.

27. Simon Veenman's extensive review of the literature on the problems encountered by first-year teachers (primarily those in public schools) shows that not only do they have instructional concerns but they are also experiencing "reality shock," or the difficulties associated with the radical transition from a teacher preparation program

Roman Catholic schools in the Archdiocese of Omaha showed that educators in these schools experience many frustrations. From their written responses the researcher identified three particular areas of concern to the new teachers: preparation and support in assuming the role of teaching as ministry, assistance in making the transition from college to workplace, and the provision of more adequate staff development opportunities. Those educators surveyed specifically asked for better orientation to the vocation of Catholic education and for additional staff development opportunities such as the provision of a mentor.[28] It is especially important to note here what the new teachers did *not* ask for: curriculum, inservice sessions, or further academic education. Their basic need was for another person to mentor them in their first year of teaching.

Karen Tye's research adds additional weight to these findings.[29] One of the common themes she found from her interviews with nineteen Presbyterian religious educators was the need for ongoing professional support. Interestingly, again in this case, religious educators were not looking for better curriculum resources or more funding but for teaching assistance and affirmation of their religious education activity. These results point to the need for a supportive mentoring structure for new religious educators.

In *The D.R.E. Book* Maria Harris focuses on some of the specific difficulties church-based directors of religious educators (DRE) encounter,

---

to a first teaching job. This is a traumatic experience that may result in changes in behavior, alteration in attitudes, or other significant differences in the life of the new teacher. See Veenman, "Perceived Problems of Beginning Teachers," *Review of Educational Research* 54, no. 2 (1984): 143–78. See also Kevin Ryan et al., *Biting the Apple: Accounts of First Year Teachers* (New York: Longman, 1980). Another problem for new educators is having "unrealistic optimism" with regard to their first year, which may make their jobs even more difficult. See Leslie Huling-Austin, "Research on Learning to Teach: Implications for Teacher Induction and Mentoring Programs," *Journal of Teacher Education* 43 , no. 3 (1992): 173–80.

28. Barbara L. Brock, "Profile of the Beginning Teacher," *Momentum* 21, no. 4 (1990): 54–57. An intense level of anxiety about teaching religious education is also documented in a study of the school system of a Canadian province by Robert K. Crocker, *Catholic Education in Newfoundland and Labrador: Report of Surveys of Members of the Catholic Education Community*, vol. 1 (St. John's, Nfld., Canada: Catholic Education Council, 1990), especially pp. 50–51.

29. Karen B. Tye, "Those Who Teach: The Local Church School Teacher's Perspective on Being a Teacher," *Religious Education* 83, no. 3 (1988): 337–48.

and she makes proposals for how these challenges can be addressed.[30] Specifically, Harris recommends that the director of religious education take on the role of guiding religious educators in their everyday professional duties.[31] She envisages the DRE teaching, assisting, encouraging, superintending, and watching the people who have been asked to teach the church community. Harris's book was written precisely because of the uncertainty in the job of DRE and the difficulties of being involved in church-based religious education work. Though *The D.R.E. Book* does not specifically discuss mentorship, the job descriptions it offers for the DRE clearly encompass a similar concept.

In her discussion of why Jewish educators need mentors, Sara Lee states a convincing reason that has marked similarity to the Christian educators' situation: The Jewish community is ultimately concerned with passing on the values and the ideas of their religious tradition. Formal Jewish institutions, therefore, should be "a reflection of what a 'Jewish community' ought to be."[32] The same responsibility to model Christian community applies to Christian religious educators. Religious educators of all faiths need to be mindful that how they initiate new professionals speaks volumes to their constituencies.

Clearly, the needs of religious educators are more for support and guidance than for academic preparation, not a surprising request when one considers that beyond academic objectives religious education is expected "to provide . . . 'a faith to live by' or 'an understanding of the meaning and purpose of life,' which can give unity to the entire educational process."[33] This "architectonic" role, as writer Basil Mitchell terms it, makes teaching religious education both difficult and challenging. This is especially true in the current cultural situation which challenges the very ideas and beliefs the religious educator has been asked to hand on. Religious educators have asked for professional assistance and their profession is attempting to respond to the call.

---

30. Maria Harris, *The D.R.E. Book: Questions and Strategies for Parish Personnel* (New York: Paulist, 1976), especially chapter 6, "Managing Managers?"

31. Ibid., pp. 104–105.

32. Sara S. Lee, "Synthesizing Individual and Institutional Aspirations: The Role of Mentoring in Institutional Life," in *Touching the Future: Mentoring and the Jewish Professional*, ed. Michael Zeldin and Sara S. Lee (Los Angeles: Hebrew Union College-Jewish Institute of Religion, 1995), p. 78.

33. Basil Mitchell, "Religious Education," *Oxford Review of Education* 6, no. 2 (1980): 134.

BENEFITS OF MENTORSHIP

Little systematic research on mentorship has been conducted, most existing literature coming from the public education sector.[34] The literature either describes current programs or hypothesizes on the value of mentorship.[35] As yet, no substantive research is available about the effects of mentorship among those involved in religious education.[36] Increasingly, professions such as business and social work have been

---

34. Researcher Judith Warren Little states, "We remain unable to assess the claims that have been made about the influence of mentoring on teachers' classroom performance, their long-term development, or their career commitment." See "The Mentor Phenomenon and the Social Organization of Teaching," in *Review of Research in Education,* vol. 16, ed. Courtney B. Cazden (Washington, D.C.: American Educational Research Association, 1990), p. 328.

35. For descriptions of current mentoring programs, see Billie Enz et al., "The Arizona Teacher Residency Program," in *Teacher Induction and Mentoring*, ed. Gary P. DeBolt (Albany, N.Y.: State University of New York Press, 1992), pp. 97–118; Nicholas G. Stupiansky and Michael P. Wolfe, "The North Country Mentor/Intern Teacher Program: A Rural Consortium," in *Teacher Induction*, pp. 80–92; Judith T. Witmer, "Mentoring: One District's Success Story," *NASSP Bulletin* 77, no. 550 (1993): 71–78.

36. Michael Zeldin and Sara Lee's *Touching the Future* (1995) contains many individual accounts of mentorship within Jewish education, but does not describe any extensive research studies. Even when religious educators do conduct an investigation into mentorship, their conclusions are often unconvincing. See, for example, Sondra Matthaei's research with a group of religious educators, in which she defines faith-mentoring vaguely as the presence of an "influential relationship" in your life (p. 15). According to Matthaei, faith-mentors can include friends, coworkers, parents, or spiritual directors. In the introduction to her book, *Faith Matters: Faith-Mentoring in the Faith Community* (Valley Forge, Penn.: Trinity, 1996), Matthaei describes faith-mentoring as "another way of dealing with the crisis of meaning" (p. 2). Her definition approximates the befriending function of mentorship that I give in this chapter. However, for me, befriending is only one component of effective mentorship. I use "mentor" to refer to professional religious education situations in which the designated mentor teaches, sponsors, encourages, befriends, and counsels the mentee. Matthaei's understanding is similar to Edward Sellner's mentor as spiritual friend in *Mentoring: The Ministry of Spiritual Kinship* (1990). It also resembles Donald G. Emler's use of the term "mentor" to mean a spiritual facilitator. See Emler, *Revisioning the DRE* (Birmingham, Ala.: Religious Education Press, 1989), especially pp. 223–25. None of these usages contribute to the professionalization of religious education nor to the refining of roles within the profession. Rather, they perpetuate the erroneous notion that religious education is a vague, undefined enterprise that defies classification and systematization.

vigorous in their research efforts to determine the value, in measurable terms, of mentorship.[37] Research has also been carried out in fields as diverse as social work, rehabilitation, retail, medicine, and nursing.[38] Given the sparsity of research in religious education mentorship, it is important for religious educators to pay close attention to the comprehensive research studies that have been conducted in public school settings. While the public school context may be different from church education settings, the reality of the need for mentorship is quite similar. In this book I consistently argue that the insights from the general educational literature can inform church-based religious education and show that the basic enterprise of teaching is the same, regardless of the situational context.

Benefits for the Mentees

There are encouraging results from those educational studies that have been conducted on mentorship. A research investigation conducted on

37. For an example from the business literature, see Gerard Roche's groundbreaking empirical study of mentorship among Wall Street business executives. Roche found of the 1,250 who responded to his questionnaire, two thirds had mentors. Those who had mentors reported greater job and career satisfaction than those who did not have mentors. "Much Ado about Mentors," *Harvard Business Review* 57, no. 1 (1979), especially "Highlights of Study," pp. 14–15. Other business examples include Nancy Brown Johnson and Terri A. Scandura, "The Effect of Mentorship and Sex-Role Style on Male Female Earnings," *Industrial Relations* 33, no. 2 (1994): 263–74. For an example of an empirical study among social workers, see Pauline M. Collins, "Does Mentorship among Social Workers Make a Difference? An Empirical Investigation of Career Outcomes," *Social Work* 39, no. 4 (1994): 413–19. Collins's research supports the notion that mentorship increases career success and satisfaction of the mentor and mentee. However, Collins found that mentorship resulted in increased income for the mentor only.

38. For an example of research from the rehabilitation field, see Sonja Feist-Price, "Cross-Gender Mentoring Relationships: Critical Issues," *Journal of Rehabilitation* 60, no. 2 (1994): 13–17. This article discusses specific strategies for making cross-gender mentorship work and points out that because males often receive mentorship serendipitously, facilitated mentorship for women is necessary. For research on mentorship in the retail industry, see LuAnn Ricketts Gaskill, "Same Sex and Cross Sex Mentoring of Female Protégés: A Comparative Analysis," *The Career Development Quarterly* 40, no. 1 (1992): 48–63. Gaskill found no significant difference in terms of benefits for cross-sex and same-sex mentorship. For medicine, see Poldre, "Mentoring Programs," pp. 183–93. For nursing, see L. M. Stachura and J. Hoff, "Toward Achievement of Mentoring for Nurses," *Nursing Administration Quarterly* 15 (1990): 56–62.

the University of Wisconsin-Whitewater teacher induction program is one such example.[39] This study shows support for the usual goals of induction programs: (1) improving retention (2) providing support and information to reduce educator concerns, and (3) providing professional development for new faculty.[40] These three benefits for the mentee, and for the profession as a whole, are encouraging findings for those churches about to undertake a mentorship initiative for religious educators. The results address crucial issues in the religious education profession: retention of new professional religious educators and adequate professional initiation.[41]

Equally positive results have been found in assessments of other mentoring programs.[42] In one inquiry, mentees were observed by an administrator at varying intervals throughout their first year, and during that time 96 percent received acceptable ratings on fifteen specifically defined teacher competencies, all of which had been emphasized in the mentoring program. Close collaboration between university and school-based personnel was identified as a significant factor in the mentoring program's success. The fact that the mentee was positively influenced to a considerable degree is important information for religious educators to know, since professional ability and competence in teaching are essential if religious education is to achieve high instructional standards, necessary for effectiveness of the educational enterprise and the credibility of the profession.

---

39. Leonard J. Varah, Warren S. Theune, and Linda Parker, "Beginning Teachers: Sink or Swim," *Journal of Teacher Education* 37, no. 1 (1986): 30–34.

40. These are the goals cited in Sandra J. Odell, *Mentor Teacher Programs* (Washington, D.C.: National Education Association, 1990), pp. 16–17. These goals are also identified in Leslie Huling-Austin, "Teacher Induction Programs and Internships," in *Handbook of Research on Teacher Education*, ed. W. Robert Houston (New York: Macmillan, 1990), pp. 535–548. Huling-Austin includes two additional goals: (1) meeting state mandated requirements related to induction and certification and (2) transmitting the culture of the system to beginning teachers. Ibid., pp. 541–542.

41. From a review of the literature, adult educator Susan Schulz makes similar claims about the benefits of mentorship for mentors and mentees. She categorizes these benefits into three areas: learning of specific skills and ideas, growth in self-awareness of professional competence, and development in psychological maturity. See her "The Benefits of Mentoring," in *Mentoring: New Strategies*, pp. 57–67.

42. Kay Hegler and Richard Dudley, "Beginning Teacher Induction: A Progress Report," *Journal of Teacher Education* 38, no. 1 (1987): 53–56.

Douglas Warring's research on a Minnesota mentor program, in which he surveyed twenty-six mentors and twenty-nine mentees, also supports the development of mentoring programs.[43] Some 68 percent of the mentees said that their teaching styles had improved as a result of the mentorship. Quite significant, as well, was the fact that some 92 percent of mentees reported that they received emotional and social support as a result of the process. Despite the positive feedback, however, the limits of self-report are evident and suggest the need for follow-up experimental studies to substantiate the reported positive results. Nevertheless, Warring's study is insightful for mentoring programs for religious educators because it provides concrete evidence of the mentees' strong positive reception of their designated mentors.

One outcome that has been proven by general educational research is the high level of personal support and professional information that mentors provide for mentees. This was evident in the Warring study, and in others as well. In one mentorship study, those who had been mentored felt more positive about both teaching and their own effectiveness as educators, compared to those who did not receive assistance.[44] Other mentoring research, tracing the influence of the mentor on the mentees over a one-year period, confirmed the degree to which mentees rely on mentors. In fact, by the end of the academic year, 80 percent of mentees were using their mentors as a means of coping.[45] Such initiation support is crucial for those in church-related educational ministries because of the rigor of their professional assignments. Having a mentor to provide educational guidance to the new religious educator will help ensure that the educational ministry perpetuates itself and that competent professionals pass on their accumulated professional knowledge and wisdom to the next generation.

43. Douglas F. Warring, "The Effects of the Mentor-Mentee Program on the Learning Environment" (paper presented at the annual meeting of the American Educational Research Association, Chicago, Ill., April 3–7, 1991), ERIC ED 333537.

44. Leslie Huling-Austin and Sheila C. Murphy, *Assessing the Impact of Teacher Induction Programs: Implications for Program Development* (paper presented at the annual meeting of the American Educational Research Association, Washington, D.C., April 20–24, 1987), ERIC ED 283779, p. 28.

45. Sandra J. Odell, "Characteristics of Beginning Teachers in an Induction Context," in *Teacher Induction*, ed. Judy Reinhartz (Washington, D.C.: National Education Association, 1989), p. 48.

Educational researchers point out that mentorship can help the mentee make the transition from being a student to being a teacher, a transition that involves many personal and professional adjustments.[46] This point is especially relevant when one realizes that a major issue in the life of a religious educator is the resolution implicit in establishing friendships and making commitments, the stage described by Erik Erikson as "intimacy versus isolation."[47] The resolution of intimacy issues will have a long-term effect on the religious education mentee, perhaps over the course of a lifetime, both personally and professionally.

There is considerable support also for the professional skills to be attained from mentorship. One empirical study showed that mentees learn risk-taking behavior, communication and survival skills, instructional skills, leadership qualities, professional attributes, and how to set high standards and achieve them.[48] Concrete professional skills are crucial for effective functioning as a competent, dependable religious educator.

The obvious recency of formalized mentoring programs makes conducting longitudinal studies on teacher retention somewhat difficult at present; nonetheless, there is reason to be optimistic. Twenty-four of twenty-five mentees in one research study remained in teaching. At the time in which the study was reported, some had reached their fourth year.[49] In another investigation, only 4.3 percent had resigned from teaching after four years, a figure significantly below the national average.[50] This potentially positive effect on retention is a very significant insight for those working with religious educators, a group for whom motivation to remain in the profession can be low. The public school success in increasing retention by providing

---

46. Fay A. Head, Alan J. Reiman, and Lois Thies-Sprinthall, "The Reality of Mentoring: Complexity in Its Process and Function," in *Mentoring: Contemporary Principles and Issues*, ed. Theresa M. Bey and C. Thomas Holmes (Reston, Va.: Association of Teacher Educators, 1992), pp. 5–24.

47. Erik H. Erikson, *Childhood and Society,* 2d ed. (New York: Norton, 1963), pp. 263–266.

48. Breda Murphy Bova and Rebecca Phillips, "Mentoring as a Learning Experience for Adults," *Journal of Teacher Education* 35, no. 3 (1984): 18.

49. Kay Hegler and Richard Dudley, "Beginning Teacher Induction," p. 54.

50. Sandra J. Odell and Douglas P. Ferraro, "Collaborative Teacher Induction," in *Teacher Induction and Mentoring*, p. 70.

mentorship is especially instructive to the church, which is in great need of a stable, continuous group of religious educators who are totally committed to the profession.

Benefits for the Mentor

The benefits that accrue to the participating mentors have also been assessed, and the positive findings constitute one of the major reasons cited for establishing formalized mentoring programs. A number of researchers have pointed out that the mentors benefit in being able to take on leadership roles, in having the opportunity to revitalize their teaching, and in fulfilling their own developmental need of generativity.[51] These positive results are consistent with insights from adult development literature suggesting that experienced educators need to nurture and find meaning in their career choice and to share this with younger colleagues.[52] The potential for adult development through mentorship is supported by researchers Mary Ann Blank and Nancy Sindelar in their report on a mentor teacher program in Illinois.[53] In the same way, religious education mentors can benefit significantly from the opportunity to induct new people into their profession. Even a perceived need to provide induction support to new religious educators serves as affirmation for more experienced religious educators that their profession is actually thinking of itself as a profession.

---

51. For a sample of the many researchers who have pointed to the value of mentorship for the mentor, see Mel P. Heller and Nancy W. Sindelar, *Developing an Effective Teacher Mentor Program* (Bloomington, Ind.: Phi Delta Kappa Education Foundation, 1991), ERIC ED 332996: p. 9; Judy-Arin Krupp, "Mentoring: A Means by Which Teachers Become Staff Developers," *Journal of Staff Development* 8, no. 1 (1987): 13.

52. See, for example, Erikson's stage theory, in which he discusses developmental needs, in *Childhood and Society* (1963). According to Erikson, generativity is "primarily the concern in establishing and guiding the next generation" (p. 267).

Roger G. Baldwin speculates on the potential of mentorship for helping aging professors work through their generative needs. Baldwin asserts that mentoring new faculty enables them to leave something behind to someone else or even to ensure that their work is carried on. See "The Changing Developmental Needs of an Aging Professorate," in *Teaching and Aging,* ed. Chandra M.N. Mehrotra, New Directions for Teaching and Learning, no. 19 (San Francisco: Jossey-Bass, 1984), pp. 45–56.

53. Mary Ann Blank and Nancy Sindelar, "Mentoring as Professional Development: From Theory to Practice," *Clearing House* 66, no. 1 (1992): 25.

A further mentor benefit is suggested by preliminary research on the use of guided reflection exercises with mentors. If carefully planned, such a process can help religious education mentors increase their conceptual complexity and reasoning ability. Though this educational research is new, it does point to the potential for the continuous lifelong learning that can be part of the mentoring process.[54] Researchers Lois Thies-Sprinthall and Norman Sprinthall have also demonstrated that the role of mentor has enormous promise for revitalizing experienced educators.[55] In documenting their experience of implementing a developmental stage theory model with mentors, the Sprinthalls point out that there is significant potential for promoting the mentor's own personal developmental growth, along with meeting the professional needs of mentees. Effective mentorship can counteract educator stagnation by promoting positive adult growth.

Mentors themselves report having experienced growth in their own teaching as a result of participation in the process. Mentors in the previously mentioned Warring study reported substantial change in their own instructional growth and development. Some 85 percent indicated that their teaching had improved because of the professional time and assistance available through mentor education.[56] Because the work of religious education is so crucial to the life and continuance of the church, evidence that mentorship can serve as a source of renewal for experienced educators is very significant. Not only do the new religious educators benefit from the mentorship but those more experienced can benefit from the enthusiasm and critical thinking generated by inducting new members into the profession.

Interviews with twenty-six mentors in an entry-year assistance study showed that all twenty-six participants indicated benefiting professionally from participation in mentorship. Some 81 percent of respondents reported that they had reexamined their own teaching

54. Alan J. Reiman and Lois Thies-Sprinthall, "Promoting the Development of Mentor Teachers: Theory and Research Programs Using Guided Reflection," *Journal of Research and Development in Education* 26, no. 3 (1993): 179–85.

55. Lois Thies-Sprinthall and Norman A. Sprinthall, "Experienced Teachers: Agents for Revitalization and Renewal as Mentors and Teacher Educators," *Journal of Education* 169, no. 1 (1987): 65–79.

56. Warring, *Effects of the Mentor-Mentee Program*, p. 18.

practices.[57] In a similar investigation of a North Carolina state-mandated program, more than two-thirds of the mentors reported that participating in the study had "definitely" assisted in their professional growth. When invited to specify the area of growth, the most significant response was "focusing on improvement of teaching skills."[58] Further research is required to determine how these changes in self-perception influence the mentors' teaching in their classes and how improvements in mentor instructional skill influence role modeling for the mentees. However, the preliminary empirical research alone is significant for religious education mentors; this promises increased educational achievement for the church.

Benefits for the Work Environment

Mentoring programs not only assist those directly involved in the relationship, they also have the potential to revitalize the entire staff.[59] Educational researchers agree that mentoring programs can have enormous potential for renewal of personnel. In a collaborative study of an induction program, Sandra Odell and Douglas Ferraro observed that the positive effects of the mentoring program tended to spill over to the rest of the educational environment in what they term "a multiplier effect."[60] If mentoring programs can have such a positive effect in a public school context, they can surely accomplish the same or more in a church-related environment, given that the latter is usually smaller and likely will have a higher percentage of

---

57. Larry B. Godley, Donald R. Wilson, and Beverly J. Klug, "The Teacher Consultant Role: Impact on the Profession," *Action in Teacher Education* 8, no. 4 (1986–1987): 70.

58. Parmalee Hawk, "Beginning Teacher Programs: Benefits for the Experienced Educator," *Action in Teacher Education* 8, no. 4 (1986–1987): 62.

59. Deanna Gordon and Margaret Moles, "Mentoring Becomes Staff Development: A Case of Serendipity," *NASSP Bulletin* 78, no. 559 (1994): 66–70. See also Cleta Galvez-Hjornevik, "Mentoring among Teachers: A Review of the Literature," *Journal of Teacher Education* 37, no. 1 (1986): 10; Krupp, "Teachers Become Staff Developers," p. 13; Judith C. Neal, "Mentoring: A Teacher Development Activity that Avoids Formal Evaluation of the Protégé," in *Mentoring: Contemporary Principles*, pp. 40–41.

60. Sandra J. Odell and Douglas P. Ferraro, "Collaborative Teacher Induction," p. 69.

staff involved in the mentoring process than the public school typically do.[61]

Nathalie Gehrke and Beverlie Hardcastle have both argued for a more spiritual dimension to mentorship, which could have positive benefits for the overall educational culture.[62] They strongly suggest that mentoring programs promote respect for the intricacies of the interpersonal relationships involved in mentorship. The deliberative fostering of the spiritual dimension of mentorship supports the notion of mentorship as aiding in the personal and professional development of participants and of enhancing the overall educational environment. If mentorship is used for the initiation of new religious educators, it is imperative that attention be given to its spiritual dimension because a purely functional and utilitarian focus to mentorship is not consistent with the professional ideals of religious educators. Mentoring programs for religious educators should include spiritual development opportunities such as reflection time and group rituals for all those involved to enable them to deepen their own relationships with God and one another.

RELEVANCE OF MENTORSHIP FOR TODAY

The existing empirical research on formalized mentoring programs, as summarized in this chapter, seems to hold out hope and inspiration for the reclaiming of the ancient concept and practice of mentorship. In the next chapter I will begin this process of reclaiming in order to assist religious educators to reach higher levels of fulfillment in their often complex professional tasks. In summary, there is reason to believe that structured mentoring initiatives can assist the religious education mentors, the mentees, and the church. This mentoring process will become increasingly essential if religious educators are to be fully

---

61. Susan F. Schulz theorizes that mentorship enriches society at large, not just the workplace. She suggests that mentorship promotes lifelong learning and self-direction, both of which enhance a society's overall quality of life. See her "The Benefits of Mentoring," in *Mentoring: New Strategies*, pp. 64–66.

62. Nathalie Gehrke says that mentorship needs to "be seen as a gift exchange phenomenon." See "Toward a Definition of Mentoring," p. 194; Beverly Hardcastle describes mentorship as "an endangered species that calls for our recognition, appreciation, and encouragement." See "Spiritual Connections," p. 208.

included in church life. This book is intended to assist the community of religious educators to find innovative ways of inducting new professionals, strengthening seasoned educators, and renewing the overall environment in which they function. In the first half of this text, chapters 1–4, I provide the religious and educational foundations for mentorship. In chapters 5–10 I offer specific suggestions on how a mentoring process can successfully be put in place and effectively monitored.

2

Mentors from the Religious Tradition

Abba, tell me a word so that I may be saved.
—André Louf[1]

The Christian tradition contains many examples of mentoring. Among the most interesting are the mentoring relationship between the *abbas/ammas* and their disciples in the Egyptian desert in the fourth century; the medieval mystics at Helfta, Germany, in the thirteenth century; and the reformers associated with Teresa of Avila (1515–1582) in the sixteenth century. In this chapter I will explore the mentoring in each of these historical cases, showing how religious mentoring in former times can illumine the mentoring of religious educators today.[2]

---

1. André Louf, "Spiritual Fatherhood in the Literature of the Desert," in *Abba: Guides to Wholeness and Holiness East and West*, ed. John R. Sommerfeldt, Cistercian Studies Series, no. 38 (Kalamazoo, Mich.: Cistercian Publications, 1982), p. 37. In the context of desert literature, the terms *abba* and *amma* literally mean "father" and "mother." They refer to the wiser, older individuals who inducted the younger disciples into the desert way of life. In many ways this parental imagery is misleading, since the elders did not assume total responsibility for the disciples. Rather, they were religious educators and counselors for the disciples, all functions identified as part of the mentoring role. (See chapter 1 for a fuller discussion of the functions of mentor.) The connection between the elder and the disciple stemmed from the expertise of the older, wiser monk and not necessarily from any emotional bond. In this text, elder will be used interchangeably with *abba* and *amma*. My usage is consistent with Louf's. See his discussion, pp. 37–38.

2. Consistent with the literature I use the term "mentor" interchangeably with "spiritual director." See Philip Rousseau's use in *Ascetics, Authority, and the Church in the Age of Jerome and Cassian* (Oxford: Oxford University Press, 1978), p. 36; and Edward Sellner's use in *The Ministry of Spiritual Kinship* (Notre Dame, Ind.: Ave Maria, 1990), pp. 9–13.

Renewed interest in spirituality since the mid-1970s has produced a voluminous literature on desert spirituality as well as on other spiritual traditions.[3] Interest is heightened by the fact that little or no attention has been given to precisely how historical figures such as Teresa of Avila were spiritual mentors, and what contemporary religious educators might learn from their example. Furthermore, the record of these mentors from the desert, mystical, and reforming traditions of the Christian past provides thick and rich description of Christian mentoring that is not found in the general education literature. This Christian mentoring is unique in its source and sustenance: mentors and mentees have a sense of religious vocation and are personally sustained by their own religious beliefs. Because this same source and sustenance applies to religious educators today, an examination of the historical characteristics of Christian mentoring will provide useful information for initiating a mentoring process for these religious educators.

Each historical example highlights different functions of the mentor: teacher, sponsor, encourager, counselor, and befriender. Though the presence of all functions in a mentor is desirable, different situations elicit the use of different functions. Where it makes sense to do so, I use the specific function to denote the action of the person who is mentoring. For instance, when one of Teresa of Avila's spiritual mentors encourages her mystical life I often use the word "encourage," not "mentor," since encourage is the specific mentoring function being employed.

MENTORING AMONG THE DESERT DWELLERS

The relationship that existed between the desert elder and the disciple in the Christian East in the fourth century highlights all the key mentoring functions. In the monastic life of the deserts of Egypt, all monks were required to have elders or directors to provide them with spiritual direction for the duration of their lives. Irenée Hausherr points out that this

---

3. Theologian Sandra Schneiders notes that when she began teaching a course on spiritual direction in 1976, she found some articles but very few books on the topic in English. However, within five years a volume of literature had been produced. "Horizons on Spiritual Direction," *Horizons* 11, no. 1 (1984):100. For a sample of the voluminous literature that has been made available by Roman Catholic and Protestant scholars, see any of the following texts: William A. Barry and William J. Connolly, *The Practice of Spiritual Direction* (New York: Seabury, 1982); Richard J. Foster,

direction must be viewed in a broad sense: in the East, spiritual guidance was guidance in a whole way of life.[4] The mentoring given and received focused as much on everyday affairs as it did on spiritual matters. The applicability of the desert elder/disciple relationship to current religious educators increases as knowledge of the breadth of the concern of desert mentoring grows. Religious education mentors are as likely to advise their mentees regarding curriculum administration as they are regarding their prayer lives.

Using the Word to Provide Mentorship

It is possible to extract a profile of the mentoring relationships in the desert from the various editions of *The Apophthegmata Patrum*, or sayings of the desert dwellers.[5] These collections of pithy sayings indicate that at the heart of the relationship was the "word" of wisdom that the *abbas/ammas* adapted to meet the needs of individual disciples.[6] The response to the request "Speak to me father that I might live" was the

---

Celebration of Discipline: The path to Spiritual Growth (San Francisco: HarperSan-Francisco, 1978); Alan W. Jones, *Soul-Making: The Desert Way of Spirituality* (San Francisco: Harper & Row, 1989); Frank C. Senn, ed., *Protestant Spiritual Traditions* (N.Y.: Paulist, 1986); Kevin Wall, "Spiritual Direction," in *Spiritual Direction: Contemporary Readings*, ed. Kevin Culligan (Locust Valley, N.Y.: Living Flame, 1983), pp. 11–17.

4. Irénée Hausherr, *Spiritual Direction in the Early Christian East*, trans. Anthony Gythiel, Cistercian Studies Series, no. 116 (Kalamazoo, Mich.: Cistercian Publications, 1990), pp. 4–5. Though the translation is sometimes difficult to understand, Hausherr's text gives an in-depth look at the role of spiritual direction in the East.

5. Two very readable collections of the sayings are Benedicta B. Ward, trans. *The Sayings of the Desert Fathers: The Alphabetical Collection*, Cistercian Studies Series, no. 59 (London: Mowbrays, 1975); Benedicta Ward, trans., *The Wisdom of the Desert Fathers: The 'Apophthegmata Patrum'* (The Anonymous Series) (Oxford: SLG, 1975). The alphabetical collection lists the sayings by the name of the speaker to whom it is attributed. The anonymous series lists the sayings in thematic groupings such as "humility" and "charity." All quotations will be from these two collections and reference will be made to alphabetical (alph.) or anonymous (anon.) collections, speaker name, and paragraph number.

6. Fifth-century bishop and historian Palladius records that "there was also a monastery of some four hundred women" in the desert, yet only three of the sayings in the alphabetic collection are attributed to women. *Palladius: The Lausiac History*, trans. Robert T. Meyer, Ancient Christian Writers, no. 34 (Westminster, Md.: Newman, 1964), p. 95. Meanwhile, nineteen of the sixty-eight sayings in the Syriac version of the sayings, *The Paradise of the Fathers,* represent women. The Syriac version

brief word of wisdom or Scripture, which was not to be discussed further; it became effective in the lives of the hearers if they were willing
to discern its meaning for their own lives.[7] Knowledge of how the
desert mentees personally integrated the elders' advice and counsel into
their own lives can inform the mentoring of current religious educators,
especially those who need assistance in framing questions about their
profession.[8] Consider the case of a first year religious educator who
wants to know precisely how to teach a second-grade Sunday school
class. Although the mentor may have specific suggestions, the mentee
has to decide how these suggestions fit a particular class.

Though not educated in a traditional sense, these *abbas/
ammas* enjoyed a reputation for wisdom and for using this wisdom to
mentor others. A foundational source of spirituality and holiness resulted from the efforts of the early monks to reflect on Scripture and
the word and to integrate this reflection into their lives.[9] Of highest
importance to the desert dwellers was obeying the commands of the
Scriptures, thereby deepening their prayer life and subsequently their
skill in discernment, necessary for giving and receiving advice. Also
important in the elder/disciple interchange was the responsibility of
the elders to provide positive example or serve as role models to their
followers.[10] For example, Psenthaisios, one of the monks recorded in

has been translated by Wallis Ernest A. Budge as *The Paradise, or, Garden of the
Holy Fathers Being Histories of the Anchorites Recluses Monks Cenobites and Ascetic Fathers of the Deserts of Egypt*, 2 vols. (New York: Duffield, 1909).

7. Benedicta B. Ward, "Spiritual Direction in the Desert Fathers," in *Traditions of
Spiritual Guidance*, ed. Lavinia Byrne (Collegeville, Minn.: Liturgical, 1990), p. 9.

8. Though brief, the word became personally so important to the hearer that one of
the elders, *Abba* Ammoe, is reported to have refused permission for his disciples to
walk with him "for fear that, after edifying words, irrelevant conversation should slip
in." Alph., Ammoe, 1. The hearer is encouraged to value the word and contemplate
how it might be applied to daily life.

9. For an extensive discussion of the importance of the word and the Scripture in
the desert, see Douglas Burton-Christie, *The Word in the Desert: Scripture and the
Quest for Holiness in Early Christian Monasticism* (New York: Oxford University
Press, 1993), pp. 112–29. See also Douglas Burton-Christie, "'Practice Makes Perfect'": Interpretation of Scripture in the *Apophthegmata Patrum*," *Studia Patristica,
XX, Papers Presented at the Tenth International Conference on Patristic Studies Held
in Oxford 1987*, ed. Elizabeth Livingstone (Leeuven: Peeters, 1989), pp. 213–18.

10. Positive role-modeling became more important as eremitical monasticism developed a communal dimension. Yet one of the paradoxes of the eremitical life was
that it too had a communal dimension and would have valued positive role-modeling

The Apophthegmata, remembers that his *abba*, Pachomius, "taught us by his actions. We were amazed by him."[11] In any era, this positive role modeling is an important characteristic. An effective mentor is one whose personal and professional role modeling of Christian lifestyle and effective teaching are evident. This role-modeling aspect is important in that the mentor ought to be seen as worthy of mentoring a mentee. It should be evident to a congregation, for instance, that the person chosen to be a mentor to a new religious educator is indeed a competent teacher who is capable of initiating another person into the profession. The active support of the congregation, required for the development of a mentoring environment, will be difficult to elicit if the mentor is not seen as credible.

Supplementary to the mentoring given by word and by example of individual elders was the discipline or structure provided by the community rule (the codified set of guidelines required for community members and the leadership of the *hegemon,* or community leader).[12] Both the leader and the rule or code of behavior for the community provided structure for desert monasticism and encouraged the interdependence and cooperation of the monks. Structural discipline is important in that it facilitates the accomplishment of desired educational goals. A mentee entering into a situation in which there is no established religious education curriculum, no dependable schedules for classes, and few dependable volunteers will have great difficulty in becoming oriented. Instead of concentrating on induction to the field of religious education, the mentor will likely spend the first three

---

from the elders. It was difficult to escape people in the desert because th emonks were host to scores of curious onlookers from the West. For further discussion, see Andrew Hamilton, "Spiritual Direction in the Apophthegmata," *Colloquium* [Australian and New Zealand Theological Review] 15, no. 2 (1983): 31. The hermit Anthony's description of the desert as a city is evidence that the monastic life was often crowded. For further reading about Anthony, see Athanasius, *The Life of Anthony and the Letter to Marcellinus*, trans. R. C. Gregg (New York: Paulist, 1980), pp. 42–43.

11. Alph., Psenthaisios 1.

12. For a variety of discussions on leadership in desert communities, see Philip Rousseau, *Pachomius: The Making of a Community in Fourth Century Egypt*. Transformation of the Classical Heritage Series, no. 6 (Berkeley: University of California Press, 1985), p. 106; Stephen Peter Tsichlis, "The Spiritual Father in the Pachomian Tradition," *Diakonia* 18, no. 1 (1983): 19; Armand Veilleux, "Pachomian Community," in *The Continuing Quest for God: Monastic Spirituality in Tradition and Transition*, ed. William Skudlarek (Collegeville, Minn.: Liturgical, 1982), pp. 51–60.

months trying to explain the unwritten rules and the general understandings of religious education that are operative in that situation. A
degree of order and discipline is essential for the effectiveness of any
mentoring process.

The Qualifications of the Desert Mentors

When choosing an *abba/amma*, the desert disciple recognized several
key attributes of the mentor. First, there was a belief that the elders
were part of a long spiritual lineage of holy men and women. The elders' behavior, therefore, was to be consistent with those holy ones
who went before; indeed, the elder had to be a disciple of such men
and women. The characteristic of holiness was particularly important,
since it affirmed the role of the elder in handing on and preserving tradition.[13] This acknowledgment of having learned from the learned
is particularly important in a religious education context because
the profession demands that the educator know and be able to communicate the acquired knowledge, affect, and lifestyle of the religious
tradition.

Second, the father/mother must also be a doer, a person of deeds as
well as words. This characteristic of holiness is integral to desert spirituality, since labor and prayer are seen as one.[14] According to the
monks' belief system, knowing the word itself is not enough, and anyone who tries to teach without having worked hard will be ineffective.
Abba Arsenius, another of the monks recorded in the *Apophthegmata*,
commends those disciples who "acquire the virtues by hard work."[15]
Similarly, religious educators need mentors who have considerable
experience in educating others. Any legitimate support process for religious educators, such as mentorship, requires experienced professionals who know sound instructional methodologies. Otherwise mentorship becomes a co-equal relationship in which both mentor and
mentee receive emotional support but neither learns. Consequently,
the mentee is not initiated properly.

Third, the *abbas/ammas* must be spiritually discerning.[16] They
must have the wisdom and insight to give the disciple the word that

---

13. Rousseau, *Ascetics, Authority, and the Church*, pp. 23–24.
14. Ibid., pp. 25–26.
15. Alph., Arsenius 5.
16. Rousseau, *Ascetics, Authority, and the Church*, pp. 26–27.

will be most helpful. This gift of right judgment is very important for a mentor because of the potential effect of bad advice on the mentee. The mentee needs to feel confident that the mentor is a person of sound judgment who tries to impart sage advice to the mentee and will be deliberate and careful in dealing with the mentee. Finally, the *abbas/ammas* must have a special relationship with God.[17] In any era the development of a strong spiritual life among mentors and mentees should be fostered by the church. Religious education mentors need to be especially attentive to God's presence in their lives if they are to serve as role models.

Mentoring in any era requires cultivation of particular spiritual qualities before one can mentor others. Though rigorous adherence to a monastic lifestyle probably will not be required of most religious education mentors today, it is reasonable to expect that religious educators meet four basic requirements: passing on their acquired religious knowledge, being actively involved in the practice of religious education, developing discernment abilities, and enjoying a personal relationship with God.

Responsibilities of Mentor and Mentee in the Desert

One of the first responsibilities of the desert elder was consenting to mentor the disciple, even if the elder was hesitant.[18] Often the disciples, when choosing the elders as mentors, recognized something in them that the elders could not perceive. One of the elders, Sisoes, is reported to have been too humble to speak when addressed, yet he was chosen as an elder.[19] Having accepted the responsibility, whether willingly or unwillingly, the elder then took on the mentoring role wholeheartedly. One of the crucial tasks of the *abba/amma* was to assist the disciples to carry their burdens by listening to them and counseling them.[20] Finally, the elders were asked to love the disciples, no matter how difficult that might be.[21] Although the intensity of this mentoring relationship likely will not be replicated today, the basic tenets of

---

17. Ibid., pp. 27–29.
18. Hausherr, *Spiritual Direction*, p. 124.
19. Alph., Sisoes 16.
20. Hausherr, *Spiritual Direction*, p. 141.
21. Ibid., p. 148.

commitment and ongoing concern of the mentor for the mentee need to be. A religious education mentor must have respect and concern for the mentee.

In turn, the desert disciples had certain key responsibilities, beginning with seeking out compatible spiritual guides. In some cases such a search constituted a formidable task and was complicated by the fact that once the disciples found guides, they were expected to remain faithful to them for life.[22] Furthermore, the desert disciples were expected to display openness of heart by disclosing their thoughts to the director. *Abba* Anthony says, "A monk ought to tell his elders confidently how many steps he takes and how many drops of water he drinks in his cell, in case he is in error about it."[23] The final responsibility of the disciple is to love the father unconditionally.[24] This obligation requires that a religious education mentor be a person who can be trusted. It also points to the need to set boundaries at the beginning of the relationship as to the amount of personal mentoring, as contrasted to professional mentoring, that the mentor can assume. A mentor who spends a disproportionate amount of time counseling the mentee on personal, nonwork-related issues has lost the focus of the relationship, namely, religious education. As in the desert, it is challenging today to identify religious education mentors. Nonetheless, with the proper supports such as a process of negotiation and discernment, effective selection of mentors can be achieved.

Observations on Desert Mentorship

Meeting the list of requirements for a desert elder or disciple was undoubtedly a Herculean feat even for the holiest of persons. The nature of the spiritual direction relationship was neither parental nor coequal, yet it bonded the partners together for life. The key to the success of the mentoring process was that the mentor and the mentee worked diligently to integrate spirituality into daily life. Similarly, today's religious education mentor and mentee need to work conscientiously at integrating their spirituality and work so that these are intricately connected. Though there are obvious difficulties with extracting directly from the desert context to mentoring, many other concepts of the

---

22. Ibid., pp. 192–93.
23. Alph., Anthony 38.
24. Hausherr, *Spiritual Direction*, pp. 208–9.

desert experience are relevant today. The quality of discernment, in particular, is integral to the mentorship role because it asks the mentor and mentee to reflect on how God is active in their lives and how they can best respond to this call from God in different situations. Furthermore, the importance attached to having an elder or mentor is significant for every era. The desert monks understood that mentorship was vital if proper induction and ongoing support for desert monasticism was to continue. Moreover, the desert elders tried to be exemplary role models for their disciples, a concept integral to effective mentoring. Finally, the one-to-one interaction is important as a model for how mentoring might occur. These are important lessons for religious education in any era.

Instructive too in this desert scenario is the connectedness, along with the separate identity, that each member of the mentoring dyad managed to maintain. The goal of mentoring in the desert was not to make the mentees replicas of the mentor. Individuality was stressed, with each disciple receiving advice that was different from the next, depending on specific personalities and the needs the *abba* detected. The challenge for the mentor today is the same: to assist the religious education mentee in developing his or her full potential as an educator.

MENTORING AMONG THE MEDIEVAL MYSTICS

Another sterling example of mentoring in the religious tradition is found in the lives of the female mystics who lived in a cloistered convent at Helfta in Saxony, Germany, in the thirteenth century.[25] The lives of these women highlight the fivefold key mentoring functions: befriender, counselor, encourager, sponsor, and teacher.

---

25. In describing the Helfta community, Valerie Lagorio writes that "strong Dominican influence, joined with the older Benedictine, Cistercian, and Bernardian spirituality, prevailed at the convent of Helfta." See "The Medieval Continental Women Mystics: An Introduction," in *An Introduction to the Medieval Mystics of Europe*, ed. Paul E. Szarmach (Albany, N.Y.: State University of New York Press, 1984), p. 167. Other scholars have debated whether Helfta was primarily Benedictine or Cistercian in character. For a more thorough discussion, see Caroline Walker Bynum, *Jesus as Mother: Studies in the Spirituality of the High Middle Ages* (Berkeley: University of California Press, 1982), pp. 174–75 n. 13.

A hallmark of this religious community was the mentorship given and received among the nuns and those whom they encountered. This mentoring process was characterized by the active support that the women gave each other, the confirmation they received from the people inside and outside the cloister with whom they interacted, and the encouragement and assistance they gave each other to make a written record of their mystical experiences. The community's three best-known mystics are Gertrude of Helfta (1256–1301/2), Mechtild of Magdeburg (1207?–1282), and Mechtild of Hackeborn (1241/42–1298).[26] A fourth woman, Gertude of Hackeborn (1251–1291),[27] abbess of the cloister, will also be discussed here because of her strong mentoring role in the life of the monastery. The mystics' writings provided witness for the whole Helfta community and gave them the assurance that subsequent generations of laity and religious would benefit from them.[28] As each nun is discussed, I will offer suggestions for how their mentoring has relevance for religious educators today.

The Mentoring Environment Created by Gertrude of Hackeborn

The abbess Gertrude of Hackeborn, sister of Mechtild of Hackeborn, while not a visionary herself, was a strong influence on all three

---

26. I will deal with these women in the same order in which they joined the community at Helfta. Thus Mechtild of Magdeburg, though the oldest chronologically, will be discussed last.

27. These dates for Gertrude of Hackeborn seem to represent the time during which she was abbess. Other dates have not been recorded.

28. Gertrude of Helfta, *The Herald of Divine Love*, trans. Margaret Winkworth (New York: Paulist, 1993); Gertrud the Great of Helfta, *Spiritual Exercises*, trans. Gertrud Jaron Lewis and Jack Lewis, Cistercian Fathers' Series, no. 49 (Kalamazoo, Mich.: Cistercian Publications, 1989) [for consistency, "Gertrude" will be used as the spelling in the text; the spelling in the notes will reflect that used in the particular book or translation being referred to]; Mechtild of Magdeburg, *Flowing Light of the Divinity*, trans. Christiane Mesch Galvani. Garland Library of Medieval Literature, no. 72, Series B (New York: Garland, 1991); Mechtild of Hackeborn, *The Booke of Gostlye Grace,* ed. Theresa A. Halligan, Studies and Texts, no. 46 (Toronto: Pontifical Institute of Mediaeval Studies, 1979, microfiche). All quotations are from the English translations of the mystics' original writings, except *The Booke of Gostlye Grace*, which is available only in Middle English. All references are to the editions given in this paragraph, unless otherwise noted. Each work will be referred to by book, chapter, and page number, and, where applicable, line number.

mystics during her forty-year tenure as abbess of Helfta.[29] Under Gertrude's mentorship the monastery flourished and became known as a center of mysticism and learning. Gertrude created a mentoring environment that nurtured the creative spirit in the nuns and also promoted teaching and mentoring. One of the most significant ways in which Gertrude provided a mentoring environment was through her support of education for the nuns. This education combined studies in the liberal arts and Scripture. Extensive quotations from Scripture, as well as a working knowledge of the writings of theologians such as Thomas Aquinas (1225–1274), in the mystics' writings attest to the thoroughness of the education system at this monastery.[30] The nuns operated a school to educate their own novices, a school that also drew students and visitors from the neighboring area.[31] This educational initiative gave the mystics the skills required to record their experiences of mysticism for other nuns and for future members of their religious community. The extensive education they received also gave them exposure to theological ideas that informed their writings and their communication with those outside the cloister whom they mentored. Likewise, high standards of professional preparation for religious education need to be required of religious educators. Mentorship itself is not meant to replace standard occupational requirements. Its function is to build on the mentee's acquired knowledge and skills in order to initiate the mentee into the profession.

Under Gertrude's leadership, the cloister environment itself provided a positive mentoring influence on the life and work of each of the three women mystics. Likewise, in the desert example, the leadership and example of the *hegemon*, or community leader, was a strong contributor to a mentoring environment that valued mysticism and writing. Both the desert and the Helfta examples highlight the fact that for mentoring to be successful for religious educators the entire

---

29. See Elizabeth Alvilda Petroff, *Medieval Women's Visionary Literature* (New York: Oxford University Press, 1986), p. 208.

30. See, for example, Gertrude of Helfta's extensive references to the Song of Songs, Hebrews, and Job, in *Herald of Divine Love* 3. 7. 160–61.

31. Sr. Mary Jeremy Finnegan, *The Women of Helfta: Scholars and* Mystics, 2d ed. (Athens: University of Georgia Press, 1991), p. x. Because girls were sometimes entrusted by their parents to the Helfta monastery at a very young age, Helfta needed to provide education for them. This monastery school was distinct from the novitiate, which was the official system of initiation for those who would profess vows to God.

environment as a whole and in each of its parts has to provide support. Furthermore, a certain amount of spiritual discipline and structure can facilitate the mentoring relationship. Though the structure of vowed life is not necessary for most present religious educators, the concept of organization and formal mentorship can be insightful. When church leaders ensure that religious educators are mentored and that both the mentee and mentor know their roles and responsibilities, the benefits of organization are evident. Church leaders need to be involved and to support mentoring by providing time for mentors and mentees to study, provide feedback on mentee performance, and work on their communication skills, all important aspects of effective mentoring.

Mechtild of Hackeborn as Mentor

The first mystic to be considered here is Mechtild of Hackeborn, sister of the abbess Gertrude, who came to live at the monastery at the age of seven and who remained there for the duration of her life.[32] Mechtild assisted her sister Gertrude with the various administrative and managerial tasks that required attention, though she herself never actually held any official administrative post such as abbess. Like all the cloistered nuns she was assigned responsible tasks in the convent, one of which was serving as director of the choir, a position to which she was especially suited because of her singing abilities.[33] Mechtild's duties also included teaching in the Helfta school and serving as director of novices. *The Booke of Gostlye Grace,* an account of her life and mystical experiences, records the many instances of counseling and direction she gave to different nuns and to a variety of people who visited Helfta for advice. These tasks are significant because they often placed Mechtild in situations where she could be a mentor to others as a regular part of her life. Similarly, current religious education mentors need to be physically close to their mentees, not in distant locations, so that the mentee can have reasonable personal access to the mentor.

---

32. Albrecht Classen, "Mechtild von Hackeborn," in *An Encyclopedia of Continental Women Writers*, ed. Katharina Wilson (New York: Garland, 1991), 1: 518.

33. Mechtild was so gifted musically that she was called "nightingale of the Lord." Theresa A. Halligan, introduction to Mechtild of Hackeborn, *The Booke of Gostlye Grace of Mechtild of Hackeborn*, ed. Theresa Halligan, Studies and Texts, no. 46 (Toronto: Pontifical Institute of Mediaeval Studies, 1979), p. 36 n.16.

Mechtild's writings show a strong emphasis on the responsibility of mentoring other individuals, especially in providing counseling for them. Mechtild believed that mentorship directly fulfilled the law of Christ in her life, a concern of paramount importance to her.[34] In fulfilling the role of mentor, Mechtild engaged in spiritual direction, offered advice, and consoled people who needed forgiveness.[35] She had strong discerning abilities that enabled her to know how to mentor the people who needed her assistance. One of the nuns with whom she shared a special mentoring relationship was the mystic Gertrude of Helfta, who held Mechtild in such regard that she is largely assumed to be the person responsible for actually writing Mechtild's book.[36]

In describing the precise nature of Mechtild's character, Caroline Walker Bynum points out that Mechtild was accessible to a wide variety of persons, including clergy, religious and laity, and that she became a "'bridge,' a 'door,' a mediator," for these people.[37] Book 4 of Mechtild's *Gostlye Grace* gives a perspective on the variety of individuals whom she mentored. Mechtild prays for the novices,[38] for a certain person who does not love God enough,[39] and an unnamed person struggling to discern her religious vocation.[40]

---

34. Hackeborn, *The Booke of Gostlye Grace* 3. 39. 487–89.

35. *The Booke of Gostlye Grace* records, "Howe owre lorde forgaffe a mane his synnes for whom sche prayede, " [How our lord forgave a man his sins, for whom she prayed]. Ibid., 4. 15. 519, lines 9–10.

36. Valerie Lagorio, "The Medieval Continental Women Mystics," in *Introduction to the Medieval Mystics*, p. 167.

37. Caroline Walker Bynum, *Jesus as Mother*, p. 211.

38. Mechtild writes, "In a tyme this maydene prayede . . . for zonge novycis" [In a time this maiden prayed for young novices], *Booke of Gostlye Grace*, 4. 7. 504, lines 16–17.

39. *The Booke of Gostlye Grace* records, "In a tyme this holye maydene prayede for a certayne persone whiche hadde grete mowrnygne in herte for sche cowth nozt luffe here God als sche schulde" [In a time this holy maiden prayed for a certain person which had great mourning in her heart for she could not love her God all she should]. Ibid., 4. 10. 510, lines 16–18.

40. *The Booke of Gostlye Grace* records, "Howre owre lorde aunswerde thys maydene when sche prayede for a persone whiche desyrede to knowe whate owre lorde desyrede moste of here" [How our Lord answered this maiden when she prayed for a person which desired to know what our Lord desired most of her]. Ibid., 4. 17. 523, lines 17–19.

In addition to seeing people in person, Mechtild also wrote letters to them and in this way provided mentorship.[41] It is obvious is that people recognized Mechtild's gift of discernment and relied on her for assistance. It is not surprising, therefore, that Mechtild's duties included directing novices. Her mentoring gifts were put to excellent use in the initiation of younger nuns. The overwhelming impression one gets from her *Booke of Gostlye Grace* is of a deeply spiritual person who mentors others and is spiritually enriched by the process. The rich evidence of the mentoring functions of befriending and counseling in Mechtild's life is instructive for any era. It shows religious educators how she was able to befriend and counsel others, functions that are also significant today. Mechtild's ability to receive mentoring as well as provide it is instructive for religious educators who may be prone to neglecting their own well-being. Mechtild's belief that she mentored others because mentoring was her responsibility is also important for religious education mentors. Mentorship is a necessity. Thus, it is reasonable to ask those who have engaged in the important work of religious education if they would consider inducting mentees into the profession. Certainly Mechtild's example of commitment to her life work is instructive for religious educators in any era.

Gertrude of Helfta as Mentor

Gertrude of Helfta, or Gertrude the Great, is often confused with Gertrude of Hackeborn, abbess and sister of Mechtild of Hackeborn.[42] According to Gertrude of Helfta's text, *The Herald of Divine Love,* Gertrude came to live at the Helfta monastery at the age of four and remained there for the rest of her life.[43] Similar to the two other mystics, Gertrude held no official administrative positions at Helfta but was generally acknowledged as having a significant role in providing spiritual advice to many mentees. Like Mechtild of Hackeborn, she makes it clear in her writing that she mentors others as a way of fulfilling her Christian commitment as a nun. Gertrude's special vocation

---

41. *The Booke of Gostlye Grace* records, "Howe this maydene sentte anothere tyme a lettere to the same womane" [How this maiden sent another time a letter to the same woman]. Ibid., 4. 35. 545, lines 13–14.

42. Gertrude is likely called "the Great" because of the depth and insight of her writings.

43. Helfta, *Herald of Divine Love* 1. 1. 52.

in mentoring other nuns is clearly evident in the role she plays in recording Mechtild of Hackeborn's revelations. In both of Gertrude's texts, *The Herald of Divine Love* and *Spiritual Exercises*, there is evidence that she has great concern for particular members of the community, even to the point of writing for them a set of spiritual exercises, namely, instructions on a life of prayer. Gertrude listened to the other nuns' troubles and filled the mentor function of counseling them, inspired by the advice she received in her mystical experiences.

Mainly because Book 1 of *The Herald of Divine Love* was written by someone other than Gertrude, we are privy to many personal details of her life that she likely would not have provided in a direct fashion. For instance, the opening chapter of *The Herald of Divine Love* points out that "she was admired by all who heard her."[44] This recognition of her special qualities is particularly evident in the number and variety of individuals who sought her out for mentorship. *The Herald of Divine Love* also discusses some of the salient characteristics of her mentees: "someone who was filled with ardent desire,"[45] someone needing to regulate his lifestyle,[46] and an illiterate person too busy to spend time in prayer.[47] The diversity of persons from inside and outside the cloister who sought Gertrude's mentorship makes it clear that she was well known for her wisdom, for her availability to laity and clergy alike, and for the concern she had for her mentees. Adhering to the Helfta lifestyle of hard work and prayer, Gertrude became involved in the religious education of the nuns, translating the Scriptures and going outside Helfta to mentor people. Though writing for the religious community members consumed much of her time, she saw these other ministries as consistent with her life vows and spirituality. It was her responsibility to provide mentorship to those who needed it. One of the insights from Gertrude's writing is that she could be a very direct mentor, cutting to the heart of the matter in a way that was less gentle than the other mentors at Helfta. This directness enhanced rather than detracted from her mentoring capacity.

---

44. Ibid., 1. 1. 52.

45. Ibid., 3. 74. 236.

46. Ibid., 3. 74. 238–39.

47. "Gertrude had pitied her [this illiterate individual], seeing her perplexed and troubled because she felt she was prevented from praying by the various duties she had to perform." Ibid., 3. 74. 242.

Commenting on the forthrightness of Gertrude's speech, the writer of *The Herald of Divine Love* reports that although Gertrude's words were sharp, they consoled many individuals from outside the cloister because they addressed problems directly and provided encouragement to the listener.[48] Religious education mentors who are not direct and honest about their mentees' teaching strengths and weaknesses will be of little long term value to the mentoring process. The profession requires teaching excellence and expects its members to support one another in upholding this standard. Collaboration is essential to the ongoing development of the religious education profession because it promotes the creative exchange of ideas and fosters the growth of all individuals, including learners.

Gertrude herself received mentoring, most notably from Mechtild of Hackeborn. In one particular instance, Gertrude sought Mechtild's advice because she was feeling a sense of worthlessness about her own self.[49] She felt confident that Mechtild would provide her with encouragement and affirmation of her faith life. A similar incident occurred when Gertrude had to consult with another person (this time unnamed, but possibly Mechtild) and ask her for prayers.[50] Gertrude recognized the need to seek mentorship and the wisdom of seeking this mentorship from other members of the community. In matters that concerned her personally, she was willing to consult others, listen to their opinions, and follow the advice they offered.[51] The mentoring relationships in Gertrude's life went beyond the usual one-on-one mentoring model and encompassed mentoring by numerous individuals and by the community as a whole. This lesson is very important for mentors because one person often cannot be expected to fill all the mentoring functions. Religious education mentees would be wise to

---

48. "It was the living efficacious word—more penetrating than any two-edged sword, reaching the very division between soul and spirit." Ibid. 1. 1. 54.

49. "When she [Gertrude] reflected on her wretched and worthless state . . . She went to Dame Mechtild of happy memory . . . . She humbly begged her to ask the Lord about the gifts mentioned . . . because she wanted to arouse in herself a greater sense of gratitude." Ibid., 1. 16. 82.

50. Gertrude asks the person to "undertake to say for me each day during her prayers before the crucifix these words: 'By your wounded heart, most loving Lord, pierce her heart with the arrow of your love.'" Ibid., 2. 5. 101–2.

51. "With humble discretion she sought the opinion of others . . . and listened to them with deference." Ibid., 1. 11. 74.

realize that they frequently need more than one mentor in the course of their work lives. At different points and with different professional needs religious educators may have to seek out new mentors or a variety of mentors.

Gertrude's mentorship went beyond face-to-face contact with her mentees. She saw herself as responsible for other significant influences in her mentees' lives, even to the point of translating Scripture from Latin to German in order for them to understand it.[52] Obviously she did not want her mentees to miss the educational and spiritual development opportunities she herself had. In addition, she sent letters to distressed persons,[53] and wrote a set of spiritual exercises identifying a concrete model of how to pursue the spiritual life. The spiritual exercises ensured that every nun had access to Gertrude's method and that the spiritual mentorship developed at Helfta would continue down through the ages. Yet Gertrude understood that she was most effective in mentoring mentees face to face. Many aspects of a religious education environment provide mentorship. Mentors not only mentor by their interpersonal communication but in the ways they contribute to the profession, sometimes by writing and at other times by providing leadership in professional associations. An abiding concern for the continuance of the profession itself can be very a strong mentoring influence in the lives of all religious educators. Along with person-to-person mentoring, such supplementary mentoring initiatives can help build a mentoring environment to support the mentoring process.

Finally, Gertrude's mentoring of males is a example of how cross-gender mentoring can be effective. The mentee's needs, not the mentee's gender, is the issue for Gertrude when she is asked for assistance. Similarly, mentors and mentees in religious education need to look beyond gender and age and focus on how the needs of the mentees can best be met. This is especially relevant for religious educators because they probably will not have a wide choice of mentors and will have to look beyond personal preferences in mentoring to the real issue of quality in the mentor.

---

52. "When she found in Holy Scripture certain passages which she thought would be of use . . . she would translate them into simpler language." Ibid., 1. 7. 64.

53. A record of Gertrude's letter writing is contained in *Herald of Divine Love* 1. 8. 66.

Mechtild of Magdeburg as Mentor

The third mystic, Mechtild of Magdeburg, is known mainly through her own account of her life and mystical experiences in *Flowing Light of the Divinity*. Unlike the other two Helfta mystics, Gertude of Helfta and Mechtild of Hackeborn, Mechtild of Magdeburg did not come to live at Helfta until old age. At the age of twenty-three she went to Magdeburg to become a Beguine, one of a group of laywomen who were structured in a loose form of community, never professing vows or following any systematic set of rules.[54] The efforts of the Beguines to care for the underprivileged people in society undoubtedly gave Mechtild adequate preparation for the life of service and counseling at Helfta, and it greatly influenced her mentoring contributions to the Helfta cloister.[55]

Mechtild came to live at Helfta when she was in her mid-sixties, quite probably in the midst of controversy and accusations that she was a heretic, a charge that the hierarchical church frequency leveled at the Beguines. Having spent most of her adult life outside a formal religious community, Mechtild did not write about her life and experiences at Helfta, nor on herself as a member of any community, even when she lived at Helfta. Rather, she focused a great deal of her attention and her writing on the world outside the cloister. For instance, in *The Flowing Light* she discusses married people, presumably those she knew and mentored before her time at Helfta.[56] Researcher Elizabeth Petroff

---

54. The Beguine movement, and its male counterpart, the Beghards, originated in the Low Countries at the end of the twelfth century. By the thirteenth century the Beguines were subject to religious persecution and restrictive legislation. For further reading, see Robert E. Lerner "Beguines and Beghards," in *Dictionary of the Middle Ages*, ed. Joseph R. Strayer (New York: Scribners, 1983), 2: 157–62. For a discussion of the Beguines' contributions to medieval spirituality, see Elizabeth Alvilda Petroff, "New Styles of Feminine Spirituality—The Beguine Movement," in *Medieval Women's Visionary Literature*, pp. 171–78.

55. Consequently, much of Mechtild of Magdeborg's text, *Flowing Light of the Divinity,* records her prayers, reflections, and advice, beautifully composed poetry, all written in low German and compiled while she was a Beguine. The text did not begin as a book and originally was little more than a heap of scraps of paper that were later collated by her spiritual adviser and mentor, Heinrich of Halle, a well-known Dominican of the time. Dominicans, or the Order of Friars Preachers, were founded by St. Dominic de Guzman and approved by Pope Honorius III in 1216. The order is primarily focused on study and preaching. See R. B. Williams, "Dominicans," in *Modern Catholic Encyclopedia*, ed. Michael Glazier and Monica Hellwig (Collegeville, Minn.: Liturgical, 1994), pp. 250–51.

56. Magdeburg, *Flowing Light of the Divinity,* 7. 1. 207.

speculates that it was Mechtild's arrival at Helfta that transformed the community from a place of learning to a place of writing.[57] Prior to Mechtild's arrival the nuns had mystical experiences and enjoyed a high quality of spiritual life but did not record these events. After Mechtild's arrival they were encouraged to begin recording the events of their lives. Mechtild's example as a writer had a tremendous impact on both Gertrude of Helfta and Mechtild of Hackeborn, influencing them to record their mystical visions. This role modeling constituted an effective mentoring strategy that had long-term positive effects in the life of the community. For religious educators, Mechtild's exemplary role modeling and encouragement are examples to be emulated, if mentoring processes are to be effective.

One of the more insightful chapters of Mechtild's text, chapter 6,[58] was likely written when she was going to live at Helfta.[59] In this chapter she discusses how a prioress should mentor subordinates, warning against the abuses of power and promoting the attitude of humility.[60] According to Mechtild, the prioress should help and comfort the disciples, giving them all the assistance within one's power.[61]

---

57. Elizabeth Alvilda Petroff, *Medieval Women's Visionary Literature*, pp. 210–211. Petroff's argument seems to make sense, given her later dating of Gertrude of Helfta's and Mechtild of Hackeborn's manuscripts. Petroff points out that Mechtild of Magdeburg's *Flowing Light of the Divinity* was written between 1250 and 1265; Gertrude's *Herald of Divine Love* was not written until 1289, and Mechtild of Hackeborn's *Booke of Gostlye Grace* was written in 1291. Ibid., p. 208.

58. Usually each section of Mechtild's *Flowing Light of the Divinity* is referred to as a book. I use the word "chapter" to avoid confusion.

59. Odo Egres, "Mechtild von Magdeburg: The Flowing Light God," in *Cistercians in the Late Middle Ages*, ed. Rozanne Elder, Cistercian Studies Series, no. 64 (Kalamazoo, Mich.: Cistercian Publications, 1981), p. 27.

60. Mechtild refers to a prioress or a prelate, not the abbess. The abbess has overall responsibility and is the leader of the whole monastery. The prioress is the person ranking next to the abbess. Mechtild's point is that all those in positions of power, regardless of rank, ought to treat their subordinates with dignity and respect.

61. See Magdeburg *Flowing Light of the Divinity* 6. 1. 167–71, for Mechtild's specific advice to wash the disciples' feet, visit their sickrooms, and watch over them lovingly. In warning her readers about the abuse of power, Mechtild says, "There lies great terror in power. When someone says: 'You are our prelate or our prior,' God knows, dear, you will be tempted to the fullest extent, so you should prostrate yourself with great humility . . . so that you may help . . . all your brothers and sisters who have been entrusted to your care." Ibid., p. 167.

This is sage advice for anyone who is in a position of mentorship. The mentor is asked to think first of the mentees and to do all that is possible to meet their needs. Mentors who put themselves first cannot be effective.[62] Presumably chapter 6 is prompted by Mechtild's own experience of directing novices, and it shows her sense of responsibility for other nuns. This chapter also indicates her awareness of power imbalances and the abuse of authority, as well as her experiences of conflict in community situations. Mechtild's sensitivities to the needs of the mentee are useful in any era. Her concern that mentors not abuse their position of power is very instructive. In a mentoring relationship there may be a temptation for the mentor to treat the mentee without due respect for the mentee's dignity. Mechtild's sage advice, born of her personal experience, is a reminder of the privileged position of the mentor and the considerable responsibilities of that position.

Mechtild's greatest contribution to our understanding of mentoring remains the intentional role modeling that she gave the nuns. Her commendable example of writing her text and of valuing and not hiding her experiences of the Divine sent a strong message to all the nuns in the cloister. Similarly, in religious education situations the positive example of experienced educators is likely to be a powerful mentoring tool. Mentors and mentees need to work on continuously developing strong discerning abilities in order to integrate sound personal and professional practices into their lives.

Mentoring Among the Helfta Mystics

Inside Helfta these nuns lived a simple yet structured life, with a considerable emphasis placed on mentoring those who entered the monastery as novices or postulants. Encouraged by the strong leadership of abbess Gertrude, they assumed responsibility for assisting one another, especially in their spiritual lives. The mentoring environment in which they lived and worked speaks to the current need to have any mentoring process include the support of the entire local religious community. The Helfta community spirit caused the cloister to flourish. Learning in the monastery school was promoted and writing on mystical encounters was encouraged. With such strong educational and spiritual foundations, conditions were optimal for the

---

62. Magdeburg *Flowing Light of the Divinity*, 6. 1. 168; 6. 1. 169.

blossoming of the community members as religious educators and mystics. Religious educators ought to note that this attention to the mentoring environment heightens the possibility that formal mentoring will be effective. Strong effective administrators are required to promote a positive learning environment. These leaders must model respect for faculty and must work collaboratively with their staff to reach decisions, improve learning conditions, and increase the overall caliber of the religious education experience.

The record of their lives and experiences that these religious women of Helfta left ensured their enduring influence on subsequent generations, including our own. The Helfta nuns, like the desert Christians, recognized that mentoring was essential to living out their vocation and to ensuring the continuance of their lifework. The nuns filled the mentoring roles of befriending, encouraging, sponsoring, teaching, and counseling. Their strong camaraderie, nurtured in this case by communal life, is no less desirable in a religious education environment today. Although vowed or cloistered life is unlikely to be the lifestyle of religious educators today, the basic characteristics of mentoring as outlined here are applicable. Careful attention to a prayer life, inducting new members, and providing a fertile mentoring environment are useful lessons for any era.

MENTORING AND TERESA OF AVILA

A third example of the religious and vocational mentor is found in the life story of Teresa of Avila (1515–1582), female mystic, writer, and reformer of the Carmelite Order.[63] She both mentored and received mentoring. The networks and special friendships Teresa established with her spiritual directors to facilitate her work were not incidental to

---

63. Teresa's compositions include *The Life*, her autobiography; *Spiritual Relations*, a work written to satisfy the demands of her confessors; *Book of the Foundations*, an account of the establishment of her houses of Discalced Carmelites; *Book Called Way of Perfection*, guidance in a life of prayer, including a contemplative reflection on the Lord's Prayer; and *Interior Castle*, a metaphorical treatise in which she describes the interior life as a mansion of many rooms. All quotations are taken from *The Complete Works of Saint Teresa of Jesus*, trans. E. Allison Peers, 3 vols. (London: Sheed & Ward, 1946); and *The Letters of Saint Teresa of Jesus,* trans. E. Allison Peers, 2 vols. (London: Burns, Oates & Washbourne, 1951). With the exception of the letters that are referred to by letter number, all references are to chapter and paragraph.

her success in reforming her order.[64] In fact, one is hard put to find a keener eye for attracting influential mentees and spiritual directors for herself than Teresa's.[65] Names such as Peter of Alcántara (1499–1562), John of the Cross (1542–1591), and Jerónimo Gratián (1545–1614) recur in her writings as individuals who exerted a significant impact on her lifework of reforming the Carmelites by setting up new houses of Discalced Carmelites, who would live a simple and austere lifestyle that was similar to the original intentions of the founder of her order.[66]

As a female in sixteenth-century society, Teresa was expected to maintain feminine decorum, have male spiritual directors and confessors, and avoid public controversy. The town of Avila would not have been sympathetic to a nun with a public role, as Teresa was well aware.[67] Furthermore, Teresa would have been hesitant to attract

---

64. Though Teresa's reform was restricted to Spain, it is helpful to situate it within the broader framework of the Catholic reform movement, the internal renewal of the Catholic Church begun in the late Middle Ages. Teresa's reform was part of much larger internal restoration movement begun centuries before, a reform movement aimed at eradicating Church dysfunction, including financial mismanagement, social stratification, church alignment with political leaders, and the gradual erosion of allegiance to religious vows to the point where only vestiges of a sense of mission remained in some communities. Catholic Reform is not to be confused with the Counter-Reformation, which describes the attempt of the Roman Catholic Church, after the Council of Trent (1545–1563), to reestablish ecclesiastical discipline and to make Catholics more religious. The definitions used here follow the usage of Erwin Iserloh, Joseph Glazik, and Hubert Jedin, *Reformation and Counter-Reformation*, trans. Anselm Briggs and Peter W. Becker, vol. 5 of *History of the Church* (New York: Seabury, 1986), pp. 431–32. Teresa's reforms were not directed at redressing the growth of Protestantism but were rather a continuation of a much longer project of internal Catholic reform begun centuries earlier. For an extended discussion, see H. Outram Evennet, *The Spirit of the Counter-Reformation,* ed. John Bossy (Notre Dame, Ind.: University of Notre Dame Press, 1968).

65. Marcel Lépée, "Spiritual Direction in the Letters of St. Teresa," in *Spiritual Direction*, ed. John Sullivan, Carmelite Studies (Washington, D.C.: ICS, 1980), p. 78 n. 1. Lépée observes that Teresa uses the term "director" interchangeably with "confessor."

66. "Discalced" (literally "barefooted") and "unmitigated" are used to denote the simpler, more austere form of life that Teresa wanted to return the Carmelites to.

67. For an extended discussion of the social, political, and economic climate of Avila in Teresa's time, see Jodi Bilinkoff, *The Avila of St. Teresa: Religious Reform in a Sixteenth Century City* (Ithaca, N.Y.: Cornell University Press, 1989). See also Bilinkoff's article, written in English, "The Social Meaning of Religious Reform:

attention to herself during this time of the Inquisition, the church's attempt to identify and eradicate religious heresy; her mysticism and mystical writing would likely have seemed suspect to this regulatory body.[68] Given this tense situation in Avila, it is understandable that Teresa would recognize the need to have strong mentors and to cooperate totally with both the townspeople and the Inquisition, to ensure that she herself was above reproach and that the reform she envisaged would continue.[69] Only by having her spiritual mentors represent her publically and by not alienating the Inquisition could Teresa ensure that her reform was accomplished. Though the political intrigue associated with Teresa is unlikely to be present in the lives of current religious educators, the importance of mentorship as a means of achieving educational success is quite relevant. Religious educators need mentors who can help them avoid unnecessary conflict and strife in their educational work.

The Case of Teresa of Avila," *Archiv für Reformationgeschichte* 79 (1988): 340–57. Bilinkoff characterizes Avila as a small town in which the landed aristocracy reigned and perpetuated an economically divided society. By endowing religious houses, the wealthy townspeople were able to ensure they had influence in Church circles. Because of her own family's social position, Teresa was granted special privileges when she entered the Carmelites, entitling her to separate quarters and servants while the other nuns were required to live in dormitories.

68. Teresa knew that an effective director could help her distinguish whether or not her mysticism was a sign of God's presence in her life. In her *Life* 19. 15, she writes that because of false reliance on one's own authority "the soul has great need of a director and of intercourse with spiritual people." For an insightful discussion of the links between mystical writing and dissent, see Steven Ozment's *Mysticism and Dissent: Religious Ideology and Social Protest in the Sixteenth Century* (New Haven, Conn.: Yale University Press, 1973). Ozment convincingly argues that sixteenth-century reformers such as Martin Luther (1483–1546) and Thomas Munster (1489–1525) were inspired to continue their reformational work by reading writings of the mystics. See especially Ozment's discussion of the influence of mystical writing on Luther. Ibid., pp.17–25.

69. Teófanes Egido,"The Historical Setting of St. Teresa's Life," in *Spiritual Direction*, ed. John Sullivan (Washington, D.C. : ICS, 1980), p. 131. Egido points out that Teresa cooperated fully with the Inquisitors. In her *Spiritual Relations* Teresa recounts her visit with an Inquisitor while he was in Avila to consult with him on the authenticity of her visions, which he declared to be valid. In Teresa' straightforward manner she reported that she was completely open, telling him everything. *Spiritual Relations* 4. 3.

Teresa's Need for a Spiritual Mentor

Teresa knew that she needed to have competent male spiritual directors who could also serve as her mentees, if her plans to reform the Carmelites were to materialize. Though every nun was required to have a director for spiritual guidance, Teresa made sure that she had able directors whom she could convince to become part of her plans for the Discalced male and female Carmelites and who would allow themselves to be mentored by her. From personal experience, Teresa was very conscious of the negative effect of incompetent spiritual directors.[70] In her estimation, it was better to be without a director than to have one who did not meet her three principal requirements: prudence, experience, and, most of all, learning.[71] Today, religious educators likewise need mentors who have all three attributes in order to maximize the opportunity for the mentee to develop as a an effective educator. No less is acceptable.

Peter of Alcántara Mentors Teresa of Avila

Before she began her reform, Teresa herself was mentored by Peter of Alcántara, an elderly and esteemed member of the Franciscan Order.[72] In her autobiography Teresa reports on her initial conversation with Peter. They exchanged thoughts on their mutual concern with reforming their orders.[73] Teresa met Peter when she was beginning the Carmelite reform and trying to set up her first new house, or foundation, of Discalced Carmelites. She was experiencing great difficulties with negotiating the purchase of this new house and had resorted to working in secret by having her brother-in-law actually make the deal for her.[74] Though her mystical visions and her awareness of the need to reform the Carmelites no doubt spurred her on, it is unlikely that Teresa

---

70. Teresa *Life* 20. 21: "It is a shame that such suffering should be caused by confessors who do not understand this." See also *The Way*, 4 (appendix). 1–5; *Life* 5. 3.

71. Teresa *Life* 13. 17–19.

72. The founder of the Franciscans was St. Francis of Assisi (1181–1226). The order, characterized by a life of poverty, preaching, and missionary work, was approved by Pope Honorius III in November 1223. See Michael Blastic, "Franciscans," in *Modern Catholic Encyclopedia*, pp. 328–29.

73. In reporting on her first meeting with Peter, Teresa writes, "When he saw that I had desires which he himself had already carried into effect . . . he delighted in talking to me about these things." *Life* 30. 5.

74. Teresa *Life* 36. 5.

would have persevered if it were not for the mentoring received from Peter. In her autobiography she described him as an old man of about sixty who had led a life of great austerity and had initiated substantial reforms in the Franciscan order.[75] Likewise, religious educators can benefit from mentoring relationships with older, possibly even retired, religious educators who generally know their field and would be willing to share their knowledge, insights, and skills with mentees.

For six years Peter was Teresa's spiritual director. He listened to her accounts of her mystical experiences and assured her that her visions were of God,[76] even going so far as to intercede for her with her confessor and with another man who doubted the authenticity of her mysticism.[77] At Peter's invitation Teresa corresponded with him until his death. Teresa's long, detailed descriptions of Peter's lifestyle, as well as her obvious awe of it, leave no doubt that she was very much influenced by his spirituality. His recommendation that every nun in her order have access to his writings is a strong indication of Peter's enduring influence on Teresa.[78] Further, frequent references in Teresa's writings to the Franciscans Clare of Assisi (1193–1253) and Francis of Assisi (1181–1226) show the overall impact of Franciscan spirituality on Teresa and on subsequent generations of Discalced Carmelites.[79] It is likely that biographies and academic writings have been influential mentoring influences on generations of religious educators. Although significant writings do provide mentorship, they cannot replace the role of living mentors.

Interestingly, Teresa's admiration for Peter's extreme austerity did not inspire her to duplicate his lifestyle model totally. For example, necessity later caused her to accept financial endowments for some religious houses, a point on which she had been opposed when she first met Peter.[80] In the final analysis, Peter's greatest influence on Teresa came when he affirmed her mystical visions. This affirmation

---

75. Teresa *Life* 27. 16–17.

76. Teresa *Spiritual Relations* 4. 2.

77. Teresa *Life* 30. 6.

78. Teresa *Constitutions* 8. St. Clare of Assisi (1193–1253) was the founder of the Poor Clares, a female order of Franciscans, an enclosed order of women. The preaching of Francis of Assisi inspired Clare to found the order. See Elizabeth Dreyer, "Clare of Assisi,"in *Modern Catholic Encyclopedia*, pp. 179–80.

79. Teresa *Life* 33. 13.

80. Teresa *Foundations* 20. 13.

strengthened Teresa's resolve and set her on a reformer's course for the remainder of her life. Mentees in any era need to know that someone trusts their experience and is willing to set them straight if they veer from the right course. This aspect of mentoring is crucial to the full professionalization of religious education.

John of the Cross

When Teresa first met John of the Cross, she was in need of someone who could initiate the reform of the male Carmelite order. At the time, John of the Cross was a young Carmelite thinking of leaving and becoming a member of the more austere male religious order, the Carthusians.[81] Though she was fifty-two and he twenty-five, Teresa recognized potential in John and decided he would be a most able reformer of the male Carmelites. Conversely, he also saw in her the ability to provide him with guidance and direction in the reform. A further appeal for John was the fact that Teresa, too, had a rich mystical life and was as committed to recording her visionary experiences as he was.[82]

Like a committed mentor, Teresa realized John's capabilities and limitations from the outset. She gave him the responsibility for establishing Duruelo, the first house for Discalced Carmelite males, in 1568,[83] but she personally oversaw the whole effort. In a letter of introduction for him on his way to Duruelo, Teresa described their relationship as containing some degree of tension. But in her characteristically diplomatic fashion, she accepted the blame for it.[84] Forever the leader of the Carmelite reform, Teresa was concerned about facilitating John's work in any way necessary. She was so concerned to induct John properly into the reform movement that she spent a considerable

---

81. The Carthusians were founded by St. Bruno of Cologne (c. 1030–1101) as a contemplative order in Chartreuse in the French Alps. The Carthusians live an eremitical (solitary) life, which is in contrast to the Benedictines and Cistercians who lead a cenobitic (communal) life . The Carthusians are the most austere order of males in the Roman Catholic Church. See Davis Bryan, "Carthusians," in *Modern Catholic Encyclopedia*, pp. 133–34.

82. The writings of John of the Cross include: *The Ascent of Mount Carmel, The Dark Night, The Spiritual Canticle, and The Living Flame of Love.* See *Complete Works of Saint John of the Cross*, ed. And trans. E. Allison Peers, 3 vols. (London: Burns, Oates & Washbourne, 1934–35).

83. Teresa *Foundations* 14. 1.

84. Teresa writes, "We have had a few disagreements here over business matters, and I have been the cause of them." *Letters* 10.

amount of time instructing him about how simply she and her re-formed sisters had decided to live. Teresa took care to provide this in-struction and preparation before he ever set out to Duruelo. In describ-ing the induction process, Teresa humbly acknowledged she had as much to learn from him as he from her.[85] This deliberate teaching en-sured that her mentee learned the principles of the reform and that he was properly prepared for his reforming work before he began it. In any era, preparation and instruction are important for mentees before they undertake specific professional tasks. Religious education men-tors would do well to follow Teresa's example of encouraging the mentees to proceed slowly at first, then offering them substantial feed-back on their progress, and, finally, supporting their independence from the mentoring relationship.

Once Teresa had given John an orientation to the reform, she con-tinued to do all that was necessary to facilitate his reform work, seiz-ing every opportunity to speak well of him in her voluminous corre-spondence. In comments made in her letter of introduction for him on his way to set up the first house of Discalced Carmelite males, Teresa writes, "He is great in the sight of God."[86] Teresa mentored John in the way Peter mentored her. Because Teresa kept detailed records of her mystical life and her reformational work, we know that not only was she a friend and counselor for John but she paved the way for his successful reforms by actively sponsoring him. We know that Teresa mentored John by writing diplomatic letters on his behalf, interceding with his superiors, trying to get him out of jail when he was impris-oned during a dispute between the Calced and Discalced Carmelites, and teaching him how to set up the new Discalced houses.[87] In turn, he helped her carry out her dream of reforming the whole order, male and female, and, additionally, he guided her spiritual life. Active spon-sorship such as Teresa displayed for her mentee is still appropriate for mentorship today, especially given the usual difficulties of religious education work. It is also relevant that though John mentored Teresa in her spiritual life, Teresa mentored him in his reformational activity. This complementarity of relationship points to the complexity of some mentoring arrangements. Teresa's and John's ability to distinguish

---

85. Teresa *Foundations* 13. 5.
86. Teresa *Letters* 10.
87. Teresa discusses John's imprisonment in 1577 in letter 246.

their roles in the spiritual and professional realm points to their maturity and cooperation. Having the ability to set boundaries is crucial for both partners in the relationship.

Jerónimo Gratián

A great deal more is known about Teresa's relationship with her spiritual director Jerónimo Gratián.[88] They met in 1575, when she was over sixty and a successful reformer with ten new Discalced Carmelite houses to her credit.[89] She was also an accomplished writer who had made great progress in her mystical life. In contrast, Gratián was thirty years old and had been a Carmelite for a few years only. Yet Teresa saw enormous potential in him as a reformer, even more than she had in John.[90] Her first meeting with Gratián lasted three weeks, but their collaboration lasted seven years.

It is quite clear from Teresa's writings that she experienced difficulties in her relationship with Gratián.[91] He was not quite the prudent and wise reformer that Teresa had initially believed him to be. Gratián often ignored her counsel, even taking advice from persons who, in Teresa's estimation, cared little for him.[92] His first catastrophe was to insist on establishing a house in Seville, an area in which the Carmelite superiors had not given them permission to reform.[93] A major disagreement between the Calced and Discalced ensued, a situation that distressed Teresa greatly.[94] During the internal Carmelite struggles John was arrested and Teresa was confined to a convent. Such rash behavior was typical of Gratián, so much so that Teresa spent a great deal of her time telling him what to do.[95] Teresa may well have overestimated his ability to effectively take direction, but theirs was a mentoring relationship she was unwilling to abandon. It

---

88. For a detailed examination of Gratián's and Teresa's relationship, see Mary Luti, "'A Marriage Well Arranged': Teresa of Avila and Fray Jerónimo Gracián de la Madre de Dios," *Studia Mystica* 12, no. 1 (1989): 32–46.

89. For Teresa's description of the meeting between her and Gratián see her *Foundations* 23–24.

90. Teresa *Letters* 71, 72.

91. Teresa *Letters* 79. Teresa tells Gratián to be gentle in his dealings with people, to be realistic in his goals, and to recognize that change takes time.

92. Teresa *Letters* 253.

93. Teresa *Letters* 71.

94. Teresa *Foundations* 28. 1–2.

95. Teresa *Letters* 232.

was through Gratián that Teresa worked to establish her houses and to enact reform. Mentors in any era will be confronted with recalcitrant mentees and will be forced to decide if they wish to continue mentoring or if mentoring is beyond their capabilities. Sometimes the decision must be made to sever the relationship, if both mentor and mentee are to emerge with their integrity intact.

Gratián accepted her guidance in his reform work and guided her spiritual life. By overseeing his reformational activity Teresa managed both to continue carrying out her plans for the establishment of a separate Discalced province or jurisdiction and to actually provide mentorship for him in his work. Though Gratián and John were her two chosen mentees, through whom she enacted reform of the male Carmelites, she worked more effectively with Gratián. She assumed the roles of adviser and guide in Gratián's life, counseling him on all the necessary diplomatic interventions in order to ensure that her goals were accomplished. She frequently wrote to him suggesting certain strategic actions such as arranging audiences with the king, with the papal nuncio, and with the president, since it was they who had the authority to set up a separate province for the Discalced, a goal of the reformers.[96] The complexity of the relationship highlights the difficulties that can occur in mentorship. The mentor and mentee will continuously be challenged to decide how they will work through their differences and if, indeed, such an effort is worthwhile.

Mentoring among Teresa and the Catholic Reformers

Great internal religious renewal was carried out in the sixteenth century by Peter within the Franciscans and by Teresa, John, and Gratián, within the Carmelites. Mentorship in all its forms was present in their relationships.[97] As with the desert and Helfta examples, these

---

96. Teresa *Letters* 224, 242.

97. Though this chapter deals only with living people with whom Teresa interacted, it is also possible to trace the influence of nonliving sources, such as books, on her spirituality. See, for example, Kieran Kavanagh, "St. Teresa and the Spirituality of Sixteenth-Century Spain," in *The Roots of the Modern Christian Tradition*, ed. Rozanne Elder, Cistercian Studies Series, no. 55 (Kalamazoo, Mich.: Cistercian Publications, 1984), pp. 91–104. Kavanagh's chapter explores, in part, the influence of church fathers such as Augustine and Jerome on Teresa's spirituality. In acknowledging her love of reading, Teresa said in *Life* 2. 1:"Unless I had a new book, I was never happy."

individuals mentored each other, not without difficulty and not in a linear fashion. Relationships that started out hierarchically became equal or even reversed themselves so that the mentor was the one being mentored. Religious educators today can look to this model as providing thick, rich detail of the actual existential circumstances of mentoring, detail that is generally underdeveloped in the public education literature.

In the case of Teresa there is evidence that largely through mentoring she was able to successfully negotiate the developmental challenges of the generativity stage in her life. Though she herself was unable to carry out all the reforms within the Carmelites, she found a way to pass on her dream or vision of the Discalced Carmelites to others much younger than herself. Through mentoring both John and Gratián she was able to fulfill her own aspirations in life.[98] Similarly, experienced religious education mentors need to be able to see mentoring as a viable way of entrusting the ideals and the future of the profession to a new generation of educators.

The presence and potential for tension in a mentoring relationship is a major theme that arises in this mentoring situation. Tension and personality differences were not avoided, if the participants could see that there was hope for resolution. Though Teresa had some difficulty with both her mentees, John of the Cross and Gratián, she was able to see that this conflict could be successfully resolved. Conflict will also arise in religious education circumstances but it may be possible to work through it.

Furthermore, this example of mentoring among Peter, Teresa, John, and Gratián shows that cross-gender mentoring can be effective. Teresa mentored men and they her, without major difficulties related to their gender. The success of this mentoring dispels the notion that mentors must necessarily be of the same gender to be effective. In fact, Teresa's mentoring shows that the unique situation one finds oneself in will have a greater influence on the quality of the mentoring given and received than the particularities associated with the mentor and mentee.

---

98. For a discussion of the psychological implications of Teresa's life and work, see Catherine Romano, "A Psycho-Spiritual History of Teresa of Avila," in *Western Spirituality: Historical Roots, Ecumenical Routes*, ed. Matthew Fox (Sante Fe, N.Mex.: Bear, 1981), pp. 261–95.

SUMMARY

Though these three historical examples are quite different, they provide a great deal of latitude to explore the myriad forms of mentorship that can exist. There are examples of cross-gender relationships, same gender relationships, cloistered individuals, public figures, people living together under one roof, people living separately, people in daily contact, and people in long-distance relationships. Some are mentored in the context of spiritual direction and some are mentored in a less structured way. Evident here, in thick and rich detail, are all the essential elements of mentoring: teaching, sponsoring, encouraging, counseling, and befriending.

Religious life, as profiled in these three historical examples, is lived by few people. The point being made is that religious educators are called to assist others in their work and to induct new members into the religious education profession. Religious educators can learn a great deal from these examples about the complexity and benefits of mentoring and they can use this information to inform current processes.

3

Educational Research Findings
on Mentorship

We will fish together now for I still have much to learn.
—Ernest Hemingway[1]

When Susan Kranger moved east six months ago to take a position at All Saints Church as the youth and education minister, she did not anticipate the problems she would have in adjusting to her new job. To begin with, the church staff is small: Susan, the pastor, Trevor, the secretary, Rena, and the pastor's wife, Marie, who directs the choir. There are numerous volunteers, but the core group of four is fairly consistent. Susan has stumbled along in her job, hoping that people like what she has to offer—Sunday school classes, youth group meetings, and a weekly women's Bible study. The most the pastor has said so far is, "Things are great." His wife, however, has had much more to say, such as, "The children were too noisy today in Sunday school," "Mrs. Sanders seems to be having difficulty with your Bible study." Marie always speaks in a lighthearted way but Susan is troubled by Marie's remarks. Susan has talked to Marie un-successfully and wishes she had a sounding board. Is there anyone she can talk to?

Susan's difficulties are no less real than those encountered by the historical characters discussed in chapter 2. Mentorship for

---

1. Ernest Hemingway, *The Old Man and the Sea* (New York: Scribner's Sons, 1952), p. 125.

beginners like Susan can be informed by insights from both religious and general educational literature. The educational sources are important because they often supply empirical research results and provide explicit practical detail about organizing and managing specific mentoring situations, which frequently are unavailable in the religious literature. In this chapter I will first draw particular attention to published insights from educational researchers about the use of mentorship in the field of education and in other contexts, such as within churches. Then I will proceed to use these educational insights to inform the practice of establishing and maintaining mentoring programs.

MENTORSHIP IN
THE EDUCATIONAL FIELD

In this section I will discuss the findings on the practice of mentorship reported in both the public education literature and the adult education literature. I will also address the educational literature on the personal and professional dimensions of mentorship. Because so many similarities exist between public education and religious education, it is entirely legitimate to extrapolate relevant findings about general education to religious education.

Indicators of Educators' Interest in Mentorship
Educational researchers acknowledge the exodus of new educators from the profession and have knowledge of the specific problems facing new classroom educators that contribute to this exodus. As a possible remedy they have devoted entire journal issues to the concerns of educator initiation and mentorship. *Action in Teacher Education*, *Journal of Teacher Education*, *Kappa Delta Pi Record*, and *ORBIT* are examples of professional journals that have chosen this route.[2] The main educational research database, ERIC, currently generates twenty-five hundred items when the category "mentors" is searched; in addition, no fewer than three digests have been issued on the topic by the ERIC Clearinghouse on Teacher

---

2. Four special-edition journals dedicated to mentorship are *Action in Teacher Education* 8, no. 4 (1987); *Journal of Teacher Education* 37, no. 1 (1986); *Kappa Delta Pi Record* 22, no. 4 (1986); *ORBIT* 22, no. 1 (1991).

Education.[3] Equally significant, the Association of Teacher Educators (ATE) regarded the induction of new educators of such importance that it formed separate commissions to investigate induction procedures and mentor educational preparation. When three thousand members of ATE were asked (944 responses analyzed) what the most critical issue in teacher education was, they ranked the provision of mentors for beginning educators as being of prime importance.[4] Significantly, numerous professional conferences and meetings have focused on educator induction and mentorship, resulting in a deluge of writing on the topic. The high level of concern for the adequate induction of school educators is paralleled by concerns within the adult education community, where the challenges are similar.

Adult Educators' Focus on Mentorship

The adult education literature on mentorship has proliferated, beginning with the publication of *Seasons of a Man's Life* in 1978 by Daniel Levinson and his associates, in which they highlighted the importance of mentors in helping individuals realize their full potential over their lifespan.[5] The value of mentorship in the education of adults was then cast in sharp relief by Laurent Daloz's vivid, book-length description of faculty mentoring of nontraditional distance students in Vermont.[6]

---

3. ERIC Digest, *Components of Teacher Induction Programs*, ERIC Clearinghouse on Teacher Education, Washington, D.C., 1986, ERIC ED 269407; ERIC Digest, *Current Developments in Teacher Induction Programs*, ERIC Clearinghouse on Teacher Education, Washington, D.C., 1986, ERIC ED 269406; ERIC Digest, *Teacher Mentoring*, ERIC Clearinghouse on Teacher Education, Washington, D.C., 1986, ERIC ED 271477.

4. Thomas J. Buttery, Martin Haberman, and W. Robert Houston, "First Annual ATE Survey of Critical Issues in Teacher Education," *Action in Teacher Education* 12, no. 2 (1990): 3.

5. Developmental psychologist Daniel Levinson's longitudinal study of forty males showed that many of them had been mentored by older men in their lives. Levinson's study revealed the importance of the mentor in helping the individuals realize their life goals or dreams. Daniel Levinson et al., *The Seasons of a Man's Life* (New York: Knopf, 1978).

6. Laurent A. Daloz, *Effective Teaching and Mentoring* (San Francisco: Jossey-Bass, 1986). Daloz again focuses on the role and function of mentorship in higher education in his chapter, "Mentorship," in *Adult Learning Methods: A Guide for Effective Instruction,* ed. Michael W. Galbraith (Malabar, Fla.: Krieger, 1990), pp. 205–24.

Though Daloz's book, *Effective Teaching and Mentoring*, is limited somewhat by its exclusive focus on positive instances of mentorship, it does provide one of the earliest insights into the actual experience of mentorship in an adult educational context. Daloz tells the stories of the men and women he mentored over a ten-year period in a community college program in Vermont. He highlights the importance of a mentor in helping these students adjust to the life transitions faced by adults who begin postsecondary education.

In recent years, numerous other works on mentorship have been produced for adult educators.[7] These books include such practical volumes as Norman Cohen's *Mentoring Adult Learners: A Guide for Educators and Trainers*,[8] which focuses on mentoring programs in higher education, business, and government, and Marie Wunsch's *Mentoring Revisited: Making an Impact on Individuals and Institutions*, which is exclusively directed to mentorship in higher education.[9] One of the most informative compilations of scholarly articles on mentorship is Michael Galbraith and Norman Cohen's edited collection, *Mentoring: New Strategies and Challenges*.[10] This book contains insightful essays on the theory, practical aspects, and research potential of mentorship in adult education. The various authors approach mentorship as a proactive, professional development strategy that has considerable benefits for adult development as well as for organizational effectiveness.

The proliferation of professional publishing among adult educators on mentorship is a strong indicator of its importance to adult development and learning. Similarly, interest in spirituality and spiritual direction, which emerged simultaneously with mentorship in the 1970s and 1980s, continues to grow. Adult religious educators are in a unique

---

7. For a fuller listing of adult education publications on mentorship, see Linda Marie Golian, "Strategies and Resources for Enhancing Mentoring Relationships," *Mentoring: New Strategies and Challenges,* ed. Michael W. Galbraith and Norman H. Cohen, New Directions for Adult and Continuing Education, no. 66 (San Francisco: Jossey-Bass, 1995), pp. 79–88.

8. Norman Cohen, *Mentoring Adult Learners: A Guide for Educators and Trainers* (Malabar, Fla.: Krieger, 1995).

9. Marie A. Wunsch, ed., *Mentoring Revisited: Making an Impact on Individuals and Institutions* (San Francisco: Jossey-Bass, 1994).

10. Michael W. Galbraith and Norman H. Cohen, eds., *Mentoring: New Strategies and Challenges* (1995).

situation because they can draw on both educational and theological sources for the development of mentoring initiatives. Typical of first-year educators is Rob Cerniglia, assigned to direct the adult religious education section of the National Bishops' Conference. Rob had years of successful administrative experience at a regional level, but the national level held many unfamiliar challenges. On 'a daily basis he faced theological and educational debates, many of which were new to him. Rob relied heavily on his colleagues in that year, particularly on one staff member who had served a term in the same adult religious education position. This woman was capable of providing the personal support and encouragement that Rob required. Her support addressed Rob's professional needs.

Educators' Attention to Personal and Professional Dimensions of Mentees' Lives

Though much of the mentoring literature is specific to the teaching field, some efforts have been made to integrate a variety of insights from other occupational areas, such as health and industry, with adult education. The most significant of these insights is found in a collection of interdisciplinary readings entitled *The Return of the Mentor*, edited by Brian Caldwell and Earl Carter.[11] Though the mentoring contexts vary from education to health to business, the empirical research tends to give equal attention to both the psychosocial (personal) and the career (professional) development of the mentee.[12] Educational research on mentoring supports the notion that education focuses on the development of the whole person.

For example, in a situation such as the one Maurice Golden finds himself, the balance of psychosocial and career mentorship is very important. Maurice operates an ecumenical retreat center that offers faith development courses and retreats for adults. Maurice is new to educational administration as well as to the center. An elder from his current congregation, Jacob Uriah, has been willing to provide advice,

---

11. Brian J. Caldwell and Earl M. A. Carter, eds., *The Return of the Mentor: Strategies for Workplace Learning* (London: Falmer, 1993).

12. The distinction between the career and psychosocial functions of the mentor follows Kathy E. Kram's usage in "Phases of the Mentor Relationship,"*Academy of Management Journal* 26, no. 4 (1983): 614. Kram points out that these two functions are quite distinctive and mentors emphasize different functions depending on the context.

counseling, and assistance to Maurice whenever he needs it. Sometimes Maurice needs help with administrative matters such as budgets (career mentorship), and sometimes he needs to discuss communication problems he is having with his retreat center staff (psychosocial). Although Maurice does not know Jacob well, he is thankful that he is only a telephone call away. Maurice's situation illustrates the growing use of mentorship in a variety of contexts, and for a number of purposes.

MENTORSHIP IN OTHER EDUCATIONAL CONTEXTS

Mentorship occurs in a variety of contexts, including churches and other informal settings. Though these contexts are not well represented in the general educational literature, they are especially relevant for religious educators. In this section I discuss both contexts and draw particular attention to special concerns relating to women and mentorship.

Mentorship within Churches

Since the 1980s, the concept of mentorship has gained considerable momentum, so much so that it is difficult to find a formal, educational system that lacks a structured induction initiative such as mentorship.[13] The adoption of mentorship in church contexts has been markedly slower, despite the fact that many parallels exist between the needs of religious educators and educators in other contexts.[14] Explanations for the absence of mentoring relationships in churches are

---

13. Attention to the extent of mentoring initiatives has been drawn in such sources as Sandra J. Odell, *Mentor Teacher Programs* (Washington, D.C.: National Education Association, 1990), p. 5. See also Ardra L. Cole, "Induction Programs in Ontario Schools: A Survey of Current Practices," *ORBIT* 22, no.1 (1991): 2–4.

14. Few sources of information on mentorship in religiously affiliated educational contexts exist. See Sandra Harris's report of mentorship in a Baptist school: "A Mentoring Program for New Teachers: Ensuring Success," *NASSP Bulletin* 79, no. 572 (1995): 98–103. See also Barbara L. Brock and Marilyn L. Grady's brief description of mentorship in Roman Catholic schools: "Keepers of the Keys," *Momentum* 27, no.1 (1996): 48–50; Michael Zeldin and Sara S. Lee, eds., *Touching the Future: Mentoring and the Jewish Professional* (Los Angeles: Hebrew Union College-Jewish Institute of Religion, 1995).

largely speculative, since little solid empirical research exists on the topic to support or deny the existence of such programs in churches. One possibility for the reluctance of churches to undertake mentorship is a perceived increase in labor and financial costs. Since church-based education rarely has a surplus of funds or staff, mentorship may seem at first blush to be a daunting undertaking. The model of religious education mentorship I offer in this book is cost-effective and can yield significant benefits for the mentor, the mentee, and the church.

Another reason that local churches have not embraced mentorship may be the paucity of rigorous writing and research on religious education mentorship. One adult religious educator identifies personal transformation of the mentee as the goal of women mentoring women.[15] Considering the more modest proposal of religious education in local church situations as a teaching and learning endeavor, the daunting task of having to transform someone else's life might deter would-be mentors. Though personal transformation in a church context might occur, the more realistic goals of typical mentoring programs for religious educators would be to focus on professional skill improvement and the successful induction of new professionals.

A further reason for the reluctance of churches to develop mentoring programs may be the belief that they are already engaged in informal mentorship. This misconception occurs because in church-related writing, terms such as "faith-mentors," "soul friends," and "spiritual kin" are used interchangeably with "mentor."[16] Mentorship in the general education literature, however, and in this book, refers to a more tangible, realistic, and goal-oriented phenomenon. Because of the casual way in which mentorship has been spoken and written of in church-related circles, it is often difficult to determine the quality and consistency of the mentorship given and received in religious education.

---

15. Janet E. Schaller, "Mentoring of Women: Transformation in Adult Religious Education," *Religious Education* 91, no. 2 (1996). See especially p. 167 where Schaller outlines the possibilities for mentorship as a means of claiming the "emerging, nascent self."

16. See the discussion in chapter 1, note 36, about Sondra Higgins Matthaei's use of the term "faith-mentor" in *Faith Matters: Faith-Mentoring in the Faith Community* (Valley Forge, Penn.: Trinity, 1996).

Some churches may have resisted mentorship because it is seen as a public education fad.[17] This is an unfortunate view, since mentorship is consistent with the Christian practice of formally inducting new members, dating back to the ancient church. In the current context mentorship is part of the professionalization process: Members of the profession know that the future of the profession depends on codes of behavior and principles that can be conveyed most effectively through mentorship.[18] Transmission of standards of professional practice requires some form of induction, and mentorship is an effective means of doing this.

Mentorship is not a replacement for formal preservice professional education, a point that has been well developed by Margaret McNay and bears repeating here.[19] McNay points out that no matter how adept the education system becomes at the induction of new educators, it needs to be careful not to allow any suggestion that initiation processes replace current university preparation programs for educators. This caution is quite timely, given the pressures of educator shortages and the concomitant temptation to bypass the lengthy and often demanding educator preparation route. In McNay's view, induction and mentoring initiatives are intended to supplement, not replace, the professional education provided by universities. All bona fide

---

17. Public school educators also wrestle with the issue of professionalism. Educational researcher Carl Glickman argues that mentorship not only initiates new educators in their first year but it also conveys to mentees that professional discussion, hard work, and attention to the initiation of new professionals are important profession-building activities. Glickman is clearly claiming that education is professional work. How new educators are inducted says a great deal about the vision of education held by members of the profession. See his preface to *Mentoring: Developing Successful New Teachers*, ed. Theresa M. Bey and C. Thomas Holmes (Reston, Va.: Association of Teacher Educators, 1990).

18. One strong proponent of the full professionalization of religious education is James Michael Lee. See *The Flow of Religious Instruction* (Birmingham, Ala.: Religious Education Press, 1973), pp. 290–91. According to Lee, the professionalization of religious instruction requires that it be equipped not only with trained personnel, a theoretical framework and a research base but also with adequate financial support and support services. I argue that if mentorship is seen as a component of educational preparation, it too is a necessary component of professionalization.

19. Margaret McNay, "Induction: Not an Alternative to Teacher Education," *ORBIT* 22, no. 1 (1991): 10–11.

professions mandate academic preparation and the field of education should be no exception.

Take, for example, the case of Jewish seminary professor Gunther Witzman, who met his mentee, second career Solomon Golstein, a student in a senior year practical theology class. He observed Solomon for the term and was thoroughly impressed with his intellectual and instructional abilities. Though they rarely spoke with each other outside class, Gunther saw in Solomon his own self at the age of thirty. In the following semester, Gunther hired Solomon to be his teaching assistant and encouraged him to apply for enrollment in a professional education program in order to prepare for a career in Jewish education. Solomon resisted because he knew that his theological background was sufficient for him to meet the typical requirements to obtain and hold a religious education position in a synagogue. Finally, however, he took Gunther's advice and completed a bachelor of education degree. At the end of his final year, Solomon was placed in a yeshiva, and his contacts with Gunther became more sporadic. Though he had learned a great deal from Gunther in the seminary, he knew his teaching skills needed further honing. This refining process would continue for years, but he would remember Gunther's teaching and example forever. The informal mentorship that Solomon received is common to other contexts as well.

Mentorship as Informal Learning

Increasingly, learning occurs outside academic institutions; the label "informal" is often used to refer to either the *site* or the *mode* of such learning. The terms "formal learning " and "informal learning" are used to refer to the learning that occurs within formal or informal contexts. One could argue that only the location or mode of delivery of education can be labeled informal or formal because these can change, whereas learning is a constant. Therefore, these adjectives cannot be paired with learning because readers will mistakenly conclude that the essence of learning is contingent on the location. Despite this problem, I use the terms "informal" and "formal" learning because they are commonly understood in educational literature, and readers of that literature will be familiar with them. My use is consistent with the remainder of this chapter, which highlights insights from the general educational literature.

Informal learning in the religious education field can include practices as diverse as mentorship, attending professional conferences, and job shadowing of religious educators. This understanding of informal learning follows with that of Victoria Marsick and Karen Watson, two researchers specializing in workplace learning.[20] For religious educators, mentorship constitutes a significant means of informal learning, especially during the professional initiation phase. When seen as a means of continuous learning, mentorship can become a positive way of highlighting the importance of collaboration and ongoing education. Because of the increasing demands placed on religious educators and the diversity of academic backgrounds from which they come, mentoring as a form of informal learning may indeed be a key contributor to their ongoing professionalization.

Take the case of first-year religious education minister Simon Roberts, who has an education degree from a traditional educational preparation program but has never taught adults. Teaching is a difficult experience for Simon; the adults in his traditional congregation have lost tolerance with his "talking down" to them in his evening seminars. Simon's teaching style is limited to lectures and the congregation is not responding positively. He knows he needs help, but he is unsure of what kind he needs. Some of the church leadership team members realize his predicament, so they recruit an elder in the congregation with effective teaching skills to mentor Simon through that first year and to help him vary his rigid teaching style to meet the needs of his audience. Simon needs to have a mentor who will befriend him and teach him how to relate and communicate with adults in a way that is respectful of them. This informal learning will advance his professional skills and knowledge. The mentorship will ensure that Simon is regularly supervised in his teaching, coached in

---

20. Karen E. Watkins and Victoria J. Marsick,"Towards a Theory of Informal and Incidental Learning," *International Journal of Lifelong Education* 11, no. 4 (1992): 287–300. See also Peter Jarvis, *Adult Learning in the Social Context* (London: Croom Helm, 1987); Peter Jarvis, "Meaningful and Meaningless Experience: Towards an Analysis of Learning from Life," *Adult Education Quarterly* 37, no. 3 (1987): 164–72; Steve W. J. Kozlowski,"Organizational Change, Informal Learning, and Adaptation: Emerging Trends in Training and Continuing Education," *Journal of Continuing Higher Education* 43, no. 1 (1995): 2–11; Victoria J. Marsick and Karen E. Watkins, *Informal and Incidental Learning in the Workplace* (London: Routledge, 1990).

specific teaching strategies, and given continuous feedback to help him grow professionally.

When mentorship is seen through the lens of informal learning, certain key dimensions must become part of the learning. Not only must the religious education mentee learn through experience but this learning must be enhanced by critical reflection.[21] Through critical reflection on specific educational experiences, both the mentor and the mentee have the opportunity to analyze their actions, identify strengths and weaknesses, think about the assumptions behind their behavior, and take positive steps to change undesirable behavior. In Simon's case, the critical reflection element comes into play when his mentor, assigned by the local mentoring leadership team, sits with him after his education session to view the class on videotape. They explore together how Simon might work toward building a more effective educational climate and have a closer personal relationship with members of the congregation. The mentor assists Simon in examining why he is afraid to delve into the deeper life questions with learners and why he will not allow silence when it is better suited to the situation. This first year of religious education ministry has forced Simon to look beyond textbooks and into himself to critically reflect on his own personal and professional strengths and limitations. When mentorship for religious educators takes on this deliberate education focus, it has the potential for revitalizing the whole church. Mentorship becomes even more effective when special considerations are given to women's needs and circumstances.

Women and Mentorship

Because women constitute the bulk of religious educators, special attention should be given to their need for a mentor. Women's need for mentoring support is consistent with emerging scholarship on female

---

21. The concept of critical reflection on action in the workplace was advanced by Donald Schön in *The Reflective Practitioner* (New York: Basic, 1983). In the educational literature the concept of reflection on action has grown astronomically. A recent discussion is provided in Terence J. Lovat and David L. Smith, *Curriculum: Action on Reflection Revisited* 3d ed. (Wentworth Falls, Australia: Social Science Press, 1995), especially chapter 11, "Towards Critical Reflection in Curriculum Work." See also Antoinette A. Oberg and Sibylle Artz, "Teaching for Reflection: Being Reflective," in *Teachers and Teaching: From Classroom to Reflection,* ed. Tom Russell and Hugh Munby (London: Falmer, 1992).

psychological needs that influence learning. Mary Field Belenky and her associates have developed the idea of women as connected knowers, as those who construct knowledge together and need others to assist them in their learning and growth.[22] Similarly, psychologist Jean Baker Miller argues that women's development primarily occurs in relationship to other people and that interpersonal connections are crucial to female growth.[23] Adult educator Mayra Bloom argues further that the many caring roles of the mentor can facilitate the positive growth and development of women.[24] A formalized mentoring program is a basic way of providing this psychosocial support that many women require for effectiveness as religious education professionals.

The empirical research conducted on women and mentorship does not confirm that women voluntarily offer mentoring support to other females. Nor does it confirm that mentorship is always effective when

---

22. Mary Field Belenky et al., *Women's Ways of Knowing: The Development of Self, Voice, and Mind* (New York: Basic Books, 1986). This book has become a standard text in women's studies curricula and in the broader canon of feminist literature. The writers have extended their conversation in an edited collection: Nancy Rule Goldberger et al., eds, *Knowledge, Difference, and Power* (New York: Basic, 1996).

23. Jean Baker Miller, "Toward a New Psychology of Women," in *Women's Spirituality: Resources for Christian Development,* ed. Joann Wolski Conn (Mahwah, N.J.: Paulist, 1986), pp. 107–8. See also Carol Gilligan, Janie Victoria Ward, Jill McLean Taylor, with Betty Bardige, eds., *Mapping the Moral Domain* (Cambridge: Harvard University Press, 1988). Gilligan and her associates report on a series of research studies they conducted at Harvard University in which they explored and contrasted male and female orientation to issues such as moral reasoning and relationships. These studies with groups such as lawyers and mothers expand and confirm to a considerable degree Gilligan's earlier research, *In a Different Voice* (Cambridge: Harvard University Press, 1982). In her original work Gilligan developed the notion that women view moral dilemmas and relationships from a lens of interdependence and *caring* more than a lens of *justice*. Gilligan's theory has helped shape the current perception that women's reasoning and judgments are based on relationships, intimacy, and caring.

24. Mayra Bloom, "Multiple Roles of the Mentor: Supporting Women's Adult Development," in *Learning Environments for Women's Adult Development: Bridges toward Change,* ed. Kathleen Taylor and Catherine Marienau. New Directions for Adult and Continuing Education, no. 65 (San Francisco: Jossey-Bass, 1995), pp. 63–72. See chapter 1 of this book, note 16, for a further discussion of the mentoring roles that Bloom identifies.

it given by one woman to another.[25] In their research on twenty-four senior female university faculty, Deborah Cullen and Gaye Luna found that senior women in academe did provide mentorship for junior female faculty but limited their mentoring to meeting career or professional goals of mentees, to the virtual exclusion of much needed psychosocial support. Cullen and Luna also point out that effective mentorship for females is very important because academic environments often are not supportive of female advancement.[26] Female religious educators who teach in seminaries and other higher educational institutes are even more likely to need mentors who champion their cause because their academic area, religious education, is frequently marginalized.[27]

Because hierarchical structures are common in many religious environments the issue of mentoring women is especially important. For example, take the case of Sr. Elsa Power, Roman Catholic campus minister at a midwestern college. Because she is not ordained, she has to invite ordained ministers to preside at Sunday Eucharist, though all week long she is the chaplain, educational lecture organizer, and the spiritual adviser whom students say they need. Despite her repeated requests, the diocese refuses to appoint a priest to the campus to work

25. Amy Saltzman, "Woman Versus Woman: Why Aren't More Female Executives Mentoring their Junior Counterparts?" *U. S. News and World Report* 120, no. 12 (1996): 50–54. Saltzman suggests that women in business management are less likely than men to mentor their female counterparts, mainly because their workplaces do not reward or encourage such mentoring relationships.

26. Deborah L. Cullen and Gaye Luna,"Women Mentoring in Academe: Addressing the Gender Gap in Higher Education," *Gender and Education* 5, no. 2 (1993): 133.

27. Likewise, Elizabeth Ervin's qualitative study of four female graduate students mentees, mentored primarily by female professors, confirms that senior female faculty experience difficulty in providing good mentorship. In allowing the individual stories of four female graduate student mentees to emerge, Ervin shows clearly the challenges of women mentoring women in academe. She describes a general malaise among female faculty as well as a tendency for female academic mentors to adopt stereotypic male ways of being in the academy. Ervin demonstrates through her case studies that the result of poor mentorship is a cadre of disillusioned graduate students who seriously question their own future in academe. The implications for the quality of university and seminary faculty and improved female status in higher education are a grave cause for concern. See "Power, Frustration and 'Fierce Negotiation' in Mentoring Relationships: Four Women Tell Their Stories," *Women's Studies* 24 (1995): 447–81.

with her. Elsa is feeling her energy drain, but the only person she can talk to is another chaplain, an ordained Presbyterian minister in his mid-fifties. Though he tries, he cannot understand Elsa's feelings of resentment toward the structural inequalities and the importance of her ministry to her. The members of the religious community Elsa lives with are supportive, but they are sometimes too busy to give her good mentoring advice.

Problems for women and female mentorship persist. Although they are confirmed in a variety of disciplines and fields, they need to be read as a challenge and not as a permanent barrier to female mentorship. The historical examples of mentorship among women, such as that among the Helfta mystics, show how much women can accomplish if mentoring relationships and a positive mentoring environment are available to them.

PRACTICALITIES OF ESTABLISHING A MENTORING PROGRAM

There are many issues associated with establishing a religious education mentoring program. One issue is the use of mentorship as a crucial component in an induction program. Other issues are how to structure a mentoring program and how to effectively involve university faculty in the process.

Mentorship as Part of an Induction Process

Religious educators should be aware that effective induction programs for new educators typically incorporate the mentor dimension and that mentors are considered to be the most important element in the induction process. From their cross-country empirical study of 150 teachers in educator induction programs in eight states, Leslie Huling-Austin and Sheila Murphy reported that the match of a mentor to a new educator may be the single most important and cost-effective induction strategy in an induction program.[28] Other strategies for inducting

---

28. Leslie Huling-Austin and Sheila C. Murphy, *Assessing the Impact of Teacher Induction Programs: Implications for Program Development* (paper presented at the annual meeting of the American Educational Research Association, Washington, D.C., April 20–24, 1987), ERIC ED 283779, p. 28. Similar findings have been reported by James V. Hoffman et al., "A Study of State-Mandated Beginning Teacher

include having orientation seminars, sending out and responding to needs-assessment questionnaires, or convening social activities for new people. However, more than two thirds of reported induction programs focus on mentorship as a key component of their initiative.[29] Religious education administrators are advised to listen attentively to this message, especially since a formalized mentorship program is a financially affordable personnel initiative that can be implemented with considerable return on the investment.

Establishing a Mentoring Program

Kenneth Kerr, Donald Schulze, and Lyle Woodward have outlined a comprehensive organizational plan for implementing a mentoring program, which is similar to the framework described in this book. The steps they include are needs assessment, identification of the target population, goal setting, appointing a program director, selecting mentors and mentees; orienting participants to the mentoring program and its expectations, matching the mentors and mentees; providing follow-up activities to support the mentoring program, and assessing the overall process.[30] Since every mentoring situation is somewhat different, however, effective mentorship requires that local congregations or leaders determine the most appropriate program planning choices within a proposed framework. Extensive preparation and clarity of

---

Programs," *Journal of Teacher Education* 37, no. 1 (1986). Hoffman et al. reported that the most important and positive component of their first-year experience was the peer or support teacher. See p. 19. See also Gail Huffman and Sarah Leak, "Beginning Teachers' Perceptions of Mentors," *Journal of Teacher Education* 37, no.1 (1986): 23. In this study of 108 new educators, 96 percent indicated that the mentor was integral to their success and survival.

29. Judith Warren Little, "The Mentor Phenomenon and the Social Organization of Teaching," in *Review of Research in Education,* vol.16, ed. Courtney B. Cazden (Washington, D. C.: American Educational Research Association, 1990), p. 321.

30. See Kenneth M. Kerr, Donald R. Schulze, and Lyle E. Woodward, "Organizationally Sponsored Mentoring," in *Mentoring: New Strategies and Challenges,* pp. 33–41. Though the steps are listed, clearer delineation of needs and contextual variables in different educational settings is required. Mel Heller and Nancy Sindelar have identified a similar set of steps involved in setting up a mentoring program: establishing a rationale, setting criteria for the selection of mentors, defining roles, inviting mentors, preparing mentors, and evaluating the program. See their *Developing an Effective Teacher Mentor Program,* Bloomington, Ind.: Phi Delta Kappa Education Foundation, 1991, ERIC ED 332996, pp. 11–15.

purpose are required for the implementation of religious education mentoring programs. Care should be taken to design a mentoring program that is suited to the needs and resources of a particular educational culture. Case studies, such as those compiled by Michael Zeldin and Sara Lee in their edited collection on informal mentoring in Jewish educational contexts, can help religious educators begin conceptualizing mentoring programs.[31]

These steps in preparation are consistent with those identified in the historical situations discussed in chapter 2. In the case of Teresa of Avila and the Carmelite reformers, care and attention was given to matching mentors and mentees for each person and providing sufficient professional preparation to enable them to do their assigned work.[32] Although there is no one set way of establishing a mentoring program, sufficient examples are available from the literature to guide DREs and other religious education administrators. Chapters 5–10 of this volume focus on the specific steps to be used in establishing a religious education mentoring program.

Role of University Programs and Faculty

Mentor programs often highlight the problems and limitations associated with preservice professional education programs. Why would a university education program graduate require induction assistance? Educational research points out that though professional preservice preparation programs play a vital role, there are many other steps that can be taken while an educator is in the field.[33] Realistically, these professional education programs cannot reasonably accomplish all that is expected of them. One only has to think of the long-standing apprenticeship model in other occupations to realize that a great deal of hands-on learning can occur only on the job. Furthermore, some researchers acknowledge that becoming a professional educator today is

---

31. Michael Zeldin and Sara S. Lee, eds., *Touching the Future* (1995).

32. Teresa of Avila insisted that her own spiritual directors be prudent, learned, and experienced and expected no less of those individuals who provided direction for the other nuns. For Teresa's list of qualifications, see her *Life* 13. 17–19, in *The Complete Works of Saint Teresa of Jesus,* trans., E. Allison Peers, 3 vols. (London: Sheed & Ward, 1946).

33. Gerald M. Mager, "The Place of Induction in Becoming a Teacher," in *Teacher Induction and Mentoring*, ed. Gary P. DeBolt (Albany, N.Y.: State University of New York Press, 1992), p. 12.

more difficult than it once was.[34] Religious education is a demanding profession and can be practiced successfully only with much support and assistance.

A realistic compromise is to require that preservice programs focus on content, classroom behavior, and management techniques, as well as on how to work with special-needs learners.[35] Induction programs can then concentrate on honing instruction skills. This compromise respects the caution that some skills can only be learned on the job, and it reminds mentor program planners that there is a limit to what one can learn about educating without actually being in an educational situation. Professional preparation programs in religious education cannot anticipate all the difficulties or challenges that individual educators will encounter. Although suggestions for taking courses in problematic areas such as discipline are certainly sound, experienced religious educators know that most functional learning occurs in the workplace.

To narrow the gap between university preservice preparation programs and concrete religious educational situations, as well as to increase communication about the needs and abilities of new religious educators, various specialists in mentoring have urged collaboration between these two entities.[36] Indeed, many examples can be cited of active collaboration between universities and here-and-now educational endeavors.[37] This collaboration should be regarded as an intrinsic and pervasive part of a continuum of lifelong learning rather than a

---

34. Ibid., pp. 12–13.

35. Ruth E. Kling and Donna A. Brookhart, *Mentoring: A Review of Related Literature*, ERIC ED 346095, p. 20.

36. Among those who support collaboration with university education faculty are Billie J. Enz, "Guidelines for Selecting Mentors and Creating an Environment for Mentoring," in *Mentoring: Contemporary Principles and Issues*, ed. Theresa M. Bey and C. Thomas Holmes (Reston, Va.: Association of Teacher Educators, 1992), p. 72; Odell and Ferraro, "Collaborative Teacher Induction," pp. 66–67; Alan J. Reiman, Fay A. Head, and Lois Thies-Sprinthall, "Collaboration and Mentoring," in *Mentoring: Contemporary Principles and Issues*, pp. 79–93 ; Lois Thies-Sprinthall, "A Collaborative Approach for Mentor Training: A Working Model," *Journal of Teacher Education* 37, no. 6 (1986): 18; Leonard J. Varah, Warren S. Theune, and Linda Parker, "Beginning Teachers: Sink or Swim," *Journal of Teacher Education* 37, no. 1 (1986): 33.

37. Examples of active collaboration between educator preparation institutes and schools include Tom Ganser, "Getting Off to a Good Start: A Collaborative Mentoring Program for Beginning Teachers" (paper presented at the annual Diversity in Mentoring Conference, Chicago, Ill., April, 1992), ERIC ED 343899; Odell and Ferraro,

series of steps or procedures.[38] Only in this way can the religious education profession actually improve and become more effective. When university faculty work with religious education practitioners in optimizing the overall induction process, many communication problems are resolved and undue repetition is eliminated. However, there is a limit to what university faculties with restricted resources can do to ease the transition. Ultimately, the local church community must assume responsibility for on-site religious education.

There is also a sense that university involvement can be more effective at some levels than others.[39] For instance, university faculty might become involved in professional preparation sessions for selected mentors and mentees while religious education practitioners mentor new professionals one-on-one. This structure has the potential for maximizing resources and expertise, as well as for increasing cooperation and channels of communication between agencies. University faculty may also be used in the design and implementation of evaluation for these mentoring initiatives.

SUMMARY

Religious educators have much to learn about the existing structures for formalized mentoring programs. A growing body of literature research points to a gradual increase in the phenomenon in church circles, though the dearth of systematic enquiry leaves religious education mentorship in a nascent stage. The practicalities of mentoring program planning have been developed sufficiently, however, to provide guidance in successfully implementing and evaluating a mentorship initiative. Religious educators with an interest in supporting and nurturing new professionals have an adequate basis on which to build mentorship.

"Collaborative Teacher Induction," pp. 51–73; Katherine Knight Wilcox, "Training Master Teachers to Mentor," in *Learning in the Workplace,* ed. Victoria Marsick (London: Croom Helm, 1987), pp. 134–48.

38. See Carol Rolheiser-Bennett, "From Campus to Classroom: What Role for Faculties of Education?" *ORBIT* 22, no. 1 (1991): 22–23.

39. For further discussion, see John M. Johnson and Richard Kay, "The Role of Institutions of Higher Education in Professional Teacher Induction," in *Teacher Induction—A New Beginning,* ed. Douglas Brooks (Reston, Va.: Association of Teacher Educators, 1987), pp. 45–59.

4

Basic Guidelines for Mentorship

Everyone carries with them at least one and probably
Many pieces to someone else's puzzle.
Sometimes they know it.
Sometimes they don't.
And when you present your piece
Which is worthless to you,
To another, whether you know it or not,
Whether they know it or not,
You are a Messenger from the Most High
　　　　　　　　　　　　　—Lawrence Kushner[1]

When the director of religious education for a large midwestern church decided to implement an adult spirituality program, he began by advertising for participants in the weekly bulletin. Two weeks after the September 1 deadline, only two people had registered. Persistent advertising through signs and announcements drew one additional participant. The DRE was devastated and was unable to identify the reason for the low level of interest on the part of the parishioners. His assessment, after the fact, helped him determine the causes of failure: the lack of needs assessment, the failure to explain adequately the purpose and content of the spirituality program, and poor timing. In other words, the planning for the spirituality program had been insufficient.

---

1. Lawrence Kushner, *Honey from the Rock: Visions of Jewish Mystical Renewal* (New York: Harper & Row, 1977), pp. 69–70.

The foregoing chapters pointed to the need to have a strong guiding basis for any program, particularly mentorship. In this chapter I draw on two sources, one educational and one historical, to present five basic guidelines that are intended to undergird the development of the specific mentoring program procedures outlined in the remaining chapters of this book. Basic guidelines are a necessary part of mentorship for religious educators because they provide professional direction and establish standards for future educational activities. If mentorship is undertaken in a haphazard way without advance planning, it becomes another educational fad that has little or no basis in research and is doomed to failure. The five basic guidelines presented in this chapter set the framework for mentorship within a research context and serve as the ecology for the practical thrust of the remainder of this book.

GUIDELINE 1: MENTORSHIP INVOLVES ACTIVE COLLABORATION

Teresa of Avila actively involved her mentees, Gratián and John of the Cross, in her decisions and actions to reform the Carmelite order.[2] Similarly strong, educationally-based mentoring programs involve all the stakeholders: university faculty, religious education administrators, mentors, mentees, and others who are affected by the mentoring initiative. The concept of collaborative leadership or coleadership is heartily endorsed by Australian writer Kevin Treston in *Creative Christian Leadership*.[3] Treston draws attention to the biblical basis for coleadership in ministry, noting that Jesus practiced team leadership by sharing power and authority with his apostles. Treston emphasizes that coleadership "is an act of faith in the creative energy of the Spirit."[4] He argues that since leadership and work are aspects of

---

2. Indicative of Teresa's willingness to collaborate and engage others in her reform of the Carmelite order is the excitement she records of her first meeting with Gratián. See *Foundations*, in *The Complete Works of Saint Teresa of Jesus*, trans. E. Allison Peers, 3 vols. (London: Sheed & Ward, 1946), 23.11: Though "he was not the first person to begin the movement, he came into it most opportunely."

3. Kevin Treston, *Creative Christian Leadership: Skills for More Effective Ministry* (Mystic, Conn.: Twenty-Third Publications, 1995). See especially, chapter 3, "Co-Leadership."

4. Ibid., p. 32.

cocreation, both aspects must be engaged in collaboratively. Humans help to develop Christian community through sharing leadership and work. In any mentoring program for new religious educators, local organizers need to give attention to identifying parishioners who will be influenced directly by the religious education initiative, especially those who regularly participate in educational programming. The identified individuals can then be involved in the process of developing and implementing a mentoring program. A collaborative approach to mentorship can foster widespread involvement, help build a strong faith community, and increase support for the induction of the new religious education professional.[5] It also can maximize enthusiasm for the mentoring program among community members who are not directly involved, especially when they hear mentorship discussed and witness positive results such as retention of new religious educators.[6] Collaboration in planning the program can assist in maintaining standards during the program's operation.

Establishing Partnerships for Planning

Some other educational researchers point out that promoting collaboration has the benefit of helping to establish a positive educational culture. They note that in an institutional context "collaboration" is a more appropriate word than "cooperation" because it denotes a fuller and more equitable involvement of all members.[7] A key way that churches can establish this collaborative culture is to have the religious education leader involve the staff in creating a religious education vision and culture.[8]

---

5. Maria Harris has developed the idea that faith communities and their activities can be effective in helping build up the body of Christ in *Fashion Me a People: Curriculum in the Church* (Louisville, Ky.: Westminister/Knox, 1989), pp. 77–78.

6. Thomas Sergiovanni describes the collaborative efforts of educators, administrators, and parents to become a community of leaders and learners. See *Building Community in Schools* (San Francisco: Jossey-Bass, 1994), especially chapter 10, "Becoming a Community of Leaders," in which Sergiovanni describes one educational institution's efforts to exercise a team leadership approach.

7. Edward W. Chance, Craig Cummins, and Fred Wood, "A Middle School's Approach to Developing an Effective School Work Culture," *NASSP Bulletin* 80, no. 576 (1996): 43.

8. There is considerable educational research to support the pivotal role that collaborative teams play in organizing and supporting new educator induction. See, for example, Peter Askey, "A System-Wide Program for Beginning Teachers,"*ORBIT* 22,

Research supports the pivotal role of the religious education leader in forming collaborative partnerships.[9] Collaboration can be extended to include a wider group that includes educators and parents. Collaboration has major concrete benefits for the religious education environment: religious educators in collaborative settings share ideas on instruction; learners in these collaborative settings perform better academically; extensive collaboration breaks down institutional barriers and supports the professional development of religious educators; and educational change is more effective in collaborative environments.[10] Most importantly, collaborative work environments are particularly helpful to new religious educators because they facilitate the introduction to the work environment and they provide a warmhearted invitation to the religious education profession.

Kim, for example, has been hired by a United Methodist congregation to direct an intergenerational religious education (IGRE) program. Kim did not fully grasp the church board's goals and objectives for the educational program because the board itself was still unclear of exactly what it wanted. Kim was assigned to help the board members in their own discernment process. She was encouraged to use a collaborative approach with representatives of the congregation to engage them in decision making around the type of IGRE program they wanted and needed. The discernment process has allowed Kim to get to know the board members and the congregants and has allowed them to work together toward establishing an educational program that satisfactorily meets everyone's needs.

The importance of collaborative involvement is also illustrated in the case of religious educator Isabelle, who was employed in a local youth ministry program. Isabelle had thirty years experience in team-based educational administration as the administrator of a private

---

no. 1 (1991): 6; Ardra L. Cole, "Induction Programs in Ontario Schools: A Survey of Current Practices," *ORBIT* 22, no. 1 (1991): 3; Ted Morrison, "Assisting New Teachers in Durham," *ORBIT* 22, no. 1 (1991): 9. Cole's survey of induction committee members indicates that in some cases school board trustees and representatives of educational organizations were also included on the mentoring planning team.

9. Donald C. Clark and Sally N. Clark develop the concept of collaborative partnerships in "Building Collaborative Environments for Successful Middle Level School Restructuring," *NASSP Bulletin* 80, no. 578 (1996): 1–3.

10. Ibid. The benefits I develop in this paragraph are based on a similar list by the Clarks.

preparatory school before coming to work in her church, so she understood the importance of widespread community support for any new activities. Not surprisingly, when Isabelle started thinking about initiating a mentoring program, she decided to hold a focus group of congregational members to promote discussion about mentoring needs for new staff and volunteers. Her potential religious education mentors and strong administrative backing emerged out of this focus group discussion.[11]

Maintaining a Standard for Operation

A crucial aspect of the overall collaboration guideline is that it infuses all aspects of the mentoring program, promoting the sharing of successes and failures of the mentoring initiative and the engagement of the creative energy of numerous people in the process.[12] Indeed, actively involving all the educational partners is a primary way of modeling collaborative planning for mentees. In a church situation, for instance, the pastor, administrators, learner representatives, and educators should be involved in establishing, facilitating, and evaluating the mentoring initiative. In a hospital, the pastoral care providers and staff committee representatives need to be included throughout the mentoring program. All religious education partners need to be part of a planning committee to determine needs, expectations, strategies, and programs, and to provide ongoing support for the religious education mentors and mentees. The mentoring pair should not be isolated. If they are to be evaluated and be held accountable for their time together, they can expect, minimally, to be given every support possible. Furthermore, the religious education mentee, in addition to the mentor, needs to be consulted and invited to have an active say in the educational preparation and development

---

11. Ronald M. Cervero and Arthur L. Wilson argue that program planning constitutes a complex process of negotiating a variety of educational interests in a responsible manner. Cervero and Wilson note that planners need ethical, political, and technical knowledge and skills. See *Planning Responsibly for Adult Education: A Guide to Negotiating Power and Interests* (San Francisco: Jossey-Bass, 1994), especially chapter 8, "Develop Skills and Knowledge to Negotiate Responsibly."

12. Adult educator Jane Vella stresses the need for continuous dialogue as a basis for adult learning in her *Learning to Listen, Learning to Teach: The Power of Dialogue in Educating Adults* (San Francisco: Jossey-Bass, 1994), especially chapter 1, "Twelve Principles for Effective Adult Learning."

process.[13] Collaboration across role boundaries can model appropriate religious education practices for the new professional in the field. The guideline of collaboration can undergird the original establishment of the program, and it can also affect ongoing aspects of facilitating mentorship: selection, preparation, evaluation, and compensation of participants.

GUIDELINE 2: SUCCESSFUL MENTORSHIP REQUIRES A MENTORING ENVIRONMENT

Collaboration among community leaders, mentors, mentees, and representative congregational members is one element in establishing a mentoring environment. However, many other factors also assist in the facilitation of a strong mentoring environment: tangible show of support for faculty, respect for differences, shared values and beliefs, and promotion of a continuous learning culture within the parish.[14] The type of mentoring environment that best suits a particular environment needs to be decided upon locally. In each of the three historical examples described in chapter 2 the individuals lived within religious communities that had built-in support for their members. In the desert example, the elders were paired with disciples and the monastic environment provided sponsorship for all of them. The entire environment offered a total mentoring environment that nurtured the life goals of each person.[15] Though an all-embracing mentoring environment

---

13. In discussing the notion of effective educational change, Michael Fullan points out that collaboration does not necessarily require consensus. Fullan argues that pretend agreement, which creates total similarity or homogeneity, is a most undesirable situation in an educational environment. See *Change Forces: Probing the Depths of Educational Reform* (London: Falmer, 1993), pp. 82–83.

14. R. Robert Cueni points out that to build a positive church climate, leaders should (1) model desirable behavior in their own lives and ministry, (2) concentrate on the positive and build on success, and (3) find ways to make people feel valued and appreciated. See *The Vital Church Leader* (Nashville, Tenn.: Abingdon, 1991), pp. 61–65.

15. I resist describing exactly what a "good" educational climate is. My decision is based on Roland Barth's insightful commentary on the use and misuse of lists. He notes that we have become a nation of list makers who believe that if only we can define the perfect educational environment, then we will have achieved it. Barth recommends that educators pay more attention to building a community of learners and renewing education through collaboration and partnership. See *Improving Schools from Within: Teachers, Parents, and Schools Can Make the Difference* (San Francisco: Jossey-Bass, 1990), especially chapter 4, "Building a Community of Learners."

such as described in the historical scenarios is probably impossible, in current situations some successful compromise can be reached by following this particular guideline.

The report of the Canadian Catholic bishops on the status of adult religious education in the whole country points out that one of the six most pressing issues is the need for a positive church climate in which to work.[16] The bishops note that such a climate for adult religious education would be marked by collaboration, oneness, mutuality, accountability, and respect.[17] Likewise, in typically nonreligious environments such as hospitals a mentoring atmosphere can be achieved with strong shows of support for religious educators and deliberate attempts to build an inclusive and vibrant educational community.

Shared Set of Values or Beliefs

Another important aspect of any large undertaking such as a mentorship program is shared core values that shape the work of the religious educators involved. In discussing how to build "community," Thomas Sergiovanni advocates starting with these core values and moving forward with them. He cautions that true community building can only occur when these core values are generated together by a "community of mind."[18] Holding core values such as a commitment to Christian ideals, belief in the value of religious education mentorship, and faith in learners is important for the development of a community of mind on mentorship. In an authentic community of mind, uniform solutions to issues and problems are not required for core values to survive. The community can accommodate a reasonable level of ambiguity and encourage a variety of solutions to problems that arise. Professional dialogue can provide a variety of answers.[19] Indeed, all mentoring

---

16. Canadian Conference of Catholic Bishops, *Pathways to Faithfulness: Developing Structures Which Support Catechetical Ministry with Adults* (Ottawa, Canada: Author, 1993), p. 35.

17. Ibid., pp. 47–50, especially p. 47.

18. See Thomas Sergiovanni, *Building Community in Schools*, pp. 94–95, in which he promotes the establishment of a common set of values or beliefs a "community of mind," p. 72.

19. Richard Sagor makes this point in "Overcoming the One-Solution Syndrome," *Educational Leadership* 52, no. 7 (1995): 24–27.

program participants need places where it is permissible to make mistakes and to start again.[20] Rob, for example, was assigned to establish an adult religious education committee in his parish in his first two months of work. He spent his first month finding out who the parishioners were, and the second month uncovering what was expected of the committee. During his first semester Robert lived in fear that the more experienced religious educators would find out how little he knew about establishing educational committees or mobilizing groups for action. Obviously, this negative type of religious education environment is not conducive to religious education. An effective mentor might have helped Rob by sharing stories of first-year challenges, connecting him with other first-year religious educators, and instructing him in educational areas in which he was weak.

A Learning Culture

A mentoring environment must be a continuous learning environment. *Pathways to Faithfulness*, the Canadian Conference of Catholic Bishops' report on the structures that support adult religious education in Canada, uses the language of "a learning parish" to refer to a parish that is involved in and supportive of continuous learning.[21] When the culture of the educational institute supports continuous learning, formal mentorship is viewed as an integral part of the learning culture, not as an additional burden in an already busy work space. A parish that is committed to learning

---

20. See, for example, Jane Vella's principle of safety or the provision of a challenging yet secure environment for learning. Chapter 4, "Safety: Creating a Safe Environment for Learning," in *Learning to Listen* (1994).

21. Canadian Conference of Catholic Bishops, *Pathways to Faithfulness*, p. 88. The language of "learning parish" echoes the use of learning organization (LO) in workplace education literature. For examples of the use of LO, see Peter Senge, *Fifth Discipline* (New York: Doubleday, 1990) and Karen E. Watkins and Victoria Marsick, *Sculpting the Learning Organization* (San Francisco: Jossey-Bass, 1993). Attention to the use of the learning organization concept in school literature is also growing. See, for example, Nancy Isaacson and Jerry Bamburg, "Can Schools Become Learning Organizations?" *Educational Leadership* 50, no. 3 (1992); 42–44; and John O'Neil, "On Schools as Learning Organizations: A Conversation with Peter Senge," *Educational Leadership* 52, no. 7 (1995): 20–23.

is one in which new initiatives, new people, and new ideas are welcome.

Churches need to recognize that implementation of formalized mentorship promotes a lifelong learning culture.[22] Learning during the mentoring phase is part of a process of professional growth that began in university education and continues with ongoing inservice and professional education throughout the religious educator's career. Mentorship does not provide a religious educator with all the substantial content he or she needs to know to be successful in the field. Learning to be an effective educator is a lifetime undertaking, even for those who are considered professional religious educators. An understanding of mentorship as part of a continuum helps emphasize realistic expectations of the formalized mentoring program. Julia established a mentoring initiative in several neighboring congregations. She began orienting pastors and congregations to the proposed program by explaining the church community's belief in a continuum of education for the mentoring program participants. She also familiarized her audience with the limits of the structured mentoring program. Julia reiterated the importance of promoting a learning culture for everyone in the congregation.

This learning culture needs to be reflected in the provision of ongoing professional development opportunities for the mentorship participants as well as access to relevant inservice in specific areas in which the mentee or mentor is weak. For instance, a religious education mentee who requires help with grouping learners for instruction needs to have access to comprehensive educational opportunities that assist him or her in developing specific skills and strategies, such as how to develop collaborative learning skills. Ongoing professional development is especially important to encourage mentees in their new efforts and work.

---

22. The potential of mentorship to contribute to lifelong learning has been discussed in depth by Norman H. Cohen and Michael W. Galbraith, "Mentoring in the Learning Society," in *Mentoring: New Strategies and Challenges,* New Directions for Adult and Continuing Education, no. 66 (San Francisco: Jossey-Bass, 1995), pp. 5–14. Cohen and Galbraith argue that mentorship contributes to an understanding of the workplace as a continuous learning environment in which there is a mutual exchange of ideas.

GUIDELINE 3: MENTORS AND MENTEES
ARE PROFESSIONALS

Initiating mentorship programs can contribute to the ongoing professionalization of the field of religious education. Though specifics vary,
mentorship is an effective means of induction for new professionals.[23]
James Michael Lee argues that religious education is a professional
activity and that a member professional "is a well-trained and adequately paid full-time employee of the local church devoting his/her
time exclusively to religious education."[24] The religious education
mentor and mentee are professionals who, as professionals, demonstrate the characteristics of professionalism in their work lives. Furthermore, consistent with a professional approach to the religious education field, the entire mentoring program benefits from planning with
attention to sound program planning principles that show respect for
adult learners.

---

23. The *Oxford English Dictionary* defines professional as "pertaining to, proper
to, or connected with a or one's profession or calling," p. 573. This definition is necessarily broad because individual professions need to determine the codes of conduct
or practice of their constituent members. Adult educator Ronald Cervero has given
much attention to the issue of what constitutes a profession. He points out that there is
no clear-cut way to determine if an occupation is a profession or not. He notes that
early attempts to define the professions used a list of characteristics of a profession to
measure whether or not an occupation constituted a profession. Cervero terms this approach "static." Proponents of a "process" perspective, in contrast, forego a yardstick-
type list in favor of asking one basic question of members of every occupation: To
what degree is our occupation professionalized? All occupations then to some degree
or another are affected by professionalism. Cervero notes that a third approach, one
that is growing in popularity, is to use socioeconomic criteria to determine what the
professions are. According to this perspective there are no permanent professions.
Rather, professionalism is determined by whatever society, through normative mechanisms such as the Census Bureau classification system, deems to be important at any
given time. See *Effective Continuing Education for Professionals* (San Francisco:
Jossey-Bass, 1988), especially chapter 1, "The Dynamics of Continuing Professional
Education." See also the discussion of the professions in Cyril O. Houle in *Continuing
Learning in the Professions* (San Francisco: Jossey-Bass, 1980), especially pp. 24–31.
In this book, I assume that by any of the three approaches (static, process, socioeco-
nomic) religious education is a profession.

24. James Michael Lee, "Religious Education Volunteers Are Very Special," in
The Complete Guide to Religious Education Volunteers, by Donald Ratcliff and Blake
J. Neff (Birmingham, Ala.: Religious Education Press, 1993), especially p. 38.

Characteristics of Those Chosen to Be
Professional Mentors

A responsible attitude should pervade all aspects of the mentoring program, especially the selection of mentors. In general, the professional religious education mentor is experienced and willing to take on the role of mentor, and is considered an exemplary religious educator. Furthermore, the professional who is chosen embodies the mission or goals of the religious education enterprise. Approachability, integrity, good listening skills, sincerity, and willingness to spend time are all characteristics identified as essential to a mentor in an educational setting.[25] These characteristics coincide remarkably well with those identified in the historical examples in that all highlight the value of good interpersonal skills.

It is important that the mentor not only be an exemplary religious educator but also a person interested in communicating the educational vision of the local religious community. Teresa wanted to enact and pass on her vision of a renewed Carmelite order. The characteristics identified in the educational literature are supportive of such commitment, vision, and competence.

Professional Mentorship Is Based on Program
Planning Principles

The professionalization of the mentoring program demands it follow guidelines for systematic program planning.[26] Rosemary Caffarella delineates an eleven-step model that can be followed to plan educational programs for adults. One of the advantages of Caffarella's model is that her proposed steps need not be followed sequentially, nor must all the steps be used.[27] This planning flexibility is desirable

---

25. These were the top five characteristics educational researcher Gary DeBolt garnered from a large-scale Delphi study of 164 mentors. See his "Mentor Suggestions for Establishing Mentor Programs," in *Teacher Induction and Mentoring* (Albany, N.Y.: State University of New York Press, 1992), especially p. 177.

26. There are many models of program planning available. See, for example, the seminal work of Cyril Houle, *The Design of Education* (San Francisco: Jossey-Bass, 1972) and Malcolm Knowles, *The Modern Practice of Adult Education,* rev. ed. (New York: Cambridge University Press, 1980).

27. Rosemary Caffarella, *Planning Programs for Adult Learners: A Practical Guide for Educators, Trainers, and Staff Developers* (San Francisco: Jossey-Bass, 1994). Caffarella puts forward an interactive model that promotes collaborative

when dealing with mentorship in religious education contexts because of the considerable variability from situation to situation. Caffarella's model of interactive program planning allows the mentoring program organizers to choose the steps that are appropriate for their mentoring program. The eleven steps include: (1) establishing a basis for the planning process; (2) identifying program ideas; (3) sorting and prioritizing program ideas; (4) developing program objectives; (5) preparing for the transfer of learning; (6) formulating evaluation plans; (7) determining formats, schedules, and staff needs; (8) preparing budgets and marketing plans; (9) designing instructional plans; (10) coordinating facilities and on-site events; and (11) communicating the value of the adult education program to be offered.

The basic quality of professionalization should guide the whole program and should set the tone for interaction among the participants. The educational and religious historical literature makes it clear that mentorship requires extensive planning and development. Every effort needs to be made to maintain a high professional standard in the program, from the initial conceptualization to the implementation and evaluation stages.

GUIDELINE 4: MENTORSHIP FOR RELIGIOUS EDUCATORS HAS A SPIRITUAL DIMENSION

As with every aspect of a religious educator's life and work, mentorship has a spiritual dimension.[28] A spiritual dimension is important because

---

planning by all those affected by the eventual program. See especially chapter 2, "An Interactive Model of Program Planning," in which she delineates her eleven steps in program planning.

28. The Rite of Christian Initiation (RCIA) process is a prime example of mentorship that is supported by ongoing growth and development. Used in the Roman Catholic Church as an adult education program to initiate adults into the church, RCIA provides a sponsor for every participant, encourages parish ritual celebration throughout the whole year to engage the entire assembly, and ensures that the whole community is involved in initiation of new members. Even after the typical one year of preparation the candidates for baptism and full communion (those who are baptized but who have not received first Eucharist, or confirmation) enter into a period of mystagogia, or postbaptismal support and nurturing. Their initiation does not end when they are baptized or confirmed. An advocate of the involvement of the full parish community in RCIA is Nancy Burkin. See "The Parish Community and the RCIA," *Insight: A Resource for Adult Religious Education* 2 (1988): 80–85.

of the nature of the content of religious education.[29] In each of the historical examples, the designated mentors were spiritually enriched by mentorship and they also spiritually enriched the lives of those they mentored.[30] Expressing spirituality in daily life is particularly desirable for religious educators because their relationships, work, and prayer life are so closely connected. For them, spirituality is the actual daily living of personally and professionally held beliefs.

Spiritual Basis of Mentorship

Mentorship can be a form of spiritual discipline or practice. In all of the historical examples (the desert dwellers, the Helfta mystics, Teresa of Avila) the mentoring relationship was founded on a belief that providing mentorship was a Christian responsibility.[31] To fortify

---

29. I am thinking here of mentorship as a means of living one's vocation. I use the word "vocation" in the sense intended by John Westerhoff. He speaks of vocation as a part of the human calling to fulfillment, not as a job. Religious education (or to use his term, "catechesis") is one means of helping people experience the presence of God in their lives or come to an understanding of their vocation. See "A Catechetical Way of Doing Theology," in *Religious Education and Theology,* ed. Norma H. Thompson (Birmingham, Ala.: Religious Education Press, 1982), pp. 229–231.

30. Our spirituality is lived out in our interactions with others, in our work and in our personal and communal relationship with God. Joanmarie Smith points out that religious educators often have the occupational hazard of being totally immersed in a religious environment that militates against nurturing a spiritual life. For one thing, religious educators often have incredibly chaotic and busy work lives, which makes allocating time for activities such as regular prayer difficult. Furthermore, the religious educator's immersion in organized religious life or the "dailyness of the sacred" may make religious practices somewhat unattractive. Acknowledging these occupational difficulties, Smith argues that religious educators have a unique work situation that can multiply present "opportunities" for spiritual growth. She notes that religious educators have the enviable situation of being able to place prayer time on their work schedules as a necessary part of their professional activity. As an antidote to an immersion in sacred images and rituals, Smith recommends that religious educators engage in practices such as centering prayer, which helps unclutter the imagination, study, which enriches the mind, and fasting, which engages the body. She notes that all three means have the potential to enrich the religious educator's professional and personal life. See chapter 4, "Ecumenical Spirituality and the Religious Educator," in *The Spirituality of the Religious Educator,* ed. James Michael Lee (Birmingham, Ala.: Religious Education Press, 1985).

31. As an example, Gertrude of Helfta, in counting her blessings, identifies the ability to mentor others. *Herald of Divine Love,* trans. Margaret Winkworth, The Classics of Western Spirituality (New York: Paulist, 1993), 1. 20. 121–25.

candidates for this mentoring task they were given opportunities to reflect, to pray, and to reflectively consider options in how to counsel their respective mentees. Similarly, ongoing spiritual development opportunities serve to support the spiritual life of religious educators. In the historical examples the mentors' ability to discern the most appropriate way springs from a rich prayer life and a singular life orientation, a major distinguishing feature that cannot be fully replicated for every religious education mentor. Prayerful discernment is a faculty that all people are called to foster in their own lives, though people's commitment to developing that capacity may be different from the historical examples. Fostering discernment in the present day is described more fully in chapter 9 of this book.

Nurturing Spirituality

The religious educator's discerning abilities can be enhanced through reflection, prayer, participation in worship services, communal prayer, Scripture reading, and growing in commitment to a religious tradition. In the Helfta example, for instance, there was ample opportunity to engage in spiritual direction, read and study about the saints, and build personal relationships with other nuns.[32] Growth in discernment can and needs to be fostered through provision of designated time for personal reflection, critical self-reflection on teaching, examination of the quality of one's interpersonal relationships with coworkers and learners, and ritualized group activity to celebrate religious education mentoring successes. The spirituality guideline undergirds all the practical components of a successful religious education mentoring program; it should infuse the selection, preparation, and ongoing support mechanisms for program participants.

Although this individual or group spirituality needs to be nurtured especially in the foundational phase, it certainly should not be limited to that phase. Examples from religious history show how important this ongoing provision is for growth in commitment and personal development in religious education. For example, Teresa of Avila continued to provide John of the Cross with spiritual and per-

---

32. See, for example, Mechtild of Hackeborn, *The Booke of Gostlye Grace*, ed. Theresa A. Halligan, Studies and Texts, no. 46 (Toronto: Pontifical Institute of Mediaeval Studies, 1979, microfiche), prologue, 42. 13, lines 5–6. Mechtild stresses the importance of observing the liturgical seasons and communal prayer.

sonal support that far exceeded their professional association.[33]
Leaders can model their approval and support of this use of educational time by voicing support for it in church meetings and by personally attending liturgies and other public mentoring events.

Religious education administrators need to take time as a group to
critically inquire into their own role in the induction of mentees,
their commitment to their program, and where they want the mentoring process to lead. This careful reflection will provide administrators with an opportunity to decide how they can most effectively
contribute to the initiation of new religious educators, and thus providing a strong message to potential religious education mentors that
religious education is taken seriously.

GUIDELINE 5: MENTORSHIP HAS A
PROCESS ORIENTATION

The type of mentorship I describe in this text is not focused solely on
the year-end outcome of retaining a new religious educator in a parish.
Equally important is the *process* of mentorship itself, the dynamic interchange involving the mentor, mentee, learners, church environment, staff, and church congregation. The mentorship described in this
book is as much about the means as it is about the ends, or the completion of the mentoring term.

Religious Education and a Process Orientation
Both Randolph Crump Miller and Helen Goggin have drawn attention
to the relationship between process theology and a process orientation
to religious education.[34] The insights of process theology include the

---

33. Teresa of Avila writes in her *Letters.* 261 that John of the Cross is the "Father
of my soul." See *The Letters of Saint Teresa of Jesus*, trans. E. Allison Peers, 2 vols.
(London: Burns, Oates & Washbourne, 1951).

34. Randolph Crump Miller deals with process spirituality in "Process Spirituality
and the Religious Educator," in *The Spirituality of the Religious Educator,* ed. James
Michael Lee (Birmingham, Ala.: Religious Education Press, 1985), pp. 66–87. Miller
avoids giving a definition of process theology but he alludes to his own understanding
when he says, "It [process theology] deals with the mystery of God and the full meaning of humanity in the presence of God. It avoids assumptions of fixed beliefs about
the nature of God, who is essentially mystery, but finds its anchor in the firmness of
ultimate commitment to a deity never fully known," p. 67.

belief that reality is ever changing and becoming, and that God is the source of this creative growth and openness to development.[35] Goggin sees three guiding principles of a process theology informing education: (1) God is involved in the cosmos, (2) "creation is an ongoing activity of both God and the world," and (3) with God, humans help to coredeem the world.[36] Among the many educational implications of a process theology is the understanding that mentors are assisting, not controlling, the learning process of the religious education mentee. Consequently, ongoing dialogue is the essence of their relationship. A mentoring process informed by process theology is open to the engagement of the creative ideas of the participants, with a view to promoting the full and unique development of each one. Facilitators of church-based mentorship need to accept the open-ended process nature of mentorship and trust that mentorship need not be straitjacketed and tightly controlled. In a practical sense, those who hold a process orientation to mentorship recognize that the participants in mentorship are active and involved in their own learning. And they believe that they are capable of giving and receiving effective mentorship. As facilitators, these process-oriented mentors prepare the groundwork for mentorship and then they allow the individual participants to do their own educational work.

Marie, for example, accepted the responsibility to mentor Angela, a new university colleague in a religious education program. Maria and Angela set mentorship goals and objectives for the year, decided together how they would proceed with their regular meetings, and agreed on how they would formalize their relationship into a mentoring covenant.[37] Maria supervised Angela's work, always challenging her to strive for further improvement and development in knowledge, skills, and lifestyle behaviors. In turn, Angela was encouraged to have input into her own professional assessment and to decide with Maria which skill sets, such as facilitation, she could focus on to improve her instruction. Both women were open to the possibility of continuous

---

35. Helen Goggin, "Process Theology and Religious Education," in *Theologies of Religious Education*, ed. Randolph Crump Miller (Birmingham Ala.: Religious Education Press, 1995), p. 127.

36. Ibid., p.136.

37. The establishment of a mentoring covenant is more fully developed in chapter 9 of this book.

changes and growth in the mentoring relationship. Although they set initial goals, they were flexible in their approach and allowed the mentoring process to evolve. Maria acknowledged she had as much to learn from the mentoring relationship as Angela.

A process orientation also assumes that process is a content of its own. In the words of James Michael Lee, "Process [content] is both the getting of a product outcome and an outcome in its own right."[38] Religious education mentorship, similarly, contains elements of product and process, both of which are important to nurture and attend to. Lee notes that process content is never quite finished or complete; "it is characterized by becomingness."[39]

Goggin argues that a process orientation means that religious educators must take seriously the notion that he or she is a cocreator of knowledge with the learner.[40] In a mentoring situation this would mean that the religious education mentor has an attitude of working *with* the mentee. The religious education mentor invests time and energy in the mentee's professional development and is open to the possibility of varying degrees of success in the relationship.[41] Process-oriented mentorship operates in a professional climate that supports inquiry and diversity but resists an inflexible framework.

Gerard, for example, works as a director of religious education in a Ukrainian Catholic parish. Gerard is mentoring a new volunteer, Mark. As a team, they set guidelines for their professional and personal relationship, established a mentoring covenant, and agreed to meet at regularly scheduled times to discuss Mark's educational progress, to review existing program goals and set new ones, and to assess the quality and ongoing productiveness of their interpersonal relationship. During each meeting Gerard and Mark spend consider-

---

38. James Michael Lee, *The Content of Religious Instruction* (Birmingham, Ala.: Religious Education Press, 1985), p. 80.

39. Ibid. Lee sees process content as consisting of not only substantive content but also structural content. Lee points out that the structure (methods of teaching, etc.) is just one part of process content. Because process content embraces the lifestyle, affective, and cognitive dimensions of education, it encompasses the totality of the teaching act. Ibid., p.107.

40. Helen Goggin, "Process Theology and Religious Education," pp.123–47; Lee, *The Content of Religious Instruction*, pp. 78–128.

41. Helen Goggin, "Process Theology and Religious Education," p. 144.

able time on Mark's professional development. They resist occasional temptations to forego the assessment of their mentoring relationship. Both men recognize that commitment to a process orientation means that they have to be concerned about more than the accumulation of skills and knowledge. They are convinced that religious education, as a profession, needs to be concerned with the personal and professional growth of both the mentor and the mentee.

Other religious educators define process as a "dynamic movement of growth and change characterizing all living organisms, including ideas and groups as well as individuals and created things."[42] According to this view, religious education mentors and mentees operate in the presence of creativity, freedom of expression, belief that God is fully present in the interchange among those involved in the mentoring initiative, and an awareness that the effectiveness of the mentoring program cannot be rigidly controlled. They understand, however, that the emphasis on fluidity in a process orientation does not mean havoc. Conversely, intensive planning and organization are necessary for genuine process to be nurtured.[43] Religious educators understand also that the ends and means of religious education are intertwined and they must work assiduously to make mentorship effective.

Process Theory of Leadership

The "prehensive leadership model" (PLM) developed by David Arthur Bickimer best represents the process orientation to leadership in mentorship intended in this book. Bickimer builds on the process theology of Alfred North Whitehead, and more particularly on Whitehead's use

---

42. Marge Denis and Brenda Peddigrew, "Preparing to Facilitate Adult Religious Education," *Adult Religious Education*, ed. Marie A. Gillen and Maurice C. Taylor (Mahwah, N.J.: Paulist, 1995), p. 177. Both Denis and Peddigrew work full-time professionally preparing educators throughout North America for the practical application of a process orientation to adult religious education. Here I am using "process" to refer primarily to process facilitation as described by Denis and Peddigrew. See also Marge Denis with Caryl Green, "What Is This Thing Called Process?" *Insight: A Resource for Adult Religious Education* 2 (1988): 45–49.

43. An excellent overview of process theology is given in a special edition of *Chicago Studies* 26, April 1987. See especially Robert L. Kinast, "An Introduction to Process Theology," pp. 3–10. Kinast identifies four concepts on which process theology is built: "(1) the essence of being is becoming; (2) subjective experience characterizes everything; (3) God is finite and changing; and (4) creation has no end" (p. 3).

of the term "prehension," defined as the whole is greater than the sum of the parts. His PLM begins with an understanding of the organization as a whole rather than an emphasis on the isolated components.[44] A PLM approach to the effective administration of mentorship would begin with the larger issue of building on the strengths of the congregation and the wider community. He would not focus immediately on providing professional or personal assistance to religious educators. Such a perspective would see collegiality as the first and foremost principle of a worthwhile mentoring program. Collegiality would mean that religious education leaders are supportive of mentor and mentee activity but avoid hands-on involvement in the day-to-day routines of mentorship. Bickimer cautions that this hands-off stance does not mean absence of responsibility or leadership but rather a keen ability to oversee without interfering.[45] A PLM approach means being consciously aware of and trusting of the presence of God in the mentoring activity.

Possible Difficulties in Dealing with a Process Orientation

A commitment to a process orientation for mentorship is challenging for those who deal best with polarities and dualities. Process implies that the mentorship is not a panacea for all the problems that religious educators, new or experienced, encounter in church-based education. A process orientation respects the individuality and uniqueness of the religious education mentors and mentees, as well as the educational contexts in which they function. Despite mentoring program planners' best efforts to positively influence the structure and the outcome of the formalized mentoring process, they need to be prepared for unpredictable elements. A process orientation prepares participants to anticipate and deal with unexpected events, such as interpersonal conflict in the mentoring situation. A process orientation to mentorship encourages participants to meet the challenge of conflict and to en-

---

44. David Arthur Bickimer, *Leadership in Religious Education* (Birmingham, Ala.: Religious Education Press, 1989), pp. 131–34.

45. On the issue of collegiality as a component of PLM, see ibid., pp. 250–52. Collegiality here means a hands-off approach that allows the religious education mentors to perform their jobs without undue interference from administrators. Bickimer cautions that he does not mean that administrators do nothing. He envisages them as being present and accessible, but not intrusive.

gage in it, if possible, as a potential learning experience.[46] Process ideally allows mentors and mentees to be who they were created to be rather than clones of one another. In practical mentoring terms, the mentee's goal is to be the best religious educator she or he can be, not a replica of the mentor. Although there are guidelines in the present volume, the ultimate form that mentorship takes in a particular situation depends on the people concerned, their needs and expectations, and the requirements of the church community. A process orientation is a belief that should influence all aspects of the mentoring program, from initial conceptualization to evaluation.

SUMMARY

The five basic guidelines that arise from the educational and religious literature are the basis of the practical components of this book. They highlight the need for a collaborative approach, the support of a mentoring environment, a professional perspective, a strong spiritual dimension, and a process orientation for any religious education mentoring program. Instead of being aligned with specific local practices, each of these basic guidelines undergirds and informs all of the procedures discussed in the remainder of this book. The same themes will recur repeatedly throughout the following chapters as I describe practical means of putting these guidelines into operation.

---

46. Walter Wink offers a creative alternative to destructive conflict: engaging the other in order to promote personal and spiritual growth and to prevent the possibility of becoming who one hates. From Wink's perspective conflict should be embraced, not avoided. Though Wink does not explicitly use the language of process theology, clearly his ideas are congruent with a process orientation to living the Christian life. See *Engaging the Powers: Discernment and Resistance in a World of Domination* (Minneapolis: Fortress, 1992), especially chapter 10, "On Not Becoming What We Hate."

5

Establishing the Basis for Mentorship

For the structure that we raise,
Time is with materials filled;
Our todays and yesterdays
Are the blocks with which we build.
  —Henry Wadsworth Longfellow[1]

All Saints Church had numerous problems retaining religious educators in their rural congregation. Approximately every two years their new educator quit, invariably citing intense professional isolation and lack of support from the congregation. When the church staffing committee decided to hire a replacement, the parish council insisted that this time they needed to do everything possible to retain the new person. The staffing committee decided to find out how to implement a mentoring program. To establish an educationally effective mentoring program for religious educators, the mentorship planners must begin with an extensive preprogram process. In this chapter I will outline a deliberate preprogram process to be implemented before specific actions such as selecting and professionally preparing mentors and mentees can be undertaken.[2] Local church communities can

---

1. Henry Wadsworth Longfellow, "The Builders," in *One Hundred and One Famous Poems,* comp. Roy J. Cook, rev. ed. (Chicago: Contemporary, 1958), p. 1.

2. The specific details involved in setting up a mentoring program have been documented by numerous educational researchers. For example, Gary P. DeBolt, "Mentor Suggestions for Establishing Mentor Programs," in *Teacher Induction and Mentoring* (Albany, N.Y. State University of New York, 1992), pp.182–84; Cleta Galvez-

96

select from the preprogram process those steps that are most relevant for their particular situation.[3]

SETTING THE STAGE

A well-thought-out mentoring program involves all the basic guidelines identified in chapter 4. Ideally, the religious education mentoring program concentrates on (1) organization of a mentorship planning team, (2) provision of adequate time for community assessment and relationship-building activities, (3) communication of the value of the mentoring program, and (4) adequate needs assessment.[4] Each of the possible steps in the religious education mentoring process is discussed here.

Organizing a Mentoring Planning Team

One of the first challenges in establishing a collaborative framework for mentorship is for a local church to decide who to involve in a religious education mentoring team.[5] I recommend including those persons who

Hjornevik, "Mentoring among Teachers: A Review of the Literature," *Journal of Teacher Education* 37, no. 1 (1986): 9; Mel P. Heller and Nancy W. Sindelar, *Developing an Effective Teacher Mentor Program* (Bloomington, Ind.: Phi Delta Kappa Education Foundation, 1991), ERIC ED 332996, pp. 11–15; Judy-Arin Krupp, "Mentoring: A Means by Which Teachers Become Staff Developers," *Journal of Staff Development* 8, no. 1 (1987): 14–15; Richard Dana Smith, "Mentoring New Teachers: Strategies, Structures, and Successes," *Teacher Education Quarterly* 20, no. 4 (1993): 15–16.

3. Rosemary Caffarella's interactive program planning model suggests careful selection of relevant program planning steps in the order appropriate to a given situation. Caffarella's model also stresses the importance of establishing a firm basis for educational programs. See *Planning Programs for Adult Learners: A Practical Guide for Educators, Trainers, and Staff Developers* (San Francisco: Jossey-Bass, 1994), especially p. 19.

4. In articulating its guidelines for adult religious education for the worldwide church, the Roman Catholic International Council of Catechesis names three similar requirements: "a good pastoral plan, the participation of the Christian community, the creation of positive experiences." See *Adult Catechesis for the Christian Community: Some Principles and Guidelines* (Ottawa, Canada: Canadian Conference of Catholic Bishops, 1991), p. 27, par. 59.

5. Kathy D. Rucker points out that Jesus himself frequently worked with groups to accomplish his mission. Structured committees have the additional advantage of modeling a strong faith community that utilizes the multiple ideas and professional skills of many individuals. See *Adult Education in the Parish: A Practical Handbook* (Cincinnati: St. Anthony Messenger, 1990), pp. 3–6.

are most directly affected by the mentoring initiative, as well as those who have educational competence. Possibilities for team membership include the following: (1) church administrators such as directors of religious education, leaders in the congregation, clergy, university deans, educational administrators, pastoral care leaders; (2) potential religious education mentors, either those who volunteer or those who are recommended through a nomination process; (3) faculty or staff, if the program is being conducted in an institutional context; (4) interested members of the local congregation; (5) participants in adult religious education activities or parents of religious education students; and (6) university faculty involved with teacher-preparation programs. Small membership churches can adjust their team membership according to their existing human resources. One viable alternate for small churches is to collaborate actively with neighboring congregations.[6]

Once the mentoring team is formed, the members need to be given clearly defined terms of reference, so that their tasks and responsibilities are clear from the outset. A sample terms of reference for the team is provided in figure 5.1.

Providing Adequate Time for the Preprogram Mentoring Activity

Mentoring organizers should set aside a definite period for community assessment and building, ideally before the arrival of the new religious educator or before the onset of the mentoring program. The amount of time designated may vary in duration from one month to a year, depending on the size of the church community and the available resources.[7] In the case of an Ontario induction initiative, a three-month period of preparation went into the planning of the mentoring

---

6. Collaborative ministry with other churches is just one of the many suggestions for religious education in small membership congregations suggested in Pamela Mitchell, "Educational Ministry, the CCD, and the Sunday School," in *Religious Education in the Small Membership Church*, ed. Nancy T. Foltz (Birmingham, Ala.: Religious Education Press, 1990), p. 91.

7. Nancy Burkin recommends this period of preprogram time before starting the Rite of Christian Initiation of Adults (RCIA) in a congregation. She argues that because the intent of RCIA is for the parish community to welcome new members, considerable time (she advocates at least a year) needs to be spent in preparation for the actual program implementation. See "The Parish Community and the RCIA," *Insight: A Resource for Adult Religious Education* 2 (1988): 80–85.

Figure 5.1
Sample Terms of Reference for the
Religious Education Mentoring Team

Length of Service

This should ideally be for two years from the date of appointment. (Renewable for one additional year.) During this time there may be different groups of mentors and mentees.

Accountability

This mentoring team reports to the leader of the community (for example, congregational elder, parish council chair, religious education committee, administrator, director of pastoral care, pastor).

Responsibilities

The faith community directs the religious education mentoring team to
1. undertake a thorough examination of the resources and commitment of the local church community for the mentoring program;
2. establish a program plan for the selection, compensation, preparation, support, and evaluation of the religious education mentoring relationship; and
3. implement the religious education mentoring program.

---

program. The mentoring planning team spent the time researching various superior mentoring programs, consulting with relevant university faculty, meeting with district personnel and committees within their educational districts, developing a mentoring model which the team then tested with local educational organizations, and providing information to new educators about their plans.[8] The preprogram time can be used to prepare the whole church community to support the mentorship of the new religious educator. Information sessions, professional retreats for concerned team members or parishioners, and focus groups on readiness to induct new religious educators can be offered. This effort is a means of focusing the local church community

---

8. Paul Moffatt, "Nipissing Welcomes New Teachers," *ORBIT* 22, no. 1 (1991): 5. Moffatt notes that the process of preparation was as important as the program itself. Educator Ted Morrison also describes an induction program that had a one-year period of preparation. Part of Morrison's team planning time was devoted to surveying the needs of new educators. "Assisting New Teachers in Durham," p. 9.

on mentorship and providing them with basic information on the mentoring program and how to support it.

This preprogram process can provide the entire staff and church community with an opportunity to prepare itself mentally and spiritually for a commitment to the mentoring project. A preprogram process is also consistent with the educational research on resistance to change, which emphasizes that enduring change occurs slowly and only when the grassroots people support it. Those involved in educational change typically experience several distinct stages: (1) awareness of the innovation, (2) request for information, (3) personal involvement and concern about how she or he will be affected, (4) management of the change, (5) concern about the consequences for the learners, (6) collaboration with others in learning to be involved with the change, and (7) refocusing of attention. The period of transition suggested here for religious education mentorship will facilitate the introduction of mentoring programs.[9] A sample schedule of meetings for the mentoring team is given in figure 5.2, and a sample of explanatory information for the initial meeting is given in figure 5.3.

Communicating the Value of the Mentoring Program

Though everyone in the community (congregation, school, seminary, university, or hospital) will not be directly involved in mentorship, there are many ways to include them indirectly and to engage their support for the mentoring process. This widespread cooperation and active collaboration may encourage qualified mentors to emerge from the local church community or staff. Educator Maureen Innes describes how her educational district worked to develop "inclusive communities" in which the entire staff, including support personnel, planned and carried out an induction program that was based on building relationships among themselves and with the new educators.[10] The goal of the district's mentoring program was not only to induct mentees but to initiate organizational and curricular change. Another way of involving the whole community is through *parish seminars*

---

9. Gene E. Hall and Shirley M. Hord, *Change in Schools: Facilitating the Process* (Albany, N.Y.: State University of New York Press, 1987), especially p. 60.

10. Maureen Innes, "A Whole–School Approach to Teacher Induction," *ORBIT* 22, no. 1 (1991): 13.

Figure 5.2
Sample Schedule of Meetings for the Mentoring Team

Initial Meeting

1. Explanation of primary information on mentorship. (Sample explanatory notes are given in figure 5.3.)
2. Consideration and evaluation of the current mission statement of the community (or the development of one).

Second Meeting

Reflection on who the religious education mentors will be. This reflection includes the delineation of desirable mentor characteristics and the development of a nomination process whereby people in the local community or staff can nominate themselves. (Chapter 6 discusses the selection of mentors and mentees.)

**Other Meetings Can Be Scheduled to Plan the
Following Parts of the Mentoring Process**

1. Preparation of mentors
2. Preparation of mentees
3. Evaluation plans
4. Communication plans for keeping the entire community informed about the religious education mentoring program
5. Schedule for periodic meetings with the mentee and mentor

(roundtables) on religious education mentorship. Such seminars might include inviting interested congregational members to come together to identify what they expect of mentorship, what they expect of religious education in their particular context, and what types of support they can offer. Another possibility is advising the community through *bulletin notices* or *staff announcements* that the mentoring discernment process is ongoing.[11] The public announcement method ensures that everyone is apprised and their input is valued. Another more traditional method of increasing involvement is to have an *invited speaker* address the whole church community on an aspect of mentorship, such as the importance of a total mentoring environment or full staff support.

---

11. Educator Richard Dana Smith advocates wide distribution of a newsletter written by mentors to keep the community informed about mentoring activities. See "Mentoring New Teachers: Strategies, Structures, and Successes," p. 15.

Figure 5. 3
Explanatory Notes on Religious Education Mentorship

1. What is mentorship?

   Mentorship is "a nurturing process in which a more skilled or more experienced person, serving as a role model, teaches, sponsors, encourages, counsels, and befriends a less skilled or less experienced person for the purpose of promoting the latter's professional and/or personal development. Mentoring functions are carried out within the context of an ongoing, caring relationship between the mentor and protégé."[12] [The definition adopted by the a local church community can be substituted here].

2. How long does a mentoring relationship last?

   The length of formalized mentoring relationships varies with the context. Mentoring relationships in educational contexts are usually organized for the mentee's first year of employment. However, after this first year, the mentor and mentee need to have a follow-up meeting to determine how the mentee is progressing.

3. What are the qualifications of a mentor for religious educators?

   A mentor must be a competent individual, have experience in the religious education profession, and be able to demonstrate superior teaching ability. In addition, the mentor must be willing to assist the mentee and must have good interpersonal skills. These qualities can be determined by the mentoring team, who may choose to nominate and vote on mentors.

4. What are the functions of mentors?

   A mentor is expected to teach, sponsor, encourage, counsel, and befriend the mentee.

5. What is expected of the local church?

   The local church is expected to support the process actively by nominating mentors, praying for their success, attending any scheduled events such as liturgies and prayer services to celebrate the mentoring initiative, and responding to requests for assistance. The mentoring team, in turn, keeps the parish informed of any major events in the mentoring program through regular references in the weekly bulletin and by other means devised by the mentoring team. The congregation's interests are represented by the mentoring team.

5. What is the financial cost of mentorship?

   The main costs in running a mentoring program include the following: substitute educator time, if the mentor or mentee need to replaced by another educator; incidental purchases, which will vary from one context to another, such as supplies for social activities, and certificates of appreciation for mentors.

6. Why is mentorship beneficial to the local church?

   The local church has much to gain from the mentoring initiative. Mentorship builds morale, ensures the supportive induction of new religious educators, and otherwise provides for the long-term professional success in religious education.

7. What is expected of this local mentoring team?

   The team will meet several times prior to and during the mentoring process to (1) identify possible mentors, (2) lay the groundwork in the local church, (3) initiate and provide ongoing support for the mentoring process, (4) provide ongoing education and support for the mentor and mentee, and (5) evaluate the mentoring program.

12. Eugene M. Anderson, "Definitions of Mentoring," unpublished manuscript, 1987, quoted in Eugene M. Anderson and Anne L. Shannon, "Toward a Conceptualization of Mentoring," *Journal of Teacher Education* 39, no. 1 (1988): 40.

One effective means of communicating the value of mentorship and promoting extensive involvement in it is for the entire staff, including church administrators, religious educators, custodians, and secretaries, to come together for one day to reflect on the needs of preservice religious educators. The information gained during the day can help prepare everyone for the arrival of the new religious educator.[13] The importance of such involvement by all individuals for planning mentoring programs is contrasted in the two following scenarios.

Situation 1: Pastor Jones has a wonderful track record of starting religious education programs in her congregation but not such a good record of finishing them. She usually thinks for a while about some ideas that interest her, primarily in Scripture study, her area of expertise from seminary days. She designs each program as a course consisting of six sessions. Pastor Jones advertises the six-session course in the weekly bulletin and facilitates the course herself on nights when she can fit it in. Sometimes parishioners attend, but more often Pastor Jones's efforts are wasted.

Situation 2: When he was appointed to his present synagogue, Rabbi Kercher realized quickly that he had more work than he could handle, especially in developing a strong adult religious education program. He spent his first year recruiting volunteers and organizing committees to establish a solid educational basis for the program. Rabbi Kercher realized that once his congregation was working with him, they could accomplish a great deal together.

Both leaders operate differently, and the results of their efforts show that collaboration often is the more effective route. Church environments in which one person or a select group continuously makes choices for the whole parish are not conducive to mentorship. In such a situation, the message that parishioners and new religious educators receive is that hierarchy is a value promoted by the church leadership and that teamwork is not important.

Determining Mentoring Program Ideas, Needs, and Expectations

One of the first functions of any religious education mentoring program is to determine which mentoring needs must be met and what

---

13. Maureen Innes implemented this idea in her educational district. See "A Whole-School Approach to Teacher Induction," p. 13.

resources the present staff have to meet these needs.[14] In their discussion of the issues that must be anticipated and managed before undertaking a mentoring initiative, British educators Chris Watkins and Caroline Whalley recommend assessment of availability of time for meetings and consultations, physical space for working alone, and availability of resource materials such as photocopiers for mentoring program use.[15] In a religious education context the needs may be those of the mentor, mentee, religious education program, or others identified by the mentoring team.

Needs assessment is a crucial aspect of planning a mentoring program because it can help match religious education mentor and mentee needs with the requirements of the local church. Furthermore, consulting congregational members about their perceptions of needs is a key means of maximizing parishioner involvement in and ownership of the mentoring program. While they are contributing to the development of the program they are themselves learning about and being engaged in the whole mentoring process. Needs assessment provides a unique opportunity for community building in program development. It sends a strong message to parishioners that collaborative planning and practice are an integral part of this mentoring program, involving the entire local church community.

There are many ways of conducting a needs assessment for a mentoring program.[16] One method is to confer with the people who have left the religious education position and ask them confidentially why they left. Another method is to ask the mentors what they need to do their mentoring job effectively or to consult members of the local community about their perceptions of what is required to make the church's mentoring program effective. Reviewing research on the needs of beginning religious educators is a key form of assessment

---

14. Needs assessment or identification of program ideas is the second step of an eleven-step program planning process outlined by Caffarella, *Planning Programs for Adult Learners*, pp. 67–78.

15. Chris Watkins and Caroline Whalley, "Mentoring Beginner Teachers—Issues for Schools to Anticipate and Manage," *School Organisation* 13, no. 2 (1993): 134–35.

16. Leon McKenzie has long argued that religious education programs require needs assessment. Among the five types of needs assessment he delineates, McKenzie includes *the subscriptive approach* in which the religious educator negotiates a match between learners' needs and the available resources. See *The Religious Education of Adults* (Birmingham, Ala.: Religious Education Press, 1982), pp. 145–47.

(see chapter 1 of this book for a review of such research). In addition, part of this needs assessment can be accomplished by exploring some of the questions outlined in the following section.

QUESTIONS FOR THE MENTORING TEAM
TO EXPLORE

Once the religious education mentoring team is ready to begin building a mentoring program, a variety of approaches can be employed. One key approach consists of exploring some basic questions in the school, church, hospital, seminary, community, or other local situation.[17] These questions could include the following: (1) Do we have a mentoring environment? (2) How does a mentoring program fit with our mission and current policies and procedures?[18] (3) How do we define mentorship for our situation and what do we expect of it? (4) What can religious history tell us about establishing a mentoring program? Researchers John Daresh and Marsha Playko underscore the importance of critical assessment of local conditions for the effectiveness of mentorship. They make clear that if certain fundamental conditions such as open and honest communication among staff are not present, a mentoring program will not be effective.[19] In the following sections I describe how a local church community can go about addressing each of these questions.

Determining if There is a Positive Environment to
Support Mentorship

Ellis Nelson describes one of the most important tasks of religious education as creating a *Christian ethos*.[20] In mentoring terms, this would

17. Nancy Burkin makes a list of challenging, reflective questions for parishes to consider before implementing an RCIA program. See "The Parish Community and RCIA," pp. 83–84.

18. Donald Ratcliff and Blake J. Neff discuss the importance of using a mission statement as a reference point for church-related planning in *The Complete Guide to Religious Education Volunteers* (Birmingham, Ala.: Religious Education Press, 1993), pp. 61–62.

19. John C. Daresh and Marsha A. Playko, "Preparing Mentors for School Leaders," *Journal of Staff Development* 12, no. 4 (1991): 25.

20. For Ellis Nelson, the activity of helping build a Christian ethos in a congregation is as much a component of religious education as facilitating a class. Nelson's view of a Christian ethos includes the congregation's understanding itself as the body

mean a nurturing environment for mentorship. One of the first questions that any local church will have to deal with is whether or not they have a positive mentoring environment to support mentorship of new religious educators.[21] The mentoring team can begin by asking the following seven questions (or related ones):

1. Are we supportive of the goals and raison d' être of mentorship of religious educators?
2. Do we have the level of commitment required to help the religious education mentor and mentee?
3. What are the possible impediments to helping the mentoring pair?
4. What resources (human, financial, educational, spiritual) do we already have to make religious education mentorship effective?
5. What resources will we need to acquire?
6. Will mentoring of new religious educators be supported by the current policies for hiring and firing church staff members or by other policies and procedures such as the selection process for adopting new curriculum?
7. Is personal support for church staff a value promoted in a clear and recognizable way by the local church?

Intensive engagement with these issues is integral to forming a cohesive mentoring program and to building a positive mentoring environment in the church. Religious education administrators must be open to extensive evaluation of current policy, procedures, and religious education programs. Educational research supports this prior assessment and management of the educational climate in which a mentoring program will be initiated.[22] Researchers point out that consideration and management of such factors as problematic

---

of Christ. See "Religious Education? Yes, Indeed," in *Does the Church Really Want Religious Education?* ed. Marlene Mayr (Birmingham, Ala.: Religious Education Press, 1988), pp. 117–19.

21. The importance of a mentoring environment has been outlined by writers such as Billie Enz, "Guidelines for Selecting Mentors and Creating an Environment for Mentoring," in *Mentoring: Contemporary Principles and Issues*, ed. Theresa M. Bey and C. Thomas Holmes (Reston, Va.: Association of Teacher Educators, 1992), pp. 65–77.

22. Watkins and Whalley, "Mentoring Beginner Teachers," especially pp. 130–34.

communication patterns and areas of conflict within the local context is very important. Specifically, religious education administrators should assess whether the goals and purposes of current policies and the proposed mentoring program are mutually compatible, and if they will support each other. Although mentorship has the potential to be a positive contributor to the religious education work environment, it cannot operate effectively if other practices, such as excessive religious educator workload, are not compatible with it.[23] For example, if an adult religious education mentee is expected to teach a class every night of the week and be available in the church office all day long, then mentorship for this person will not flourish. Religious education leaders need to establish a fair system of administration and policies that contribute to an effective workplace. As with the element of collaboration, religious education leaders can set the tone for the mentoring environment by giving tangible signs that they endorse the mentoring educational program.[24] Concretely, they can recognize and celebrate the achievements of individual religious educators, support them publicly and privately, provide encouragement, show they care, and act fairly. These explicit actions demonstrate that religious education leaders promote a climate of appreciation and gratitude for their faculty members.[25] When administrators do not actively support the mentoring program, the results can be disastrous.[26]

In one case, administrators established an induction program and assigned mentees unreasonable workloads in their first year, a

---

23. See Ann Kilcher's assessment of factors that impinge on the success of mentoring programs. "Mentoring Beginning Teachers: Guidelines for Practice," *ORBIT* 22, no. 1 (1991): 19.

24. Linda Phillips-Jones recommends specific strategies for administrators in "Establishing a Formalized Mentoring Program," *Training and Development Journal* 37, no. 2 (1983): 38–39.

25. My list of suggestions for how religious education leaders can support their faculty is derived from a slate compiled in Jeffrey Winter and James Sweeney, "Improving School Climate: Administrators are Key," *NASSP Bulletin* 78 , no. 564 (1994): 65–69. Winter and Sweeney identified these behaviors from their interview study with thirty-two urban educators.

26. Some mentoring researchers argue that the leadership role is vital enough to require specific educational preparation for those who administer mentorship. Ruth E. Kling and Donna A. Brookhart, *Mentoring: A Review of Related Literature*, 1991, ERIC ED 346095, p. 18.

combination that resulted in negative assessments of the mentoring program.[27] A contrast is the situation that religious educator Maura finds herself in: She has been given adequate financial, human, and material resources to operate her mentoring program for new volunteers. The parish council gives her verbal support for the mentoring program, she has a listening ear from church administrators, and she has been provided with the independence to complete her program work. Such concrete actions in a mentoring initiative can greatly enhance the probability of its success.

Religious education leaders, through their attitude, policies, and educational practices, are a critical determinant of the success of mentorship. Initiating mentorship in parishes where the pastor is a dictator who rigidly controls the mentoring process and allows no flexibility in the mentee's schedule is a pointless activity. The mentoring team should pay close attention to existing styles of leadership and make careful decisions about the probability of success of a mentoring program before proceeding further. Joanne, for example, is director of adult faith development in her parish. She has been asked by her pastor, Father Hynes, to start a mentoring program in their parish. Joanne is surprised by the request because when she herself raised the possibility at a parish council meeting last year, she was flatly refused by the pastor. But Father Hynes has just returned from attending diocesan meetings where he discovered that many of his colleagues in other parishes have started mentoring programs. Joanne agrees, if somewhat warily. She rationalizes that if mentorship is the pastor's own idea, he may more readily support it. When Joanne begins by gathering a committee of people to serve on a parish mentoring team, Father Hynes becomes

---

27. James Hoffman et al., "A Study of State-Mandated Beginning Teacher Programs," *Journal of Teacher Education* 37, no. 1 (1986): 20. From their study of two state-mandated induction programs, Hoffman and his colleagues argue credibly that even the best of programs could not help the educators overcome the negativity they faced when they were given unrealistic workloads. Alvah Kilgore and Julie Kozisek similarly have recorded the negative outcomes when the entire environment was not supportive of the program. They found that lack of administrative assistance was a major source of dissatisfaction for mentoring program participants. See "The Effects of a Planned Induction Program on First-Year Teachers: A Research Report," in *Teacher Induction*, ed. Judy Reinhartz (Washington, D.C.: National Education Association, 1989), pp. 108–12. When administrators support mentorship, they are less likely to expect inductees to perform at the same level of efficiency as a veteran educator or to be capable of handling situations that even the most experienced could not.

quite irate, wondering why she requires a team when adult faith development is her responsibility. Finally, he reluctantly agrees to the formation of the team. The mentoring plans move along smoothly until Joanne's team initiates the preprogram plan. Father Hynes tells her to forego any extensive preparation process and to just call a meeting of the potential mentors and get the program launched. After all, he tells her, the neighboring parish has almost finished a full-year mentoring program. Joanne realizes that collaborative ventures such as this one cannot succeed in a parish where the pastor interferes with team decisions and sabotages well-laid plans. Further discussions with Father Hynes meet with similar responses that impede collaboration.

Evaluating the Mission and Identity and Its Congruence to Mentorship

One of the important purposes of the preprogram meeting time is to examine the current mission statement of the context in which the religious educator is working, be it a church, seminary, community, hospital, or school.[28] A thorough examination of the mission statement can be accomplished through a series of meetings. I recommend periodic reexamination by the local church community to help them assess their goals and vision. An existing mission statement might read: "We are intent on reaching out to support and educate our seniors this year. Next year we will focus on educating and supporting young families." Another sample mission statement and a reflection process are given in figure 5.4. If no mission statement exists, then the local church community needs to look to general church guidelines for ministry, perhaps given by a larger sponsoring body such as a national church conference.[29] Otherwise, they can attempt to identify the

---

28. Kevin Treston discusses the importance of measuring actions and effectiveness against the mission statement. See Treston's discussion of the importance of the creation of a "shared vision" in *Creative Christian Leadership: Skills for More Effective Ministry* (Mystic, Conn.: Twenty- Third Publications, 1995), p. 35.

29. An example of a leadership statement on ministry is the Canadian Conference of Catholic Bishops' "Responsibility in Ministry: Statement of Commitment," *ORIGINS: CNS Documentary News Service* 25, no. 38 (1996): 633, 635–36. This statement outlines the basic responsibilities of all those in ministry (clergy, religious, married and single laypeople) to (1) those to whom they minister, (2) their colleagues, (3) the diocesan and universal church, (4) the wider community of Christians and those of other faiths, and (5) themselves.

Figure 5. 4
Sample Mission Statement and Reflection Process

Mission Statement

To work toward more fully including single parents in our congregation.

Reflection Questions

1. Do we actually use this mission statement in all our planning activities? Have we read and evaluated this mission statement as a faith community in the past year? If not, do we need to write another mission statement?
2. In general, are we a welcoming community?
3. Since developing this mission statement, how specifically have we worked toward including single parents? Whom exactly have we included?
4. Does our religious education ministry actively reach out to address the needs of single parents?
5. What are some concrete ways we might work toward improving our current record of inclusion of single parents?
6. How does our intended religious education mentoring program fit with our current mission statement? Can the program and mission statement inform one other?
7. Any other points . . .

"unwritten" vision and energy that every system contains.[30] Articulating the vision and the mission likely will give mentoring team members guidance for proceeding with their religious education activity. If the mission statement is continuously being examined in light of mentorship, chances increase that there will be congruence between the overall ecology of the church and the mentoring program. The ideas presented here for examining a mission statement point to the need for a thorough institutional assessment before a religious education mentoring program is undertaken.

---

30. Donald Eugene Miller points out that all congregations have an operational vision and energy, even if these are functioning at low levels and even if these have not been identified consciously. Miller argues that good leadership can "recover and enrich the vision, release and concentrate the energy." See "Centers of Vision and Energy," in *Congregations: Their Power to Form and Transform*, ed. C. Ellis Nelson (Atlanta: John Knox, 1988), p. 140. Further, Fayette Breaux Veverka points out that congregations continuously educate through their routine activities and practices, which give them a unique character and an identity. See "Congregational Education: Shaping the Culture of the Local Church," *Religious Education* 92, no. 1 (1997): 81.

The congruence between the mission of the local church community and the proposed religious education mentoring program needs to be explored. A statement of mission and belief will help the local community regroup and focus on the induction of new people and on the ongoing formation of others already active in religious education. All church staff need to become clear on their own identity, mission, and mandate before they can engage in religious education mentoring. Clarification can be fostered through structured workshop days, through professional and spiritual retreats, and through dialogue with each other. This may involve an opportunity for individuals to assess their commitment to the ideals of religious education and to identify areas they are willing to work on.

Defining Mentorship and Setting Realistic Expectations

Every local church community planning a religious education mentorship program should decide on a definition of mentorship that suits their particular context.[31] The question they need to ask themselves is, What will mentorship mean in our context? The definition of mentorship (see fig. 5.3) can be used as a starting place for any local church team trying to start a religious education mentoring program. A discussion on the meaning of mentorship probably will lead to determining limits for the mentoring program. For instance, the team members may decide in advance that the mentoring program will be extended beyond the one-year period. A localized definition can also be used to decide which goals and objectives fit a particular program. Questions to help consider goals include the following: What do we as a team want to accomplish by being involved in a mentoring enterprise? What are the benefits?

Realistic expectations for the outcome of mentorship need to be set early on in the process.[32] A mentoring program will not result in the development of expert religious educators in one year, nor can it

---

31. Educator Frank Clifford notes the importance of defining what mentorship means in a particular educational context. See "A Policy Perspective on Teacher Induction," *ORBIT* 22, no. 1 (1991): 7.

32. Adult educators Mechthild Hart and Deborah Horton discuss the immense difficulties involved in building a learning community that embodies spirituality. Hart and Horton caution enthusiasts to have realistic limits in mind about the educator's and the learner's depth of commitment to the spiritual development process. See "Beyond God the Father and the Mother," in *Adult Education and Theological Interpretations,* ed. Peter Jarvis and Nicholas Walters (Malabar, Fla.: Krieger, 1993), p. 256.

renew a whole church community. In this respect the mentoring program envisioned here differs from the mentoring experienced by the historical figures discussed in chapter 2. Mentorship in the case of the Helfta mystics, for instance, sometimes lasted a lifetime and resulted in the blossoming of the religious community as a center of learning and mysticism.[33] The mentors and mentees built up a very strong relationship and gave each other substantially more support than can ever be expected in a current religious education environment. Despite its legitimate promises, mentorship cannot single-handedly accomplish reform, but it can contribute a great deal toward positive change. A realistic set of program goals could include any or all of these seven:[34]

1. To provide the religious education mentee with a structured introductory experience that invites and encourages professional learning
2. To enable the religious education mentee to reach a satisfactory level of mastery in teaching that meets professional standards
3. To assist religious educators in developing a personal philosophy of teaching
4. To facilitate the religious education mentee's learning of new teaching strategies and the reinforcement of previously learned techniques
5. To develop an individual teaching style that is based on observation, discussion, and consultation
6. To encourage and enable new educators to develop a commitment to continuous professional learning
7. To orient the mentee to the culture of religious education in its local context

These goals are by no means exhaustive, but they do help the mentoring team set realistic limits on the mentoring relationship.

---

33. Many of Mechtild of Magdeburg's mentees, for instance, were people she knew for an extended period of time during her life as a Beguine. See *Flowing Light of the Divinity*, trans. Christiane Mesch Galvani, Garland Library of Medieval Literature, no. 72, Series B (New York: Garland, 1991), 7. 1. 207.

34. This list of goals was derived from two sources: Louise Stoll, "Evaluating Induction Programs: Do They Work?" *ORBIT* 22, no. 1 (1991): 20; Leonard J. Varah, Warren S. Theune, and Linda Parker, "Beginning Teachers: Sink or Swim," *Journal of Teacher Education* 37, no. 1 (1986): 31.

Religious History Can Inform Mentorship

It is important for organizers and participants in a Christian mentorship program to know that mentorship has its roots in religious history. Interestingly, many local induction initiatives specifically include information on the history and philosophy of the educational district, and they make an attempt to introduce new personnel to the community. A religious education mentoring program has the decided advantage of being able to draw on historical precedent for mentorship of new religious educators.[35] In a religious education context the information component would include a synopsis of the religious history of mentorship, as outlined in chapter 2. The historical content can be presented to team members and, later to mentors and mentees to assist them in recognizing the legacy of mentorship in religious history and the potential for mentorship to continue into the future. A concerted effort to trace the past and be informed by it is an improvement on many present educational system ventures, which frequently start with program details. An attempt needs to be made to make religious history come alive for the participants so that they can find their own connections between the past and the present.

ADDRESSING MYTHS ABOUT MENTORSHIP

Many writers on mentorship have addressed the myths that surround the mentoring experience.[36] The reasons for the growth of these myths

---

35. An example of a program that included information about the local educational context is Ralph Kester and Mary Marockie, "Local Induction Programs," in *Teacher Induction—A New Beginning*, ed. Douglas M. Brooks (Reston, Va.: Association of Teacher Educators, 1987), especially p. 27.

36. See, for example, Bernice Sandler, "Women as Mentors: Myths and Commandments," *Chronicle of Higher Education,* 10 March 1993, sec. B, p. 3. Sandler identifies common myths about mentorship, including (1) the best way to succeed is to have a mentor, (2) mentorship is always beneficial, (3) the mentor should be older than the mentee, (4) mentorship exists explicitly for the benefit of the mentee, (4) mentees should wait to be invited by mentors, (5) males mentoring females necessarily leads to a sexual relationship, (6) men are better mentors for women, and (7) mentors always know more than mentees. Sandler argues that rather than concentrate on all the things that can go wrong, it is more educationally productive to consider each mentoring situation individually. There is no one way to be an effective mentor—particular religious education contexts (home, school, hospital, church), for instance, will demand different professional strengths. According to Sandler, once each of the myths is debunked, successful mentoring relationships are possible.

is unclear, though it may be linked to the fact that little systematic research has been conducted on mentorship. The resultant confusion and uncertainty has led to misinformation and unfounded fears. Because it is impossible to list them all here, five of the more prominent myths are identified and discussed briefly.

The first myth is that women cannot be mentioned by men or vice versa. In fact, though there is considerable academic discussion on this point, there is little empirical evidence to support resistance to matching males and females in mentoring relationships.[37] Cross-gender mentorship can be negotiated effectively by providing a well-organized program, matching compatible personalities, allowing participants to withdraw for valid reasons, and ensuring that program evaluation is continuous.[38] (This point will be discussed further in chapter 6 of this book.)

The second myth is that mentorship is essentially a means of preparing religious educators for administrative positions. In fact, mentorship is generally not designed for the grooming of church leaders. Its purpose is to enhance the religious educator's initiation to a new environment, and to provide ongoing support for mentees.[39]

---

37. Ibid. Sandler argues that the myth of the impossibility of effectiveness in cross-gender mentoring needs to be dispelled. This myth is also addressed by Sonja Feist-Price,"Cross-Gender Mentoring Relationships: Critical Issues," *Journal of Rehabilitation* 60, no. 2 (1994): 13–17. However, Feist-Price cites five problems that cross-gender relationships can present: (1) collusion in stereotypical roles, especially when female mentees assume a supportive role for male mentors; (2) limitations of role modeling, since males and females encounter different challenges in the workplace; (3) intimacy and sexuality concerns; (4) public scrutiny that limits social contact between the mentor and the mentee; and (5) peer resentment if one woman receives mentorship by a male superior who is perceived to have power. Nevertheless, Feist-Price argues that a well thought out program can address these concerns.

38. Ibid., p. 16. Feist-Price draws on the work of M. G. Zey, *The Mentor Connection* (Homework, Ill.: Dow Jones—Irwin, 1984) in identifying seven ways to build strong mentoring programs that are supportive of cross-gender mentorship.

39. The bulk of the educational literature on mentorship concerns the orientation to teaching activities conducted in a formal setting such as in a classroom. The issue of mentoring administrators is occasionally addressed in the literature but not to the extent that mentorship of new professional educators is. For some references on mentorship of administrators, see Daresh and Playko, "Preparing Mentors for School Leaders," pp. 24–27; Heinz Luebkemann and Jacqueline Clemens, "Mentors for Women Entering Administration: A Program that Works," *NASSP Bulletin* 78, no. 559 (1994): 42–45.

The third myth is that mentorship is a lifelong process. In fact, although some mentoring relationships do last a lifetime, most structured mentoring situations are designed for a specified period of time that is agreed to beforehand by the mentor and mentee. Formal mentoring relationships in religious education contexts, such as the ones described in this book, are usually organized for a one year period. Informal mentoring relationships, in contrast, typically last from three to eight years.[40]

The fourth myth is that mentorship is a means of producing new religious educators who are the same as their mentors. In fact, if mentorship is facilitated properly, religious education mentees are neither encouraged nor required to become replicas of their mentors. Rather, they are asked to reflect on their own professional experiences and the professional example of their mentor and to integrate new learning into their own professional practice.[41] One of the key indicators of success in mentorship is that mentees become more proficient practitioners of religious education.

The fifth myth is that conflict in a mentoring relationship should be avoided at all costs. In fact, conflict needs to be dealt with by the most appropriate means available. Religious education without dissenting opinions is extremely problematic, mainly because it does not encourage creativity, openness, or the possibility of new ideas. Researcher Norman Cohen discusses the responsibility of the mentor in challenging the mentee to change ineffective behaviors and roles.[42] Cohen advises the mentor to assess the mentee's readiness to accept suggestions or advice before confronting the mentee. Clearly, conflict and

---

40. Kathy Kram, "Phases of the Mentor Relationship," *Academy of Management Journal* 26, no. 4 (1983): 608–25. For a concise summary of the typical mentoring phases and the duration of the mentoring relationship in business settings, see especially p. 622. In contrast to Kram's model, most of the educational mentoring relationships last for one year. Kram's stages are discussed more fully in chapter 9 of this book.

41. See, for example, the compelling stories of the four women who sought to define their own lives and experiences as distinct from those of their mentors in Elizabeth Ervin, "Power, Frustration, and 'Fierce Negotiation' in Mentoring Relationships: Four Women Tell Their Stories," *Women's Studies* 24, no. 5 (1995): 447–81.

42. Norman H. Cohen, *Mentoring Adult Learners: A Guide for Educators and Trainers* (Malabar, Fla.: Krieger, 1995), especially chapter 6, "Engaging in Constructive Confrontation."

confrontation can be integral to the effectiveness of mentorship if they lead to clarification on different educational issues and change approaches to practices. The ability to discuss professional differences, such as varying adult education philosophies, and to confront and consider alternative ways of practicing religious education is an important step in one's development as a professional. (Specific strategies for dealing with conflict are given in chapter 9 of this book.)

Though many myths can surround the development of a religious education mentoring program, the action and presence of so many effective programs is proof that difficulties can be addressed, that myths can be challenged, and that religious education programs can operate smoothly.

SUMMARY

A successful mentoring program requires setting the stage prior to commencing the mentor-mentee interaction. Active collaboration among a local mentoring team or community and setting aside time to prepare are important, as is the development of terms of reference for the mentoring team. These terms of reference should be tied into the local church's sense of mission. The religious education mentoring team's deliberation on a set of prepared questions can help set the stage by clarifying the anticipated operation and outcome of the mentoring program. Preparation can promote a positive environment in which the new mentor feels welcome and valued and does not feel alienated. An extensive preparation program can help establish a positive basis for mentorship that increases the opportunities for success and helps dispel the misguided fears and myths that commonly surround mentorship.

6

Recruiting, Selecting, and Matching Mentors and Mentees

We share our sacred stories,
sift through our graced experience,
and discover common ground,
create our creeds of courage
and our paradigms of praise.
We hear one another into being,
laugh into life our sterile dreams,
support the choice taking shape within us.
　　　　　　　　—Miriam Therese Winter[1]

There are different ways of recruiting religious education mentors. The following scenarios describe three different cases and highlight several models of mentorship, including one-on-one and multiple mentoring:

1. When the Afton Presbyterian School decided to develop a mentoring program to induct new religious educators, its staff knew that it had to attract volunteer mentors. So the administrator posted signs around the building, highlighted the benefits of mentorship at faculty meetings, and offered information sessions to encourage potential mentors to volunteer.

---

1. Miriam Therese Winter, "A Psalm for Women Church," in *Woman Word* (New York: Crossroad, 1990), p. 30.

2. When the Human Resources Department of United Hospital directed the pastoral department to initiate a mentoring program, the pastoral staff were unsure of where to begin. They decided to meet internally, discuss possible strategies, and plan a series of weekly meetings for a one month period to generate ideas. One key decision they made at the end of the first meeting was to invite congenial colleagues from a neighboring hospital to work with them in recruiting mentors and in establishing a joint mentoring program.

3. When a local parish, St. Gabriel's, decided to provide mentorship for an incoming religious education director, they formed a small mentoring team that decided to develop a multiple mentoring program. Of the five people on the parish staff, four decided they would volunteer themselves as comentors for the new director of religious education. They would work together to mentor the new professional.

The various ways of recruiting religious education mentors illustrated in these three cases also are present in the examples from religious history that are outlined in chapter 2. In the last chapter I discussed how a preprogram process for mentorship can be developed. In this chapter I will look at specific effective strategies for recruiting and selecting mentors and for matching religious education mentors and mentees.

RECRUITMENT

The strategies chosen to entice and solicit religious education mentors depend on the dynamics of different church-related environments. In this section I will discuss several strategies for recruitment and examine the role of the local mentoring team in the overall mentor recruitment process. Because the recruitment strategy influences the type of mentor who will be attracted to the religious education mentoring program, it is important that recruitment procedures be carefully thought out and implemented.

Identifying Potential Mentors

There are three major ways of identifying religious education mentors: self-selection, recruitment, and selection by the mentee.[2] Any strategy or combination of strategies can be used, depending on the religious education context. For instance, a secondary denominational school with sixty educators may be large enough to encourage all three identification strategies. A local church with eighty parishioners and three staff members, however, may have to recruit religious education mentors from a neighboring congregation. Obviously no one method will work for all religious education situations, and local mentoring teams will have to decide which choice is most appropriate for them. Each strategy for determining religious education mentors is described below.

Self-Selection for the Religious Education Mentor Role: Soliciting volunteers for the religious education mentor role will be challenging for the local mentoring team. To encourage potential mentors to volunteer, the team should circulate a clear job description consisting of roles, responsibilities, and expected time lines.[3] Volunteers can be sought by inserting notices in a weekly newsletter or by speaking publicly on the value of the religious education mentoring role, both of which encourage potential religious education mentors to come forward.[4] Other effective recruiting strategies include the distribution of promotional materials, well-designed posters, and brochures, as well as the public endorsement of mentorship by administrators, possibly through pulpit announcements.[5] Some researchers on mentorship argue that creating a positive environment is the best way to have

---

2. These three means of identifying mentors have been identified in Margo Murray with Marna A. Owen, *Beyond the Myths and Magic of Mentorship: How to Facilitate an Effective Mentor Program* (San Francisco: Jossey-Bass, 1991), p. 70. Among a variety of mentoring models that the authors present are a generic model that is a composite of the others. See pp. 67–72.

3. Nancy T. Foltz points out that religious education volunteers often become discouraged because the tasks to which they are assigned are frequently vague and confusing. Foltz argues that ensuring clarity of roles and responsibilities for religious education volunteers is one effective way to encourage them. See "The Context of Wanting: A Methodist Perspective," in *Does the Church Really Want Religious Education?* ed. Marlene Mayr (Birmingham, Ala.: Religious Education Press, 1988), p. 180.

4. Kathy D. Rucker suggests that advertising in a variety of ways is crucial to capture parishioners' attention. *Adult Education in the Parish: A Practical Handbook* (Cincinnati: St. Anthony Messenger, 1990), p. 24. Some of the means Rucker suggests are posters, flyers, paid advertisements, and newspaper articles.

5. Norman H. Cohen, *Mentoring Adult Learners: A Guide for Educators and Trainers* (Malabar, Fla.: Krieger, 1995), p. 129.

potential mentors emerge.[6] This positive environment can be developed by using educational seminars, social functions for the entire church and educational staff, and a welcoming attitude to promote mentor self-selection. The development of a positive environment as a means of volunteer recruitment is also supported by religious educators Don Ratcliff and Blake Neff in *The Complete Guide to Religious Education Volunteers*.[7] They discuss the value of creating a "high-touch" environment: one that is supportive and welcoming, that is not demanding, and that does not promote guilt for noninvolvement.

Being Recruited for the Religious Education Mentor Role: Besides encouraging self-selection, nominations can be sought for the religious education mentor role by advertising the mentoring position and asking directly for recommendations or by personally encouraging potential mentors to come forward.[8] The nomination process may serve as a useful public-relations tool for the mentoring program by giving it visibility, highlighting the desirable characteristics of the religious education mentor, and raising in the local church community an awareness of the importance of welcoming new members. A sample call for nominations form is given in figure 6.1.

Some mentoring researchers support mentor nomination by administrators.[9] These researchers believe that mentors should be invited by an educational administrator to assume the mentoring role. They argue that such selection conveys the positive impression that the mentor role is an honor and a reward for educational excellence and contributions to the profession.

---

6. See the positive process of mentor recruitment which is discussed in Judy-Arin Krupp, "Mentoring: A Means by Which Teachers Become Staff Developers," *Journal of Staff Development* 8, no. 1 (1987): 12–15.

7. Don Ratcliff and Blake J. Neff, *The Complete Guide to Religious Education Volunteers* (Birmingham, Ala.: Religious Education Press, 1993), especially chapter 9, "Encouraging Them to Volunteer." In their discussion of a high-touch environment Ratcliff and Neff build on the work of John Naisbitt, *Megatrends* (New York: Warner, 1982).

8. Wayne A. Babchuk and Sean Courtney, "Toward a Sociology of Participation in Adult Education Programmes," *International Journal of Lifelong Education* 14, no. 5 (1995): 391–404. Babchuk and Courtney note that the reasons for volunteering and for participating in adult education programs are closely related. From a review of existing studies, they demonstrate that "personal influence" or face-to-face contact is a primary means by which adults become volunteers.

9. Mary Ann Blank and Nancy Sindelar, "Mentoring as Professional Development: From Theory to Practice," *Clearing House* 66, no. 1 (1992): 24.

Figure 6. 1
Call for Nominations

Martin Luther Parish invites nominations for the role of mentor to the incoming religious educator. While the whole congregation is asked to support the new professional on staff, the local mentoring team would like to designate one person to be the official religious education mentor. Guidance in developing the skills of mentorship will be provided. The person you nominate ought to exhibit the following characteristics or show promise of being able to develop them:

1. Professional expertise in religious education
2. Commitment to the concept of mentorship
3. Good interpersonal skills
4. Ability to organize
5. Time to fulfil the mentor role
6. Flexibility and creativity
7. Ability to be a spiritual companion

I believe that _____ has the characteristics of a religious education mentor.

I have _____ (have not _____) spoken to the person about his or her willingness to undertake this role.

Your Name_____

Being Chosen for the Religious Education Role by the Mentee: In some cases, religious education mentees will be familiar with the local church before starting their position and therefore may be able to identify a potential mentor themselves.[10] An example is a mentor and a

---

10. Maria Harris describes the professional influence of her informal mentor Mary Anderson Tully. As a faculty member at Union Theological Seminary, New York City, Mary Tully's attention to the aesthetic had a lasting effect on Harris's own educational style. See "A Pedagogical Model," in *Teaching and Religious Imagination: An Essay in the Theology of Teaching* (San Francisco: Harper & Row, 1987), pp. 119–41. Harris also pays tribute to Tully's mentorship in *Fashion Me a People: Curriculum in the Church* (Louisville, Ky.: Westminster/Knox, 1989), pp. 40–41. Tully and Harris's mentoring relationship arose informally and spontaneously in the context of a seminary educator-learner situation. In contrast, the mentoring situations described in this book are much more formalized and structured. It is precisely because some religious educators such as Harris do receive informal mentoring and benefit professionally from it that I argue here that some form of mentorship needs to be made available to all religious educators.

mentee who worked together in a congregation previously and developed a strong professional rapport. When the new religious educator was hired, she naturally gravitated to her former mentor, and their mentoring relationship was renewed.[11] Mentee selection of a mentor is a common means of informal mentorship, especially after a person has been working in a new context for a short period of time. However, most religious education mentees do not know colleagues or possible mentors, so the recruitment method that is chosen is ultimately the decision of the local mentoring team. Along with recruitment, this church team has a number of rights and responsibilities.

Rights and Responsibilities of the Local Mentoring Team

The local mentoring team can exercise certain rights and privileges with regard to religious education mentor recruitment. To begin with, the team has the right to set selection criteria. On the basis of those criteria the mentoring team can accept or reject religious education mentor candidates. Furthermore, the local church mentoring team has the right to cancel the mentor's appointment at any time in the relationship, if justifiable causes such as irreconcilable differences are involved. In cases where the religious education mentor and mentee request a no-fault separation, the organizers will have to evaluate the relative merits of the situation and make a final judgment.[12] However, local mentoring team members, acting in a professional manner, know that interference is a tactic of last resort.

In addition, the local mentoring team may have to play an intermediary role in assisting the religious education mentor and mentee to resolve difficulties that might arise. Maya, for example, has begun mentoring a volunteer religious educator. About two months into the academic year, one of her religious education mentees begins to miss scheduled planning meetings for team teaching. Maya immediately realizes that her mentee is avoiding her and is not living up to her

---

11. A similar example is given in Helen Spence and Patricia Hayes, "Prophets in Our Own Land: The Role of Mentors in the Carleton Board's Pilot Induction Project," *ORBIT* 22, no. 1 (1991): 15.

12. The concept of a no-fault separation is suggested by Norman Cohen in *Mentoring Adult Learners*, p. 141.

agreed-upon responsibilities. All Maya's attempts to address the problem with the mentee prove ineffective, so she decides to request an intervention from the mentoring team. When Maya explains her troubling situation, a team member volunteers to step in and confront the negligent mentee. As in this instance, availability to religious education mentors and mentees is one of the roles of the local mentoring team. Yet another role for the mentoring team is determining the desirable characteristics of a religious education mentor.

Characteristics to Look for in Religious Education Mentors

Mentoring program goals are always determined before the actual mentor selection takes place. Goals form a handy reference point for deciding on the desirable characteristics of the religious education mentors. Although many desirable mentor characteristics are dependent on the local church context, others are universal. They include the following: professional expertise in religious education, commitment to the mentorship program, good interpersonal skills, organizational ability, time to fulfil the religious education mentoring role, flexibility, creativity, and ability to be a spiritual companion.[13]

Professional Expertise in Religious Education: Professional expertise is obviously important because the religious education mentor will require it to facilitate the mentee's professional development. The definition of qualified obviously will vary from situation to situation, but it minimally includes adequate academic preparation in religious education and two years' professional experience in the field.[14] Though identifying "qualified" religious education mentors may be

---

13. These are based on lists given in Ann Kilcher, "Mentoring Beginning Teachers," *ORBIT* 22, no. 1 (1991): 18 and Judith T. Witmer, "Mentoring: One District's Success Story," *NASSP Bulletin* 77, no. 550 (1993), p. 72. For a few other samples of the voluminous literature on desirable characteristics of mentors, see Beverly Hardcastle, "Spiritual Connections: Protégés' Reflections on Significant Mentorships," *Theory into Practice* 27, no. 3 (1988): 206–7; Sandra J. Odell, *Mentor Teacher Programs* (Washington: D.C.: National Education Association, 1990), p. 11; Sandra J. Odell and Douglas P. Ferraro, "Collaborative Teacher Induction," in *Teacher Induction and Mentoring*, ed. Gary P. DeBolt (Albany, N.Y.: State University of New York Press, 1992), pp. 63–64.

14. For a discussion of religious education as a profession, see chapter 4 of this book.

challenging, particularly where small church staffs are concerned, the local mentoring team needs to try every means possible to recruit them. The need for professional expertise is clearly illustrated in the case of the new religious education director, Robbie, who is young, energetic, and equipped with an adult education degree. But she is a beginner in practitioner skills such as instruction and administration. To facilitate Robbie's induction, the local mentoring team asked the director of youth ministry from the same congregation to mentor Robbie through the first year. Specifically, the assigned mentor is asked to tutor Robbie in facilitation skills for conducting small groups such as an adult Bible study.

Commitment to Mentorship: The religious education mentor chosen needs to be committed to the educational enterprise, to want to be a mentor, and to show interest in the personal and professional development of the mentee. A high level of commitment is essential if the newly instituted mentoring program is to be effective; without it, the high degree of personal integrity that the new religious education professional brings to the mentoring situation may wane. Mentors who have commitment to religious education mentorship believe that only the highest quality mentorship is acceptable for persons new to the profession. For example, Sadie Parker, a religious educator, informally mentored her niece Josephine during the first year that Josephine home schooled her children. Sadie set her professional expectations for Josephine quite high. She treated the mentoring relationship as extremely important, and she provided Josephine with as much attention as she might give to a formal mentoring relationship with any other junior educational colleague in an institutional setting.

Good Interpersonal Skills: The chosen mentor needs to have good interpersonal skills, such as the ability to listen and deal with differences of opinion, and be able to use these communication skills to promote the religious education mentee's personal and professional growth and development. Mentors with good interpersonal skills enjoy the time spent with the mentee and work diligently to find ways of affirming the mentees' professional abilities while stretching them to their fullest potential. For instance, Amarit, a university faculty member who mentors Sualla, knows that Sualla has been ineffective in holding the learners' attention in class. Amarit is challenged to continuously encourage Sualla to find strategies to solve her classroom interest problems rather than attack or blame her for this problem. The task is challenging and it requires many extra hours, but he is gratified by the positive results.

Time to Fulfill the Mentor Role and Accessibility: The effective mentor has to have considerable time to devote to frequent interactions with the mentee and to critically observe the mentee's teaching. Availability needs to extend to assisting mentees in a crisis situation, regardless of when the crisis happens. Religious education mentors must be in close physical proximity to their assigned mentees. Take the case of Kevin, a local director of religious education, who mentors Bob, a volunteer catechist in the parish religious education program. Because there is little flexibility in Bob's teaching schedule and Kevin has numerous work commitments, they often have to struggle to find agreeable meeting times for dialogue and inclass observations. If Bob has to consult Kevin, he often has to wait for quite some time, which increases his own frustration. Essentially, the time constraints have rendered their mentoring relationship ineffective. Mentees and mentors need to work in the same building, spend a great deal of time together in class, and have ready access to one another.

Flexibility and Creativity: The religious education mentor needs to be flexible enough to tolerate and appreciate the uniqueness and individuality of the mentee. This flexibility allows the mentor to encourage the mentee's development of abilities in areas he or she might not have known existed. For example, José's mentor Pedro encouraged José to develop his storytelling abilities, which might easily become José's strongest asset as a religious educator. Pedro himself is not an experienced storyteller. He has heard arguments that too much instructional time is lost in telling stories. Nonetheless, he encourages José because he recognizes the ability to tell stories as the key in José's religious educational successes. Pedro has sufficient confidence in his own religious education instructional ability not to be threatened by José and not to transform José into a replica of him. Pedro's flexibility and creativity help make the religious education mentoring relationship effective.

Spiritual Companionship: Effective religious education mentors often understand the interconnectedness of all people and the intricate bonds humans share. Successful mentors realize that they are companions, not authoritarian dictators, for their mentees. They earnestly try to understand their professional struggles and are determined to stand

by them in times of difficulty.[15] Take the case of Maria. She mentored
Carmella through her first year, cheered her on, was concerned that
she become an effective educator, and knew that her presence in
Carmella's professional life made a significant educational contribution. Maria wanted her to do well, listened to her, and developed a
great deal of patience in supporting her struggle to deal with her religious education difficulties.

These characteristics of desirable religious education mentors are
evident in the historical literature that is discussed in chapter 2. The
record of the desert elders, for example, shows the older monks' experience in the monastic way of life, commitment to inducting new her-
mits, and ability to be spiritual companions to their mentees.[16] Likewise, the Helfta mystics were examples of commitment to novices,
good interpersonal skills, and accessibility to their mentees.[17] Teresa
of Avila not only was a spiritual companion to John of the Cross but
also demonstrated the keen ability to be flexible with her many
mentees.[18]

---

15. Current research on mentorship supports the notion of reciprocity and mutuality in mentorship. See, for example, William Cutter, "Hierarchy and Mutuality: Mentor, Protégé and Spirit," in *Touching the Future: Mentoring and the Jewish Professional*, ed. Michael Zeldin and Sara S. Lee (Los Angeles: Hebrew Union
College-Jewish Institute of Religion, 1995), pp. 46–52.

16. As an example of the desert dwellers' identification of experience as a qualifi-
cation to mentor neophytes, see *Abba* Arsenius's praise of the monks who "acquire
the virtues by hard work." Arsenius 5 in Benedicta B. Ward, trans., *The Sayings of the
Desert Fathers: The Alphabetical Collection*, Cistercian Studies Series, no. 59 (London: Mowbrays, 1975).

17. Among the Helfta mystics there was an understanding of mentoring as service.
The nuns exercised humility and patience when they mentored others. Mechtild of
Magdeburg, for instance, cautions those in authority to "prostrate yourself with great
humility . . . . so that you may help . . . all your brothers and sisters who have been entrusted to your care." *Flowing Light of the Divinity*, trans. Christiane Mesch Galvani.
Garland Library of Medieval Literature, no. 72, Series B (New York: Garland, 1991),
6. 1. 167.

18. Teresa of Avila displays the high regard she has for experienced mentors when
she records her meeting with her own mentor Peter of Alcántara. She notes, "When he
saw that I had desires which he himself had already carried into effect . . . he delighted
in talking to me about these things." *Life* 30. 5. See *The Complete Works of Saint
Teresa of Jesus*, trans. E. Allison Peers, 3 vols. (London: Burns, Oates & Washbourne,
1951).

Voluntary Participation

One of the premises on which a sound religious education mentoring program is built is the voluntary nature of the structured mentoring relationship. (A sample application form for potential mentors to complete is given in figure 6.5.) This voluntary dimension applies to mentees as well as mentors. No level of coercion to participate is acceptable, especially since some new religious education professionals may not require a formal mentoring program. For instance, religious educators who have extensive experience in other church education environments may not benefit directly from a mentoring relationship. If a formalized mentoring program is instituted, it must be voluntary for mentees as well as mentors. If new religious educators do indeed choose to have an assigned mentor, they need to become involved in personally assessing their own readiness to receive educational direction. Personal preparation will enable them to collaborate with others so the mentor-mentee matching can be done effectively.

For example, Rev. Boutilier, an assistant pastor, was assigned to mentor several Sunday school religious educators. Reverend Boutilier was intimidated, at first, but as with any other work assignments given him in that first year in the congregation, he took on the mentorship task with enthusiasm. Until he completed his own self-assessment for mentorship he did not fully realize that he had been coerced into a job that was beyond his professional capabilities. Voluntary participation in religious education mentorship needs to be one of the key considerations in selecting from among potential mentors.

SELECTING FROM AMONG THE POTENTIAL MENTORS

Once potential religious education mentors have been identified and nominated, or have volunteered, there are several means of screening them: self-assessment, in-depth interviews, or a combination of both. In this section I will discuss each of these specific means. Ultimately, particular contextual factors such as small church staffs and time constraints will strongly influence the means chosen for assessment.

Self-Assessment

Though it is infrequently formalized, self-assessment often is part of the intricate process of deciding to become a religious education mentor. Potential religious education mentors need to think carefully about the following desirable characteristics: (1) professional expertise in religious education; (2) commitment to mentorship; (3) good interpersonal skills; (4) time to fulfill the mentor role, and accessibility; (5) flexibility and creativity; and (6) ability to be a spiritual companion. Then the potential mentor can decide whether or not to accept the nomination for religious education mentor. Educator Norman Cohen points out that the willingness to volunteer as a mentor should generally be seen as a positive indicator of the individual's professional commitment. Cohen also provides a comprehensive inventory to be used with prospective mentors or returning mentors.[19] The local mentoring team can use such a self-assessment inventory to formally screen applicants for the mentoring role. Figures 6.2, 6.3, and 6.4 contain self-reflective exercises that religious education mentors and mentees can be asked to complete as part of their self-assessment. The entire mentor self-assessment process may be followed with an in-depth interview.

Interviews

The personal interview strategy is advocated by many general education writers on mentorship.[20] Interviews are also recommended by religious education writers Ratcliff and Neff, who provide detailed interview protocols on recruiting religious education volunteers. Citing the work of Mark Senter, Ratcliff and Neff offer the following guidelines: interview the volunteer privately, give an advance copy of the interview questions to the candidate beforehand, and follow a standard format for all volunteers.[21] One significant recommendation they make is to ask volunteers specific questions on their individual strengths and

---

19. Norman Cohen, "Principles of Adult Mentoring Scale—Postsecondary Education," *Mentoring Adult Learners*, appendix A (1995), pp. 159–70.

20. See, for example, Judith T. Witmer, "Mentoring: One District's Success Story," *NASSP Bulletin* 77, no. 550 (1993): 72.

21. Mark Senter III, *Recruiting Volunteers in the Church*, rev. ed. (Wheaton, Ill.: Victor, 1990), cited in Ratcliff and Neff, *Complete Guide to Religious Education Volunteers*, pp. 98–99.

weaknesses. Other writers and resources on interviewing can also be used to guide this mentor screening process, though it is advisable for the local church mentoring team to use their independently constructed mission statement and definition of religious education mentorship to direct the content of the specific questions that are asked. In a religious education context the following questions are suggested as criteria for preparing the interview format:

1. Does the religious education mentor's experience and ability fit each of the desirable characteristics (professional expertise in education, commitment to mentorship, good interpersonal skills, time to fulfil the mentor role, flexibility, creativity, and ability to be a spiritual companion)?
2. Does the religious education mentor have the ability to fulfil each of the desired mentor roles (befriender, counselor, sponsor, teacher, encourager)?
3. Do the religious education mentor's self-assessment questionnaire responses (beliefs about professional mentorship, communication skills, and ability assessments) provide adequate information from which to make a decision?
4. Does the religious education mentor assent to the mission statement of the local church community?

Though the self-assessment and interview processes can be quite time consuming, they also can be effective ways of screening potential religious education mentors. A comprehensive process can help ensure that new religious education professionals receive the best mentorship possible. Once the qualified mentors have been selected, the local church mentoring team can then address the complex issue of finding mutually satisfactory matches for mentors and mentees.

MATCHING MENTORS AND MENTEES

Although the whole faith community (congregation, school, hospital, seminary, university, or home) is asked to provide mentorship for the mentees and contribute to a positive mentoring environment for them, one religious education mentor is usually selected for each mentee. Matching religious education mentors and mentees involves being mindful of individual differences between the personal and

Figure 6.2
Beliefs about Religious Education Mentorship

(This form is to be completed by potential mentors.)

1. My own belief about the purposes of religious education mentorship is

   _____ .

2. What I have to offer to a new religious educator is

   _____ .

3. The amount of time I am willing to commit to formal mentorship is

   _____ .

4. I am motivated at this time to become a religious education mentor
   because _____

   _____ .

professional backgrounds of each. It also involves being fully aware of mentee needs and the work responsibilities of their assigned partners. Effective matching is extremely challenging and will require considerable attention to the designated characteristics of the mentor and mentee, beginning with their potential for compatibility.

Compatibility Considerations

The basic concern of compatibility is matching religious education mentors and mentees who have similar timetables, work responsibilities, physical proximity, and personal affinity.[22] Whether or not the two have personal compatibility is not easily determined. Writers Margo Murray and Marna Owen suggest the use of personality inventories such as the Personal Skills Map and the Personal Profile System

_____

22. Helen Spence and Patricia Hayes, "Prophets in Our Own Land," p. 15. These points are supported by Kilcher, "Mentoring Beginning Teachers," (1991), p. 18. Significantly, Kilcher acknowledges the considerable difficulty involved in successfully determining compatibility of participants when new educators are involved.

Figure 6.3
Communication Skills for Religious Education Mentors

(This form is to be completed by potential mentors.)

This form is for your own assessment and self-selection for religious education mentorship.

Most people I work with would say that:

1. My listening skills are.

.... average .... good .... above average.

2. My ability to explain ideas is

.... average .... good .... above average.

3. My conversational skills are

.... average .... good .... above average.

4. My willingness to help other people is

.... average .... good .... above average.

5. My ability to say no, when necessary, is

.... average .... good .... above average.

6. My ability to give constructive feedback is

.... average .... good .... above average.

---

as a means of matching the mentor and mentee.[23] Other researchers recommend a form of psychosocial matching whereby potential mentors and mentees complete a leadership inventory.[24] The goal of such a test is not to find identical matches but to heighten mentoring

---

23. Margo Murray with Marna Owen, *Beyond the Myths and Magic of Mentoring*, pp. 144–45.

24. John C. Daresh and Marsha A. Playko, *A Method for Matching Leadership Mentors and Protégés*, 1992, ERIC ED 344315.

Figure 6.4
Self-Assessment for the Role of Mentor

Religious Education Mentoring Roles	How I Have Played This Mentoring Role Previously	What Challenges Me about Playing this Mentoring Role	The Skills I Require to Be More Effective in this Role
Role model			
Befriender			
Sponsor			
Teacher			
Counselor			
Encourager			

program participants' awareness of their individual leadership styles and to use this information to negotiate their strengths and weaknesses. Leadership inventories, however, only make sense in church situations where both mentor and mentee are employed in leadership positions such as religious education directorships.

One possible method of matching is to have religious education mentors and mentees complete a standard personality inventory and then have them discuss the information that the completed inventories yielded. Among the more well-known personality inventories are the Myers-Briggs Type Indicator and the Keirsey and Bates Temperament Sorter, both of which are based on the psychological theory of Carl Jung.[25] The purpose of both instruments is to foster mutual self-understanding of how you and others in your environment (school, home, or work) function best and to use these commonalities and

---

25. The Myers-Briggs, and Kersey and Bates typologies are described in Toni La Motta, "Using Personality Typology to Build Understanding," in *The 1992 Annual: Developing Human Resources*, ed. J. William Pfeiffer (San Diego: Pfeiffer, 1992), pp. 263–74. The Keirsey and Bates typology is available in a brief, accessible format: D. Keirsey and M. Bates, *Please Understand Me* (Del Mar, Calif.: Gnosology, 1984).

differences to build productive relationships. Another type of individual assessment that can be used for matching religious education mentors and mentees is the Van Tilburg and Heimlich Teaching Beliefs Scale, which assesses personally held attitudes about the role or function of the educator.[26] Of course, the purpose of these inventories is not to select same-type matches but to use the differences and similarities to strengthen the religious education mentor-mentee relationship. Learning how to appropriately use the data gathered from these diverse forms can be a challenge.

Use of Data from Self-Assessment Forms

Mentor and mentee self-assessment, followed by individual interviews with the local mentoring team, may be enough to determine who would be a good match for whom. The more similar the professional tasks of mentor and mentee, the more beneficial the mentoring relationship will be for both. By soliciting input from the religious education mentor and mentee, the mentoring team can increase the chances of effectively pairing mentors and mentees.[27] Educator Judy Clarke carries personal involvement in selection a step further by describing a unique mutual selection by mentor and mentee.[28] According to Clarke's plan, the mentees are invited to a lunch soon after their hiring to meet other mentees. The same mentees are invited back in several months and asked to bring with them another staff person whom they have identified as a possible mentor. One advantage of this process is that it encourages the religious education mentee to become

---

26. E. L. Van Tilburg and Joe E. Heimlich, "The Van Tilburg/Heimlich Teaching Beliefs Scale," in *Developing Teaching Style in Adult Education*, ed. Joe E. Heimlich and Emmalou Norland (San Francisco: Jossey-Bass, 1994), pp. 207–9. This scale measures the respondents' beliefs about their roles in teaching. Those who work in professions other than teaching are asked to complete the inventory from the perspective of how they think an educator should answer. Another inventory of Heimlich's that would be useful for this exercise is the Norland/Heimlich Teaching Values Scale, ibid., pp. 210–15.

27. In reporting on their experience of developing a mentoring program for educational administrators in Singapore, Allan Walker and Kenneth Stott attest to the value of the intensive involvement of mentor and mentee in the matching process. See "Preparing for Leadership in Schools: The Mentoring Contribution," in *The Return of the Mentor: Strategies for Workplace Learning*, ed. Brian J. Caldwell and Earl M.A. Carter (London: Falmer, 1993), especially p. 90.

28. Judy Clarke, "Changing the Odds," *ORBIT* 22, no. 1 (1991): 24.

acclimatized to the new religious education environment before having to begin a formal mentoring relationship.

Caution about Demographic Considerations

The professional educational literature has given considerable attention to demographic factors that affect the matching of mentors and mentees. In chapter 5 I discussed some warnings that have been articulated about matching males and females. Concerns about cross-gender pairing stem from the possible development of a sexual relationship or the potential for gossip. There is no possible way to completely guard against liaisons or gossip, but developing a well laid out plan for religious education mentorship can help by promoting professionalism in the formal mentoring program.

Writers of some of the earliest mentoring literature assumed that the mentor should be older than the mentee. Daniel Levinson and his associates, for instance, asserted that effective mentors should be a half generation older than the mentees.[29] Many subsequent educational writers agree with Levinson.[30] The strengths of age and wisdom do tend to support considering an age differential when pairing religious education mentors and mentees. However, there does not appear to be any convincing empirical research to indicate that retaining older mentors is crucial for mentoring program success. Since younger people often acquire expertise early in their careers, the need for ensuring an age differential is conjectural at best. Likewise, calls for racial and ethnic compatibility have not been convincingly connected to substantially increased success of the formal mentor-mentee relationship.[31] One possible solution is to encourage the religious education mentor and mentee to explore the implications of personal differences and

---

29. Levinson and his associates suggest that whereas many mentors in informal mentoring relationships are older, there may be situations where a person of the same age or younger can be an effective mentor. Daniel Levinson et al., *The Seasons of a Man's Life* (New York: Knopf, 1978), p. 99.

30. From their reviews of the literature, Cleta Galvez-Hjornevik and Peeter Poldre conclude that many subsequent writers agree with Levinson and his associates. See Cleta Galvez-Hjornevik, "Mentoring among Teachers: A Review of the Literature," *Journal of Teacher Education* 37, no. 1 (1986): 8; Peeter A. Poldre, "Mentoring Programs: A Question of Design," *Interchange* 25, no. 2 (1994): 187.

31. Ibid. Poldre is one of the writers on mentorship who support drawing attention to ethnic and racial compatibility in mentor-mentee matching.

Figure 6.5
Application Form for Religious Education Mentors

Name ————————————————————————————————

Address ——————————————————————————————

Telephone number —————————————————————————

Background questions ————————————————————————

Religious education experience ———————————————————

Educational background ————————————————————————

A statement (100 words) of why you would be an effective religious education mentor ————————————————————————————

————————————————————————————————————

————————————————————————————————————

————————————————————————————————————

————————————————————————————————————

References ——————————————————————————————

————————————————————————————————————

similarities in areas such as age and ethnicity, instead of emphasizing
homogeneous grouping.[32] Matching issues are very significant in religious education where a shortage of religious education mentors is
likely to exist. As a consequence, I recommend that program planners
remain open-minded about possible matches, given that little convincing research exists to support setting limits and restrictions.

SUMMARY

Religious education mentor and mentee recruitment, selection, and
matching are challenging aspects of the formal mentoring program

---

32. Cohen, *Mentoring Adult Learners*, pp. 148–50.

development process. Attention to detail in each of these areas will help develop a solid mentoring program that has committed, professional mentors. There are other recommendations for the process such as attending to personal similarities and differences between religious education mentors and mentees, as well as carefully planning and implementing the selection process. Effective matching for religious education mentors can be accomplished by a combination of interviewing and self-selection. Furthermore, promotion of the positive aspects of the actual match can help dispel any uninformed speculation about the relationship. An informed public is often a supportive community.

7

Preparing Mentors and Mentees

He called to him the twelve, and began to send them out two by two.

—Mark 6:7

"Gosh, this is difficult," Margaret remarked to her coplanner, Steve, as they met to discuss the more important elements to include in their mentoring preparation program. Though they had read the recommended professional literature on mentorship, they felt little further ahead than when they began. Margaret and Steve discovered what many mentoring planning teams have already realized: Though there is little empirical research on the design and content of mentoring preparation sessions,[1] there are numerous mentoring program descriptions available. This educational research can be adapted readily to the needs and resources of the congregation, hospital, home, semi-

---

1. Mia Gladstone concluded from her review of nine mentor workshops and the analysis of data from three hundred mentor satisfaction questionnaires that careful planning and preparation are essential for successful mentoring programs. Yet neither she nor the other mentoring researchers seem to have given in-depth attention to the questions of how long the professional preparation sessions should last, what the sessions should consist of, how they should be conducted, and what the effects of different types of educational preparation are. See *Mentoring as an Educational Strategy in a Rapidly Changing Society* (Quebec City, Canada: Quebec Department of Education, 1987), ERIC ED 288028.

Similarly, Gary DeBolt confirms the importance of preparation for the mentoring role; yet he offers only a one-day workshop format for mentor preparation. In his workshop format DeBolt lists items to be covered, such as communication skills, tran-

nary, or educational institution. However, the question of what constitutes adequate preparation for participation in a particular mentoring program ultimately needs to be decided by the local mentoring planners. In this chapter I will develop a program design for planning and implementing a professional preparation program for religious education mentees and mentors.[2]

RECOMMENDED PREPARATION
PROGRAM DESIGN

My preparation program design is influenced by a similar process developed and documented by Katherine Knight Wilcox.[3] The process elements of her framework design that I am adapting include: (1) deliberate responsiveness to the needs of mentors, (2) specific tailoring to mentor preparation for a one-year formalized mentoring relationship, (3) rootedness in adult education principles and practices. Unlike Wilcox, however, I extend the mentorship preparation design to include both religious education mentors and mentees. First, I discuss Wilcox's program design (which she calls a model), and then I outline my own mentor and mentee preparation plan.

---

sition to the position of leader, conferencing skills, and giving effective feedback. This type of description is typical of the available research literature. See "Mentor Suggestions for Establishing Mentor Programs," in *Teacher Induction and Mentoring* (Albany, N.Y.: State University of New York Press, 1992), pp. 182–84.

William and Marilynne Gray have argued for a more in-depth orientation to their five-level Helping Relationship model, which they maintain gives comprehensive information for mentors to help mentees progress through five levels of development. (In their model, level 1 is a state of dependency whereas level 5 is a state of independence.) Despite the fact that Gray and Gray say that their model provides in-depth professional preparation, there is little indication that the educational preparation offered in the Helping Relationship model surpasses the one-day workshop model. See "Synthesis of Research on Mentoring Beginning Teachers," *Educational Leadership* 43, no. 3 (1985): 37–43.

2. The issue of providing preplacement education for religious education mentors is especially important, since church-related environments are notoriously lax in giving adequate preservice support to employees. R. Michael Harton argues that churches lose volunteers to other community groups who are more willing to provide adequate preparatory education. See "Working with Educators of Adults," in *Handbook of Adult Religious Education,* ed. Nancy T. Foltz (Birmingham, Ala.: Religious Education Press, 1986), p. 140.

3. Katherine Knight Wilcox, "Training Master Teachers to Mentor," in *Learning in the Workplace*, ed. Victoria Marsick (London: Croom Helm, 1987), pp. 134–48.

The Wilcox Program Design

Wilcox operated a mentor training program that prepared retired educators to mentor inductees.[4] With a team of mentoring program planners composed of professional educators from the local education board and university faculty with expertise in education, Wilcox developed and implemented an eighteen-hour preplacement program that trained a group of mentors for the tasks of mentorship. Her team began by having the trainers themselves observe the interactions between current mentors and mentees in their work environments in order to identify the issues that seemed most challenging for participants. The trainers then used this information to plan and structure their own mentoring preparation program. The training they subsequently designed for mentors involved in-class sessions on the transition from educator to the role of mentor, as well as opportunities to develop strategies for changing undesirable behaviors. Wilcox's organizing team first invited the designated mentors to participate in a four-day preplacement program. The team followed this intensive introduction with three supplementary mentor sessions that were interspersed throughout the academic year. They addressed ongoing problems the mentors were encountering. These continuing professional preparation sessions resulted in an additional nine hours of training for mentors.

Basing Mentor Preparation on
Adult Education Principles

My professional preparation program design is based on adult education principles, specifically on the six basic premises of Malcolm

---

4. My use of the word "training" in this particular section is consistent with Wilcox's usage. In the remainder of the chapter and elsewhere in this book I use the term "professional preparation" because the program I recommend for religious education mentors and mentees is a combination of education and training. For an argument supporting the use of training, see W. L. Day, L. Hommen, J. Johnson, J. Ottoson, H. Schuetze, and A. Thomas, who point out that for too long the adult education literature has relegated training to the acquisition of narrowly defined skills in an instrumental fashion, and subsequently to second-class status. They argue that there can be no training without education, or the enabling of learning. Likewise, there can be no education without training. See "Adult Education and Training: Two Solitudes" (paper presented at the Canadian Association for the Study of Adult Education, University of Saskatchewan, Saskatoon, Sask., Canada, May 1992), p. 109.

Knowles's concept of andragogy (a set of assumptions about how adults learn).[5] Applied to adult religious education, the six premises assert that both mentors and mentees (1) are self-directed in their learning, (2) have a vast wealth of experience to bring to their learning, (3) are interested in learning to solve real life dilemmas, (4) want to apply what they have learned to their personal and professional lives, (5) need to know *why* they are learning something before they learn it, and (6) respond more to intrinsic motivators (increased self-esteem and quality of work life) than to extrinsic motivators (better wages, promotions).

Paying attention to these andragogical assumptions results in a religious education preparation program that fully involves the participants and prepares them to be colearners in the formal mentoring process. Using adult education principles increases the likelihood that religious education mentoring programs will meet participant needs and will respect learners as professionals.[6] For example, a preparation session facilitator[7] asks potential religious education mentors to identify and fully describe the most distressing incident they can remember from their own first year as an adult religious educator. What factors about the incident made it so distressing? What specific educational issues did it raise? What or who helped you to resolve the problem? How were others able to assist you? What might your colleagues have done to help you even more? This critical incident exercise has the potential of sensitizing religious education mentors to the

---

5. Knowles's original description of andragogy was composed of the first four assumptions cited here. See *The Modern Practice of Adult Education: Andragogy Versus Pedagogy Practice* (New York: Association Press, 1970), pp. 39–49. His argument was that andragogy (a way of thinking about working with adults) ought to be distinguished from pedagogy (a way of thinking about working with children). Knowles describes all six assumptions in *The Making of an Adult Educator: An Autobiographical Journey* (San Francisco: Jossey-Bass, 1989), pp. 83–84.

6. The principles of adult learning have been applied to religious education in Nancy T. Foltz, "Basic Principles of Adult Religious Education," in *Handbook of Adult Religious Education*, pp. 25–58.

7. I am using the term "facilitator" in the sense intended by R. E. Y. Wickett, *Models of Adult Religious Education* (Birmingham, Ala.: Religious Education Press, 1991), p. 40. Wickett broadly defines a facilitator as anyone who assists individuals to learn, either directly or indirectly. Facilitation can include teaching, planning, and evaluating learning.

learning experiences and needs of their own mentees.[8] It also provides room for everyone's experience to be heard and valued within an educational setting, an essential component of a positive adult education environment.

One of the main aims of the religious education mentor preparation program is to encourage the designated mentors to examine their own beliefs and assumptions about mentoring, teaching, and learning so that they can be better equipped to meet the professional needs of their mentees. Though no mentoring preparation program can familiarize participants with every possible mentorship challenges, as a minimum, preparatory programs should equip potential mentors to think critically about challenges they may encounter and to identify and practice strategies for analyzing and dealing with them. Such professional preparation should encourage religious education mentors to critique their own professional behavior and assumptions in order to ready them for their interactions with mentees.

A series of steps to follow in the mentor and mentee professional preparation process includes: making decisions about the preparation process, planning and implementing the preparation sessions, and designing and implementing a series of ongoing professional development sessions.

DECISIONS ABOUT THE PREPARATION PROCESS

As with any facilitative design for adults, there are numerous questions that need to be asked when planning preservice sessions for religious education mentors and mentees. I recommend using Wilcox's eighteen-hour preplacement program design and implementing it over a four-day period, with each day consisting of four and one-half hours.[9] I choose this distribution of time because I believe the

8. Stephen D. Brookfield has popularized the use of critical incident exercises in adult education. See *The Skillful Teacher* (San Francisco: Jossey-Bass, 1991), pp. 31–34.

9. Katherine Knight Wilcox, "Training Master Teachers to Mentor," p. 136. There is considerable variation in the duration of different mentoring preparation sessions. For instance, Mary Ann Blank and Nancy Sindelar advocate only four to five hours of preparation for the mentor. See "Mentoring as Professional Development: From Theory to Practice," *Clearing House* 66, no. 1 (1992): 24.

preparation is sufficiently intense to require a concentrated block of time. Further, the shortened days will accommodate those who need considerable opportunities to process independently the session content. In this section I will discuss substantive content and choosing an adult religious education facilitator who can lead the professional preparation sessions.

Who Decides on the Educational Content

Local mentoring planning teams need to consider the issue of who will determine the religious education content not only of the orientation sessions but of subsequent continuing preparation sessions. Arguably, seeking input from all those who have a stake in the program is the most effective way of implementing a religious education mentoring program.[10] This option will allow the mentoring preparation process to remain open enough to accommodate problems and issues as they arise for the mentoring pair.[11] An example of an inclusive decision-making process would be a local congregation that hires a new religious educator with substantial theological background but little facilitation experience. The mentor and mentee consult with the local mentoring planning team. They conjointly recommend that the professional preparation sessions respond to the mentee's identified need for more practical, skills-based content. Another resource in the content selection and design of a preparatory program is university faculty who have knowledge of, and expertise in, adult education and mentorship.

Deciding Who Facilitates the Preparation

The local mentoring planning team also has to decide if it will facilitate the preparation program or engage another person for this function. Employment of a facilitator does not mean the team will no longer be active. In fact, it needs to be included in a significant portion of the professional preparation session schedule. For instance, the team members are in the best position to familiarize the religious

---

10. This suggestion is provided in Lois Thies-Sprinthall, "A Collaborative Approach for Mentor Training: A Working Model," *Journal of Teacher Education* 37, no. 6 (1986): 13-20.

11. See Ann Kilcher, "Mentoring Beginning Teachers,"*ORBIT* 22, no. 1 (1991): 19.

education mentor and mentee with the details of the preprogram stage of preparing the local church community for the formal mentoring program. The team can inform participants about the locally developed understanding of the concept of religious education mentorship and the stated goals and expectations for the mentoring program. Evidence from the evaluation of previous mentoring programs supports providing religious education mentors with flexibility to clarify appropriate roles for the particular context in which they are working instead of having clearly defined roles from the very beginning of the preparation process.[12]

In larger settings such as universities, the numbers of participating mentees and mentors may warrant the hiring of a facilitator for the preparatory stage. In the Wilcox example, the school district and a neighboring university cooperated to develop and facilitate a mentoring program. However, in many religious education settings smaller staff numbers and fewer funding resources will require the local mentoring planning team to search for other alternatives, such as working collaboratively with neighboring congregations to launch the preservice sessions together and using internally available facilitators together. This cooperative effort is more likely to occur in locations where a central administrative unit exists, such as a diocesan office, regional health board, or national church office.

If no one person is employed to facilitate the professional preparatory sessions, then the existing resource people in the faith community can be used. For instance, experienced volunteer facilitators can be recruited and prepared or seasoned religious education mentors from previous years might be invited to be part of the planning process.[13] Whoever actually facilitates the professional preparation sessions

---

12. See Gary P. DeBolt's research with mentors from twenty-eight programs in New York state. These mentors identified flexibility concerning role identification as important for the efficacy of their mentoring programs. "Mentor Suggestions for Establishing Mentor Programs," p. 182.

13. It is important that the persons chosen be religious educators, not theologians. Leon McKenzie points out that religious educators of adults lack credibility because often they pretend to be theologians rather than educators. As a result they are isolated from adult education as a field and they do not use communicative language in their practice. McKenzie's critique highlights the need for a religious education facilitator who is solidly grounded in educational theory and practice. See *The Religious Education of Adults* (Birmingham, Ala.: Religious Education Press, 1982), p. 70.

should be an integral part of the decision of whether to prepare the religious education mentors and mentees together or separately.

Whether to Prepare Mentor and Mentee Together or Separately

Many existing preparation designs assume that mentors, not mentees, receive preparation for their role.[14] However, the possibility exists for including the religious education mentees in sessions with the mentors, though designing a conjoint program presents challenges such as how to effectively meet their respective preparation needs.[15] The potential benefits of learning about the expectations of religious education mentorship together outweigh the difficulties of organizing and planning for the sessions.[16] A modified preparation design that includes independent and combined sessions may solve the problem of how to meet mentor's and mentee's needs simultaneously.[17] For instance, the first nine hours of the preservice orientation to the religious education mentoring program and to the local mentoring planning team's expectations can be offered to both religious education mentors and mentees. This conjoint session will provide the participants with time to become familiar with each other, to begin building a working relationship, and to participate together in general mentoring sessions that are relevant to them both. Following this initial nine-hour orientation, mentors and mentees can divide into two groups so that the last nine hours are used to address their respective needs. This separation is intended to foster collaboration among mentors and among mentees. It will provide a needed opportunity for groups of common concern to discuss issues such as the problems new professionals encounter. I recommend that during the academic year mentors and

14. Katherine Knight Wilcox, for example, does not include any preparation sessions for the mentees. See "Training Master Teachers to Mentor."

15. Louise Bay Waters and Victoria L. Bernhardt, "Providing Effective Induction Program Support Teachers: It's Not as Easy as It Looks," in *Teacher Induction*, ed. Judy Reinhartz (Washington, D.C.: National Education Association, 1989), p. 56.

16. See Ann Kilcher, "Mentoring Beginning Teachers, " p. 19.

17. An alternative to full involvement of the mentee in preparatory education would be to use Margo Murray and Marna Owen's suggestion of designing an orientation session specifically for mentees. See *Beyond the Myths and Magic of Mentoring: How to Facilitate an Effective Mentoring Program* (San Francisco: Jossey-Bass, 1991), p. 70.

mentees continue to separate for concurrent inservice sessions. The mentor and mentee can attend seminars together when topics of common concern, such as communication skills, arise.

The professional preparation program proposed here has elements of preservice and continuing professional development. This framework assumes that substantial preparation is required for religious education mentors and mentees and that ongoing professional development sessions will be used to supplement and inform the initial preparation period. Whereas the initial preparation program will provide an orientation to the formal mentoring process, the continuing preparation activities will offer ongoing support for religious education mentors and mentees as well as an opportunity to meet with their colleagues to deal collectively with individual problems encountered in the formal mentoring situation.

PLANNING THE PREPARATION SESSIONS

Planning for the professional preparation sessions is necessarily comprehensive. I give attention in this section to preparing the facilitators of these sessions, orienting the religious education mentors and mentees together, providing preparation for the designated mentors, and outlining the structure and content of the continuing professional development sessions. The first concern is preparing the session facilitators.

Preparing the Facilitators

A variety of ways can be used to develop a preparation program for mentoring program facilitators. In the Wilcox program design, the facilitators visited current mentors and mentees to observe the interchanges between them. They also identified from their site visits the issues and problems that seemed most difficult for the mentors and mentees. The facilitators learned from experienced mentors and documented the issues and problems they seemed to be encountering. For instance, Bert and Ronald have visited Holy Rosary Parish several times in three weeks to meet with the mentors and mentees in the religious education program. Two of the mentors, Elsie and Cyril, have reported that the pastor's decision to begin the program halfway through the year has caused insurmountable problems. Specifically, their mentees had already found sources of support or were exceedingly discouraged. Likewise, Elsie and Cyril felt the time pressure of having only five months left in the academic year to provide an adequate mentoring experience to their charges. Taking this information, Bert and Ronald revised their own time schedules and moved forward expeditiously to plan their orientation sessions. Localized concerns such as these can be balanced with those documented in the literature, which I discuss below.

The Common Orientation Session

The joint preparation of religious education mentors and mentees can begin with combining both groups for the opening orientation session (nine hours). The mentoring pairs will have an opportunity during this time to discuss their respective interests and goals for the mentoring program. Optimally, the entire eighteen-hour orientation needs to occur away from the work site so that both mentor and mentee have time away from regular religious education responsibilities to build a personal relationship. The session also provides an opportunity for them to clarify any misunderstandings or limitations before the mentoring relationship begins. For instance, when Ralph and Wilf met for the first time in their mentorship orientation session they spent a great deal of time becoming acquainted with each other. They also engaged in the structured preparation process that included analyzing the aspects of the religious education field they enjoyed most and the goals they each had identified for participating in the formalized mentoring program.

Substantive topics to be covered in a preplacement religious education mentoring program include:

1. A general overview of the mentoring program, with attention given to the local religious education context. This overview should include specific insights from the preprogram phase in which the concept of mentorship is introduced to the congregation, school, hospital, seminary, or home. These insights might concern the chosen operational definition of mentorship, relationship of the mission of the local church to the religious education program, agreed-upon goals and limits for the program and expectations of it, compensation allocated for mentors, proposed evaluation procedures, particular situational concerns, and available resources.

2. Brief explanations of the expectations and requirements of mentorship for religious educators. These explanations might include a discussion of mentorship in historical contexts, delineation of the concept of spiritual companionship, roles of mentors and mentees in religious education contexts, limits and boundaries for mentoring relationships, phases of mentoring relationships, adult development theory, and typical mentoring activities such as routine meetings and on-site observations. (Sample explanations of mentorship are given in chapter 5, figure 5.3.)

3. Attention to the identified needs of new religious educators. This section might include a review of the educational research findings on the needs of first year religious educators, as outlined in chapter 1 of this book.

4. Negotiation and completion of a mentoring covenant. The discussion could include issues of confidentiality, proposed format of the covenant, and reasonable limits for the mentoring relationship. Covenants will be more fully discussed in chapter 9.

5. Congregations may also want to include local concerns such as how to work effectively with volunteer religious education personnel, a common component of most religious educators' intra-parish work.

Planners' sensitivity to local mentor concerns is demonstrated in the case of Angela, a new director of religious education for a large parish. She worked with religious educators previously, but on a much smaller scale than in her present placement. Angela's current concerns are learning how to cope with a larger bureaucracy and how to delegate responsibilities. When the preplacement facilitator discovered Angela's real requirements in a routine needs analysis, she modified her agenda to accommodate them.

Alternative Structures for Common Orientation

Though the number of religious education mentors and mentees being prepared may be insufficient in some cases to justify full-scale preplacement seminars and workshops, professional preparation for the mentoring roles is still required. Alternate preparation techniques include an equivalent amount of time in one-on-one tutoring with an experienced religious education mentor or a formal consultation with the local mentoring planning team to help the candidate become familiar with the hopes and expectations of their particular mentoring program. Another alternative is to use the example of St. James United Congregation, whose designated mentor/mentee group was too small to justify its own orientation program. Instead, the pastoral staff co-organized a professional mentoring preparation program with a neighboring congregation that was also inducting a new religious educator. Regardless of the size of the congregation, the provision of preparation for mentors and mentees is essential. For the second half of the orientation (remaining nine hours) mentors and mentees can be divided so that their distinctive needs are addressed.

Proposed Outline for Preplacement Mentor Sessions

The mentor preparation program can focus on concerns that mentors experience in their new role.[18] Mentor preparation programs typically address a number of topics, some of which focus on the mentor's adult development and some of which focus on the mentor's direct interaction with the mentee:[19]

1. Focusing on the religious education mentor's role. This discussion might involve each religious education mentor's identifying past experiences of being a mentor, remembering his or her first year as a religious educator, assessing strengths and weaknesses for assuming the mentoring role, and planning how to build on personal strengths for the upcoming year.

---

18. To support the preparation sessions, educators Mary Ann Blank and Nancy Sindelar advocate giving mentors a handbook of policies and procedures. This suggestion obviously would be more important for larger settings with a significant organizational structure than for smaller ones. See "Mentoring as Professional Development," p. 24.

19. This list is derived from Gary P. DeBolt, "Lessons and Questions from School-Based Collaborative Programs," *Teacher Induction and Mentoring*, p. 194. See also John Daresh and Marsha Playko, "Preparing Mentors for School Leaders," *Journal of Staff Development* 12, no. 4 (1991): 24–27. Daresh and Playko describe a three-day educational design consisting of five emphases: (1) orientation to mentorship, (2) instructional leadership skills, (3) human relations skills, (4) mentor process skills, and (5) contextual realities and district needs. The strength of their choice of topics is the emphasis on contextual factors such as the needs, expectations, and conditions of the local educational environment. Attention to context ensures that religious educators receive important information early in their job placement.

2. Learning from other religious education mentors. If a mentoring process has already been initiated locally, experienced religious education mentors might be invited to be present and to offer suggestions for success and failure in the mentoring role.

3. Focusing on strategies and tactics for working with the religious education mentee in the first phase of the mentoring program. This section might include review and practice of communication and observation strategies, constructive feedback techniques, and listening skills. The emphasis here is on feedback because the mentors need to hone this skill in order to have effective interactions with their mentees.

4. Phases of adult development. The focus in this portion of the orientation is on the mentor's developmental needs and concerns. For instance, if the majority of mentors are late-career professionals, then the facilitator might concentrate on professional transitions and on the opportunity to "pass on" acquired skills and knowledge to the new educational professional.

5. Ways to improve religious education mentee skills. In this section, the preplacement facilitator can focus on specific strategies and techniques to improve mentee skills in areas such as instruction and interpersonal communication.

Mentoring planning team members need to bear in mind that religious education mentors at the orientation stage are probably not yet focused directly on the mentee nor on potential incidents and situations. Simulation exercises are often useful because of the absence of concrete situations to work with. Once the mentor has had practical experience with the mentee, the inservice sessions can draw on actual experiences and problems to be solved.

One effective strategy for these preplacement sessions is a critical incident process whereby the mentors are encouraged to remember their past experiences of teaching, examine their assumptions, assume new roles, and experiment with new ways of teaching and interacting in religious education.[20] Procedures used include brainstorming, role-playing, and problem identifying. In the preparatory sessions religious education mentors practice positive mentor behaviors such as active listening, in both small and large group sessions. By role-playing a

20. Stephen D. Brookfield, *The Skillful Teacher*, pp. 31–34.

variety of religious education mentorship scenarios and by having the other participants examine the mentor roles that are exhibited, intense discussion tends to result. This dialogue facilitates examination of mentorship attributes and activities that are effective and those that are inconsistent with mentoring of religious educators.

An example of how to use the critical incident process would be to have two religious education mentors role-play the following scene: Denise stayed home from work for four consecutive days and Jane, her mentor, suspected the absenteeism was due to her inability to cope with troublesome teenagers in a confirmation preparation program. Jane's task is to deal with this situation constructively. When Denise finally returns to work, she asks Denise a number of questions. Why she is at home so often? Is she experiencing family problems? Following the role play the whole group of prospective mentors discuss Jane's solution to the problem. Some of the mentors challenge Jane to think about personal boundaries and how to reframe her questions in a nonthreatening manner. The session participants affirm Jane's mentoring role and assist her in thinking about new ways to approach the problem of mentee absenteeism. This critical incident procedure can also be utilized with religious education mentees in a variety of scenarios.

Proposed Outline for Preplacement Mentee Sessions

Religious education mentees' preparation session can run concurrently with the mentors' sessions during the second half of the orientation program. The mentees' session can begin with a focus on the mentee's role in the mentoring relationship and then move on to specific instructional concerns. A sample list of topics for the nine-hour preplacement program is listed here:[21]

1. Focusing on the role of mentee and on the religious education mentee's past experiences of being mentored informally. What can the mentee offer the relationship? What are some strategies

---

21. For a list of potential mentee-preparation topics, see Ted Morrison, "Assisting New Teachers in Durham," *ORBIT* 22, no.1 (1991): 9. Educational researchers Nicholas Stupiansky and Michael Wolfe have suggested similar topics for mentee professional development. See "The North Country Mentor/Intern Teacher Program: A Rural Consortium," in *Teacher Induction and Mentoring*, p. 87.

of benefiting from mentorship? Though answers will probably be solicited from the group, the facilitator may present several suggestions, including openness to the mentor's ideas, willingness to practice recommended instructional strategies, and ability to request and receive assistance.

2. Learning from other religious education mentees. If a mentoring process has already been initiated locally, mentees from previous initiatives may be present to offer suggestions for success and failure in the mentoring role.

3. Phases of adult development that are peculiar to mentees. This section could focus on adult developmental phases that provide a lens through which mentees can understand their particular situation. Religious education mentees could be invited to explore various phases and to determine which they identify most with, as well as how they could best use that knowledge to learn and grow continuously

4. Concentrating on the concerns of new teachers and on effective strategies for coping with the new religious educational assignment. Considerable education literature, such as is discussed in chapter 1, is available to inform this discussion.

5. Focusing on identified areas of professional weakness, such as instructional skills, curriculum design, evaluation and record keeping, and dealing with special learners. Religious education mentees need to realize that their professional education is ongoing and does not end with their university education.

As with the mentor preparation sessions, the facilitators ought to keep in mind that the mentees' religious education professional experience will be limited in the orientation stage. Specific examples of educational difficulties are not yet formed in most mentees' minds and might be more appropriately dealt with later in the academic year. Therefore the orientation process might be more facilitator led than mentee generated. The critical incident process suggested above can also be used, though with a simulated religious education situation. Mentees can be encouraged to recall their own experiences of being a learner, to examine their assumptions, to assume new roles, and to try out new ways of teaching and interacting in religious education.[22] The

---

22. Ibid.

same procedures of brainstorming, role-playing, and problem identifying are recommended. Religious education mentees can practice positive mentee behaviors such as active listening and careful consideration of the mentor's practical advice.

Using the critical incident process, two mentees could role-play the following situation: An elderly parishioner, Mr. Powers, participates in a religious poetry study circle. He constantly disrupts the group with monologues that are off topic. Susan, the leader, tries gently at first to listen to what Mr. Powers is saying and then realizes that he is diverting the group from its purpose. She needs to find a way to meet Mr. Powers's needs and those of the group. The mentees discuss this situation and Susan's solution (opening the next session with a minilecture about the purpose of the group). The mentees debrief the situation and Susan's solution and offer her suggestion for how to handle this situation more effectively. More specific concerns can be addressed in the ongoing professional development sessions.

PROVIDING ONGOING PROFESSIONAL DEVELOPMENT

The continuous learning culture recommended in this book requires constant attention to the many ways in which the church can sponsor and promote a learning culture for mentor program participants. Furthermore, the mentoring preparation program outlined here provides ongoing professional preparation sessions for both religious education mentors and mentees.

Mentor Sessions throughout the Year

The three continuing preparation sessions for mentors can be interspersed throughout the mentoring year. These three sessions take nine hours and focus on problems the mentors identify as being difficult to address in their workplace. This structure focuses on religious education mentors' needs, providing them with ongoing guidance in their mentoring role. Because the same mentors continue to meet throughout the year, trust in the group is often high, a condition that facilitates openness among them, as well as personal development and learning. The topics that the subsequent mentor preparation sessions might include are illustrated in the following three sessions:

Session I Topics:

1. Examination of specific religious education mentor experiences of working with mentees. Examples include positive encounters with mentees as well as more challenging interactions. Sharing experiences builds the group's trust and sense of common identity as mentors.
2. Dealing with specific problem areas in being a religious education mentor. For example, all mentors are asked to identify specific issues they encounter, such as how to encourage a mentee to persevere in implementing collaborative learning strategies even after negative experiences. The mentor discusses how he or she dealt with the troubling situation and is given helpful feedback from the facilitators and from experienced colleagues on alternative strategies.
3. Identifying topics for the next mentor preparation session, such as negotiating interpersonal issues of authority with mentees, in a formalized mentor program.

Session II Topics:

1. Sharing of religious education mentor experiences. Discussion could center on individual experiences and challenges of working with designated mentees.
2. Honing skills in how to be an effective mentor. For example, this section could include using role play to develop effective communication skills. Mentors are encouraged to utilize experiences from their mentoring encounters and to use these as the content of the professional preparation sessions.
3. Identifying topics for the next mentor preparation session, such as how to deal with conflicting messages from religious education administrators about mentor autonomy or how to cope with mentee overdependence.

Session III Topics:

1. Preparing for separation from the religious education mentee. This session might include identifying methods of assisting

mentees in becoming more independent in their professional decision making.

2. Assessing personal strengths and weaknesses in providing religious education mentorship. A constructive strategy for mentors would be to self-assess whether they had successfully fulfilled the conditions of their learning covenant. (See chapter 9 for a discussion of learning covenants.)

3. Providing feedback to the local mentoring team planners on the formalized mentoring program. Because mentors have had first-hand experience they are in a unique place to offer participant evaluation, which can be used for the improvement of the present program.

These topics are suggestive only. The strength of facilitating these mentor-centered sessions throughout the year is that the topics can emerge from the actual mentoring contexts. The effectiveness of this developmental planning approach in mentoring professional development will depend largely on the degree of cooperation and support received from the religious education mentors involved.

Mentee Sessions throughout the Year

Local mentoring planning teams also need to regularly schedule continuing professional preparation sessions for mentees throughout the year. These sessions can focus on those areas of religious education in which mentees need assistance. Mentees can benefit from the opportunity to discuss problems of mutual concern and frustrations that they may have with their mentors or their specific professional tasks. A suggested outline of session topics is given here:

Session I Topics:

1. Examination of specific mentee experiences of working with the mentor. This might include identifying individual problems that mentees are encountering in their religious education work. Sharing experiences builds the group's trust and sense of identity as new professionals.

2. Dealing with specific problem areas in being a religious education mentee. For example, all mentees identify problematic issues they encounter, such as how to deal with an overly enthusiastic

mentor who sets project goals beyond reasonable limits. The mentee discusses how he or she dealt with the situation and is given feedback from the facilitators and from her colleagues that affirms her current response or suggests alternative strategies.

3. Identifying topics for the next mentee preparation session, such as designing and implementing effective collaborative learning procedures.

Session II Topics:

1. Sharing religious education mentee experiences. This session could include a task of highlighting individual experiences with religious education mentors and examining possibilities for dealing with them constructively in the future.
2. Honing specific religious education instructional skills. This section could include using role play to develop communications skills with learners. Religious education mentees could access experiences from their actual teaching experiences and use them as the content of the continuing preparation sessions.
3. Identifying topics for the next mentee session. Examples include how to work constructively with church administrators who oversupervise the mentee.

Session III Topics:

1. Preparing for separation from the mentor. This session might include individually identifying examples of overdependence on the mentor and practicing specific strategies for dealing with the issue.
2. Assessing personal strengths and weaknesses in the mentoring relationship. This session might include self-assessing whether the mentee had fulfilled the commitments named in the mentoring covenant. (See chapter 9 of this book for a discussion of the mentoring covenant.)
3. Providing feedback on the mentoring program and making program suggestions for the next year. Like mentors, mentees have had firsthand experience and consequently are in a unique place to offer participant evaluation, which can be used for the improvement of the present program.

The topics listed here are only suggestive. Particular congregations will want to focus on their own mentee's needs and concerns. The mentee inservice sessions, for instance, could be held collaboratively with a neighboring congregation, especially if the mentees express a concern about professional isolation. Another proposal is for a religious education mentee in a church situation to meet with at least two other mentees in the local area once every six weeks for a combined dinner and continuing education meeting. The three mentees could take turns inviting a facilitator to guide them through the meeting and provide professional insight into the issues they identify. In the first six months they could plan to host a university faculty member in the field of education with expertise in educational induction, a retired seminary religious educationist, or a practicing pastoral counselor. Some of the facilitators will be more beneficial than others, but the consensus is that mentor meetings are worthwhile. Other religious education mentees have benefited from more structured educational initiatives organized by central church bodies and school boards. Whatever the format, the continuing professional development of religious education mentees is crucial.

SUMMARY

Providing adequate preparation for mentors and mentees requires a thorough assessment of needs and current resources. No universal means of preparing mentors and mentees suits every situation, nor is a universal solution desirable. Individual groups will have to decide what works best for them in a particular context. However, several basic guidelines in designing a mentoring program preparation apply. All preparation program designs ought to be responsive to mentors' and mentees' professional needs, be based on adult learning principles, include time for mentors to be educated separately and apart, include an immediate preparation initiative, and incorporate an ongoing professional development plan.

8

Compensating
the Mentors

A little onward lend thy guiding hand
To these dark steps, a little further on.
—John Milton[1]

Patrick and Angela's mentoring program plan was in place in June, to be implemented in September when their mentee participants would officially start teaching in the parish religious education program. As a means of bringing closure to the planning stage, Patrick and Angela asked a colleague in a neighboring congregation to review their comprehensive plan. Having spent considerable time reading through their documentation, the colleague asked, "Where is the compensation for the religious education mentor?" Patrick and Angela learned quickly that one of the key supports for an effective mentoring program is a well-developed compensation structure that provides incentives for participation and acknowledges the worthiness of the mentoring role.[2] The primary reward experienced by the desert elders was the apostolic satisfaction for having served one's religious community and one's

---

1. John Milton, *Samson Agonistes* in *Paradise Regained, the Minor Poems and Samson Agonistes,* ed. Merritt Y. Hughes (New York: Odyssey, 1937), p. 542, lines 1–2.

2. Recruitment and compensation are closely linked concepts. Refer to chapter 6 of this book for a discussion of the issues involved in recruiting religious education mentors.

God.[3] In present educational situations, such compensation is still applicable, though the life circumstances of religious education mentors vary considerably. There is substantial and open-ended discussion about how to give adequate appreciation to and how to highlight the religious education mentor's contributions.[4] In this chapter I will discuss some current issues implicit in compensating religious education mentors. Then I will offer practical suggestions for structuring an appealing compensation package.

A VARIETY OF WAYS TO
COMPENSATE MENTORS

Nancy Foltz argues that too often religious leaders fail to give religious education volunteers adequate appreciation for their contributions of time and professional expertise.[5] In her view, this significant oversight contributes to a reluctance to volunteer. Consequently, a shortage of competent personnel is created. The mentors' personal and professional investment in the mentoring relationship needs to be recognized, though there may be some debate over the most effective type of acknowledgment. On the one hand, personal satisfaction for having contributed to one's chosen profession can provide considerable reward for a religious education mentor. On the other hand,

---

3. *Amma* Theodora, for example, describes the ideal desert mentor as "patient, gentle and humble as far as possible; he must be tested and without partisanship, full of concern, and a lover of souls," in *The Sayings of the Desert Fathers: The Alphabetical Collection*, trans. Benedicta B. Ward. Cistercian Studies Series, no. 59 (London: Mowbrays, 1975), no. 5.

4. Supporters of mentor compensation include Sandra J. Odell, "A Collaborative Approach to Teacher Induction That Works," *Journal of Staff Development* 11, no. 4 (1990): 14; Ann M. Schnieder, *Understanding Context: A Key to the Design of Formalized Mentor Programs to Induct Beginning Teachers* (paper presented at the annual conference of the National Council of States on Inservice Education, Orlando, Fla., November 16–19, 1990), ERIC ED 327523, pp. 5–11; Delores M. Wolfe, "Designing Training and Selecting Incentives for Mentor Programs," *in Mentoring: Contemporary Principles and Issues,* ed. Theresa M. Bey and C. Thomas Holmes (Reston, Va.: Association of Teacher Educators, 1992), pp. 106–8; Nancy L. Zimpher and Susan R. Reiger, "Mentoring Teachers: What Are the Issues?" *Theory into Practice* 27, no. 3 (1988): 179.

5. Nancy T. Foltz, "The Context of Wanting: A Methodist Perspective," in *Does the Church Really Want Religious Education?* ed. Marlene Mayr (Birmingham, Ala.: Religious Education Press, 1988), pp. 180–81.

external compensation such as certificates of appreciation are a tangible way of communicating the importance of the service to the ongoing development of the profession. Such external rewards signal to the congregation that mentorship is a valuable undertaking that is integral to the growth of the church. The entire congregation can offer its thanks and communicate its appreciation to mentoring program participants by providing these rewards. Ways and means of compensating the religious education mentor need to be examined thoroughly.

The most important guideline for mentoring team organizers in identifying appropriate forms of compensation is to frame the various alternatives in terms of the rationale for ministry. All compensation should be tied to service and to the continuation of religious education as a professional ministry. Rewards need to reflect the value placed on being a contributing member of one's chosen vocation. Commercializing mentorship by offering financial honoraria to mentors, for instance, may convey the impression that mentorship is a stepping-stone to financial and career success.[6] Rewards for mentorship in church-related contexts, in contrast, highlight the individual's contributions to the educational profession. They function as a positive means of recruitment for future mentoring projects. Mentoring team organizers should choose their reward structure with care in order to impress on all religious educators that inducting new members is a valuable service. As with many professionals, religious educators want to pass on what they have learned to the next generation.

Educational researchers have pointed out that the need to provide extrinsic compensation is important for the success of a formalized mentoring program.[7] However, the type of reward mentoring program organizers decide on is often less important than the public

---

6. In contrast, educational researcher Ann Schnieder concluded from her ethnographic study of a mentoring program that the greatest impediments to successful implementation of the program were structural and that a major difficulty was that no financial incentives were given to the mentors. In Schnieder's view this was a violation of the local cultural norm and indicated a disregard for the context in which the educational initiative was being implemented. See her "A Key to the Design of Formalized Mentor Programs," pp. 16–20. I argue in this chapter that religious educators typically choose to work in environments that do not compensate them well financially. Mentors' motivations for being involved in the religious education profession are typically not utilitarian; therefore, the compensation structure should reflect this reality.

7. Odell, "Collaborative Approach to Teacher Induction," p. 14.

acknowledgment of the religious education mentor's role in induction of new educators. One way to attract competent and experienced people is to include a combination of tangible and intangible rewards, such as released time, financial compensation, professional development opportunities, luncheons, and ceremonies of public recognition. The key is to provide a variety of alternatives from which to choose.[8] In an inner-city Baptist congregation, for example, the religious education mentors decided that the best compensation for them for this year's mentoring contributions was to have ground transportation provided to a practical theology conference in a neighboring county. Those mentors who volunteered in subsequent years chose different alternatives, namely, released time from regular class schedules and mentorship inservice opportunities. Both cycles of mentors, however, subscribed to the idea of mentorship as service to this church profession and their judicious choice of rewards reflected this generous thinking. The Baptist pastor and his mentoring team knew that the religious education mentors could be relied on to develop an equitable system to reward themselves.

Maintaining a delicate balance between celebrating and rewarding the religious education mentor and alienating other church staff, such as a Sunday school director who may not be directly involved in the mentoring program, is also an important consideration. Because religious educators typically work in positions that rarely lend themselves to job promotions or other incentives, they may be more sensitive to perceived inequalities in treatment among their peers.[9] The potential for unreasonable mentor compensation to create havoc and interpersonal conflict on a church staff is especially noteworthy given that the maintenance of a supportive, nurturing environment is crucial for the success of the church-based mentoring program. Establishing incentives that are inviting but not overwhelming presents a continuous challenge for church administrators. In the case of the Baptist congregation cited above, the first inclination of the mentoring team was to

8. Wolfe, "Designing Training and Selecting Incentives," pp. 106–8. Wolfe's conclusions are supported by educators Mary Ann Blank and Nancy Sindelar, who, in reporting on their mentoring program, point out that financial rewards have not been necessary. See "Mentoring as Professional Development: From Theory to Practice,"*Clearing House* 66, no. 1 (1992): 25.

9. Helen Spence and Patricia Hayes, "Prophets in Our Own Land: The Role of Mentors in the Carleton Board's Pilot Induction Project," *ORBIT* 22, no. 1 (1991): 17.

offer to pay conference registration fees for their volunteer mentors. The church governing committee overruled this suggestion because they perceived it to be a possible source of tension among other employees. When the local mentoring team considered this reason, its members were quite receptive to changing the initial compensation plan.

In the remainder of this chapter I describe a variety of forms of mentor compensation: (1) released time from regular schedules, (2) public announcements, (3) opportunities to share mentoring experience, (4) recognition of knowledge and skills, (5) provision of social activities with other mentors, (6) professional recognition, (7) ritualized celebrations of mentoring contributions, and (8) professional development activities. None of these rewards is more effective than the others in all educational situations. Rather, each alternative fits different church-related environments at different times.

SUGGESTIONS FOR COMPENSATION OF MENTORS

Mary Hatwood Futrell's suggestion to involve educators in constructing a fair and equitable reward system seems reasonable given the collaborative approach to religious education mentoring programs recommended in this book.[10] Active collaboration can begin once the local church mentoring team has identified potential mentors. Mentoring teams should have some reasonable alternatives, including combinations of possibilities, available before they ask religious education mentors for their views. One key means of providing adequate compensation is to make released time available to religious education mentors.

Released Time from Regular Schedules
Anyone who has been a religious educator for a short period of time knows the importance of released time in completing professional assignments above and beyond one's regular instructional duties. The released time could come in the form of a lightened teaching load or through the provision of a replacement educator for specific

---

10. Mary Hatwood Futrell, "Selecting and Compensating Mentor Teachers: A Win—Win Scenario," *Theory into Practice* 27, no. 3 (1988): 225.

days devoted to continuing professional development for the religious education mentor and mentee. Released time signals that the designated mentoring task is important and that religious education administrators are supportive of it, both significant messages in promoting the success of a mentoring initiative. Take, for example, educator Diemut Schaller, who has taught in a private girls' college for twenty-one years and has been asked to articulate her experience as a mentor to new educators. Diemut's first response was to say that the released time at the end of every second day made her feel as though what she was teaching her mentee, Sally, was important. In all her years in religious education and chaplaincy she had never been made to feel that she was a valued professional. The released time to carry out mentor functions was an affirmation of her educational responsibilities and an acknowledgment that as a professional she could be counted on to use the time wisely. Diemut's comments really touch the essence of the professional life of many educators: They are given many assignments in addition to their classroom activities and subsequently the new assignments cause difficulties for them. When released time is allocated to spend on the additional responsibilities, religious educators know they are respected as responsible professionals whose knowledge, skills, and attitudes are of value. The released time signals to church colleagues that mentoring work is viewed as an essential service to the faith community.

Public Announcements

A key means of soliciting and retaining religious education mentors is to publicly acknowledge their performance. Public acknowledgment of mentors could take the form of news articles, with accompanying photographs, posted in church newsletters. Mentor Alia Cadinouche observed in her written evaluation of the pastoral care department's mentoring program that seeing an article on her individual contributions to the mentoring program in the hospital newsletter and having photocopies posted on staff bulletin boards greatly improved her personal and professional relationship with hospital coworkers. Colleagues who had not attended the departmental staff meetings where mentorship was discussed finally realized what a time commitment mentorship entails. The newsletter item took pressure off Alia to justify her released time from pastoral visitations. Public announcements affirm the religious educator's efforts and inform the faith community that the mentor service is valued. Public announcements positively acknowledge the mentoring role, give it considerable status, and signal that mentorship is indeed an integral part of religious education and of the life of the entire church.

Public announcements also serve the function of legitimating the religious education mentoring activity as a professional undertaking. So-called soft skills that mentors utilize, such as the ability to communicate, are often devalued in the faith community. Announcements in public places indicate that mentorship is time consuming, demands effective communication skills, requires a theoretical and skill-based knowledge and can be used to further the religious education profession. In fact, supporting mentors is an integral part of actively contributing to the ongoing life of one's chosen profession.

Opportunities to Share Mentoring Expertise

The expertise that a religious education mentor acquires from coaching a mentee can be utilized to improve or initiate other church-related mentoring programs. Religious education mentors who have been successful in one academic year should be given the opportunity to function in a similar capacity in subsequent years, as well as to become educators of new volunteer mentors. Religious education mentors with a positive track record can also be invited to collaborate with other congregations in establishing a mentoring program. The referral and recognition of the experienced mentor is a concrete way of recognizing educational excellence and of maximizing the transfer of acquired mentoring skill from one church situation to the next. For instance, Florence was asked by the pastor of a Mennonite congregation in another district to assist his congregation in building a mentoring program. Florence began by forwarding him a detailed plan of the mentoring program she helped design and implement. She also agreed to meet with the pastor on several occasions and to make oral presentations to his Mennonite organizing team. The recognition of her professional mentoring skills encouraged Florence to persist with her extensive involvement in mentorship in her home congregation. Florence continued her mentoring leadership role, became involved with orienting new team members, and began the process of revising the existing mentoring program.

Recognition of Knowledge and Skills Gained through Mentorship

Consistent with the continuous learning culture promoted throughout this book is the notion that skills gained in mentorship should be continuously identified and acknowledged.[11] Such recognition may serve as an adequate form of compensation for some mentor recruits. For instance, a volunteer mentor may have enhanced skills in communication and one-on-one instruction as a consequence of involvement in the religious education mentoring program. Team organizers can highlight the fact that the volunteer mentor has further developed competence in these specific areas by writing a professional report on the mentor's skill progression and by including letters of professional support in the mentor's personnel file. For instance, Margaret Powell has been part of the mentoring program for three years. Chosen primarily for her expertise in group facilitation skills, Margaret stated at the beginning of the mentoring program that she specifically wanted an opportunity to develop her professional skills in one-on-one instruction of other adults. To record her skill development progress, Margaret stated that the mentoring program director occasionally supervise her practice and that her assigned mentees provide periodic reports of their observations. Margaret also conducted her own self-evaluation to continuously monitor personal improvement in her teaching skills. At the end of the academic year, any considerable changes in skill level and knowledge were recorded in Margaret's personnel file. Margaret, meanwhile, planned to use the reports as part of her professional portfolio in applying for an adult faith development position at the diocesan level.

Social Activity as Part of the Mentorship

Another reason for religious educators to participate in challenging learning experiences, such as mentorship, is to enlarge their social

---

11. In a study of twenty-eight African-American women, researchers found that one of the greatest rewards for volunteering were the informal opportunities for learning that were made available to participants. Voluntary activities provide unique situations in which individuals have the opportunity to develop personally and to practice communication skills. Organizers of mentoring programs should be aware of the reported value of such learning and use it to promote involvement. See Jovita M. Ross-Gordon and William D. Dowling, "Adult Learning in the Context of African-American Women's Voluntary Organizations," *International Journal of Lifelong Education* 14, no. 4 (1995): 306–19.

network. The opportunity to participate in a variety of social events during which they can meet new people is adequate compensation for involvement in mentorship for some volunteer participants. Church suppers, picnics, or banquets are satisfactory means of compensation for these volunteer mentors.[12] Beyond personal enjoyment, invitations to participate in select church social occasions can be used to single out the volunteer mentors for meritorious service. If such social events are held in conjunction with several local congregations or hospitals, religious education mentors will have the opportunity to meet others with common interests and beliefs, as well as to exchange mentorship ideas and experiences with them. Angus, for instance, enjoys being part of a cadre of semiretired mentors who are invited to attend a coffeehouse function several times a year. The coffeehouse provides a suitable occasion for these volunteer mentors to exchange professional experiences with each other and to plan to improve their mentee feedback skills. For instance, last year at one of the coffeehouse functions Angus met a colleague from another parish who was also mentoring a parish nurse. Together they developed a set of criteria to assist them in continuing to instruct the nurse mentees on the religious educational dimensions of the parish nursing profession. Every time Angus and his colleague meet they compare notes on their respective successes and failures. They are affirmed by the fact that other professionals are striving hard to refine their mentoring practice. Social opportunities constitute a significant reward for them.

Professional Recognition

Official professional recognition is another effective means of compensating volunteer mentors. Institutions, in particular, have established forums whereby religious education mentorship can be recognized in meaningful and ceremonial ways. Mentoring team organizers in universities and seminaries, for instance, can lobby to have involvement in a staff development activity, such as mentorship, considered as a valid criteria for faculty promotion. A prime example is a seminary mentor, Pete Gonzalez, who came to the realization that organizing mentoring activities had consumed a great deal of his professional

---

12. For a variety of ways of compensating volunteers, see Donald Ratcliff and Blake J. Neff, *The Complete Guide to Religious Education Volunteers* (Birmingham, Ala.: Religious Education Press, 1993), pp. 140–41.

time for a considerable number of years. When assembling his academic portfolio for consideration by the employee advancement committee, he included a great deal of information on his contributions to mentorship. The seminary administration recognized this service to the faculty as valuable and agreed to consider it when evaluating his case for promotion. Other organizations, such as churches, can reward religious education mentors by nominating them for staff appreciation rewards. Because religious educators generally do not receive financial distinction for their work, any form of accolade that celebrates their contribution to the profession is valuable to them. Rewards for performance excellence and educational service are key to recognizing the positive investment mentorship makes to the profession. Such recognition assists in the continuous process of professional self-definition and particularly in prioritizing the main issues that are important for any profession at different stages of growth. Once the primary emphasis in the religious education profession was on mandating adequate academic preservice education for all functioning religious educators. Now the principal emphasis should shift to the provision of mentorship for new members. Therefore, official recognition should be afforded to concerted efforts to support and develop religious education mentorship initiatives.

One of the characteristics of a profession is that the members continuously evaluate its status and contribute to its continuous process of self-definition. Recognizing the value of mentorship for the growth of the profession is one primary way of contributing to religious education. Official recognition of mentorship serves as a clarion call to the profession that religious educators value a variety of forms of knowledge beyond those provided by academic institutions. Awards for mentorship highlight the behaviors that members of the profession regard highly—providing service, offering support, and sharing knowledge, skills, and lifestyle behaviors with new members. Eligibility for performance awards has an additional benefit of bringing visibility to religious education, among other church-related professions.[13] The religious education profession creates a positive perception when it utilizes the desirable behaviors operative in other professional bodies.

---

13. Studies with older adults, for example, show that many are motivated by achievement and affiliation. They prefer purposive incentives such as the satisfaction that comes from having contributed to a worthwhile cause. See, for example, the

Ritual Celebrations of Mentorship

Another public vehicle for acknowledging the contributions of the religious education mentor is to organize public rituals that bring attention to mentorship, signal its importance, and provide a significant opportunity for the entire congregation to become actively involved in the initiative. Commissioning ceremonies and closing liturgies at year's end are two church-related rituals that can be used to publicly acknowledge the professional endeavors that the mentor is involved in. Ritualizing participant contributions to religious education mentorship involves the entire faith community and provides it with an opportunity to formalize its commitment to support the formal program.[14] Because rituals are a usual means of publicly celebrating significant turning points in people's lives, they can be used in mentorship to mark the induction of the new religious educator and also to mark the progression of the mentor into a wisdom or senior position in the profession. Commissioning rituals, in particular, highlight the religious educator's competence and selection by peers for educational excellence. Inviting as many congregational members as possible to all formal rituals will also raise the profile of the mentoring program. Egon, a pastoral care worker, described the commissioning ceremony as a time when he felt blessed and affirmed in his mentoring role. Egon understood the ritual as a message from his congregation telling him to continue living his religious educational vocation of service through mentorship. Attended by his family and friends, the commissioning event was a significant affirmation of Egon's chosen life path.

Mentoring celebrations also fulfill the innate human need to ritualize key moments in one's life. Theologian Tom Driver contends that participation in ritual is so integral to living fulfilled lives that "to lose

---

research conducted with a group of two hundred adults, all over fifty years of age, who volunteer with youth and adult organizations. Of this group, 81 percent responded to a mailed survey. Shirley B. Rouse and Barbara Clawson, "Motives and Incentives of Older Adult Volunteers," *Journal of Extension* 30, no. 3 (1992): 9–13.

14. For a comprehensive theological discussion of the value of ritual see Tom Faw Driver, *The Magic of Ritual: Our Need for Liberating Rites that Transform Our Lives and Our Communities* (San Francisco: HarperSanFrancisco, 1991). Driver observes, "We need them [rituals] to give stability to our behaviors and to serve as vehicles of communication" (p. 23).

ritual is to lose the way."[15] Rituals are time-honored means of recognizing individual people and of celebrating achievements. Driver notes that people all over the world have always performed rituals. Humans not only create rituals but are created by them, making the exercise of them crucial to full human development. Rituals such as commissioning celebrations and year-end closing celebrations serve as public acknowledgments of the great respect the faith community has for involvement in mentorship. Participants in the commissioning ritual become implicated in mentorship by visibly showing their support, commitment, and appreciation for the contributions of the religious education mentor and mentee.

Commissioning and closing rituals can be organized by the local mentoring committee in cooperation with the mentoring program participants. Typically, rituals include elements of music, readings, and symbolic acts such as prayers over the commissioned mentors. All members of the congregation can be invited to attend, with the leader of the congregation presiding, as a sign that the entire faith community wholeheartedly endorses the mentorship of religious educators. As an indication of unity and as a means of creating links with those outside the immediate congregation, other congregations could be invited to take part or to join in and plan rituals for their mentors.

Professional Development Opportunities

Another tangible means of compensating religious education mentors is by offering professional development opportunities to them. Lectures, courses, or conferences in religious education or related fields would be attractive to many volunteer mentors. Such adult education opportunities have the additional benefit of contributing to the development of a continuous learning culture in the parish. They extend the religious education that began in undergraduate academic settings and

---

15. Ibid., p. 4. He acknowledges, however, the existence of some negative rituals such as religious rites that oppress women and ritual sacrifice (p. 8). Kathleen Hughes and Barbara Quinn, "The Transfer and the RCIA: Process and Ritual," *Review for Religious* 52, no. 1 (1993): 91–92. Hughes and Quinn also note that "ritual is a powerful medium of expression which publicly marks boundary or threshold moments in people's lives, clarifies and intensifies the experience being named and celebrated, expresses change of status, establishes new relationships, alleviates some of the peril of the unknown, and gives permission for new ways of being and acting as one continues on the journey" (pp. 91–92).

contribute to ongoing professional development. The opportunity to engage in new learning situations provides religious educators with ready access to current professional knowledge, skills, and attitudes. One mentor, Koo Sung Lee, relates that the professional development days really pressured him to expand his thinking on religious education generally. The time allocated to continuing professional education rejuvenated him considerably and encouraged him to volunteer again in the new year. Professional education opportunities contribute to the development of a learning congregation and they signal that access to educational events is an appropriate reward for the instruction of new colleagues. Professional development opportunities highlight the value of the mentor's contribution and signal the importance of participating in continuing education.

The availability of opportunities to develop professionally and to be publically rewarded for contributions to the profession may motivate religious educators to become mentors. The incentives outlined in this chapter are not exhaustive, but they do offer a variety of alternatives to a financial reward scheme for participation in educational mentorship. Local mentoring team planners can make use of these possibilities and create more of their own. Whatever choices individual congregations make, the existence of a comprehensive system of incentives and rewards is integral to the professionalization of mentorship within church-related environments.

SUMMARY

The educational literature overwhelmingly favors compensation for the mentor, though there is diversity of opinion on whether this compensation must be financial. The conclusion I draw is that although compensation is necessary, it may indeed include alternatives such as peer distinction, released time, or official professional religious education recognition. Furthermore, careful consideration of local cultural norms and religious educator expectations are the best indicators of the type of reward necessary in a given situation.

9

Maintaining the
Mentoring Relationship

If you'll let a guide direct you who only has at heart your get-ting lost.

—Robert Frost[1]

The United Church congregation had gone through three religious education directors in as many years, but this year the staff composition seemed stable. The current DRE was married and had a family. She indicted that she was planning to remain with the congregation for at least a five-year period of commitment. She would immerse herself in rural religious education, and her husband would try to find contract work in the community development field. The situation appeared to be stabilizing until her assigned mentor, a retired educator in the congregation, suffered a heart attack in their second month together. The mentoring program organizers were shocked. What would the planners do? They decided to discuss the matter with the DRE mentee, determine her needs, consider their own human resources, and proceed from there. It was evident to the mentoring planners that the religious education mentor and mentee not only need professional preparation for their mentoring roles but also ongoing assistance in maintaining their demanding relationship.

---

1. Robert Frost, "Directive," in *The Poetry of Robert Frost,* ed. Edward Connery Lathem (London: Cape, 1971), p. 377.

In this chapter I will deal with the intricacies of making the mentoring process effective. Specifically, I will discuss the use of a covenant as a formal phase to increase the commitment of religious education mentors, mentees, and administrators. I recommend the use of a covenant as a continuous reminder of the rights and responsibilities inherent in a mentoring relationship.[2] I will then discuss the informal phases of mentoring relationships.[3] Yet problems can arise even if the planning process has been carried out fully. I will touch on issues of conflict in mentoring relationships as a way of alerting participants to

---

2. I have deliberately chosen to use the word "covenant" rather than "contract." My usage follows the argument of R. E. Y. Wickett, *Models of Adult Religious Education Practice* (Birmingham, Ala.: Religious Education Press, 1991). Wickett defends his choice of terms by stating that "covenant" is more appropriate in a religious context because it reflects the common language and heritage of a religious community. See chapter 13, "The Learning Covenant." See also Wickett's discussion in "Contract Learning and the Covenant," *Adult Education and Theological Interpretations*, ed. Peter Jarvis and Nicholas Walters (Malabar, Fla.: Krieger, 1993), p. 214. Wickett describes the parties to a covenant as responding to a vocation or call. Another attribute of a covenant that I favor is that it challenges participants to live up to their articulated ideals. In a mentoring context, covenants not only serve as reminders of invitation and response but also as a means of enabling mentor and mentee to call one another to accountability.

3. Other mentoring researchers have focused exclusively on the mentor's own phases of growth. Katherine Knight Wilcox, for example, has delineated four phases in growth of understanding of oneself as a "mentor." The first phase is the orientation pre-relationship phase, which occurs before the first contact of mentors and mentees. During this phase, the mentors are usually eager and enthusiastic, but they are not yet centered on the needs of their religious education mentees. The second phase, initiation and relationship-building, occurs during the initial contact with the mentee. During this time, mentors try to build personal relationships with their mentees and address their professional deficiencies. In the third phase, role consolidation, the mentor focuses on the mentee's needs and is involved in refining strategies for dealing with mentee concerns. The final phase is collegial collaboration between mentors and mentees, a time during which mentors are preparing for separation from the mentee. Wilcox's four phases provide a useful framework for religious education mentorship because they show the typical progression of identity and focus over a one-year, formalized mentoring relationship, which is the standard length for educational mentorship. Though the four phases may not apply in all instances, they provide general indicators of mentors' needs and development. Familiarity with the typical phases of mentorship allows local mentoring planners to more easily design effective and responsive mentor education experiences. See "Training Master Teachers to Mentor," in *Learning in the Workplace,* ed. Victoria Marsick (London: Croom-Helm, 1987), pp. 140–44.

the potential ups and downs of mentorship. I will also identify proactive mentee behaviors. Finally, I will discuss specific administrative supports that can promote maintenance of the mentor-mentee relationship, such as opportunities for the integration of spiritual concerns for mentorship and organizational flexibility.

PHASES OF THE MENTORING RELATIONSHIP

Agreement on a covenant is one means of organizing a formal mentoring relationship. Following mutual consent to a covenant, the relationship roles can be fully acted out. Once the religious education mentor and mentee initiate mentorship, several predictable phases in their relationship can be observed.[4]

Covenanting the Relationship

A covenant among the religious education mentor, mentee, and administrator identifies what each signatory is obliged to commit to the mentoring relationship. Covenanting can be used to sanction the mentoring relationship and to hold the partners mutually accountable. This covenant needs to include specific meeting times, parameters of casual contact, and intentions of the mentors, mentees, and administration, as well as time lines for beginning and ending the relationship. The standard length of time for educational mentoring relationships is one year, though the phases described below reflect the progression over a five-year period. Though there are no specific guidelines on

---

4. Phases of the mentoring relationship have been discussed in numerous professional educational sources. For instance, Norman Cohen identifies four stages of mentorship. In the first or early phase, the mentor and mentee begin to build their professional relationship. In the second or middle phase the mentor determines the mentee's needs. In the third or later phase the mentor challenges the mentee to change undesirable work habits. In the fourth or last phase the mentor encourages the mentee to think critically about how best to meet personal goals. See *Mentoring Adult Learners: A Guide for Educators and Trainers* (Malabar, Fla.: Krieger, 1995), p. 16. Other writers who have documented mentor phases include Judy-Arin Krupp, "Mentoring: A Means by Which Teachers Become Staff Developers," *Journal of Staff Development* 8, no. 1 (1987): 12–13; Allan Walker and Kenneth Stott, "Preparing for Leadership in Schools: The Mentoring Contribution," in *The Return of the Mentor: Strategies for Workplace Learning*, ed. Brian J. Caldwell and Earl M.A. Carter (London: Falmer, 1993), pp. 81–84.

how often the mentor and mentee should meet, many programs use the guideline of once every two weeks and other times as agreed upon.[5] Mentors and mentees can begin with this biweekly schedule of meetings, increasing it if their situation warrants more frequent contact (such as in the case of a mentee who is struggling professionally). Periodic assessment of the mentoring partners' satisfaction with the timing of meetings, quality of relationship, and professional progress of the mentee will help ensure that the covenant is functioning effectively.

Mentor program planners can ensure that the mentoring covenant is being respected through regular feedback from mentoring participants. Religious education administrators can request regular verbal reports from the participants in regard to meeting times, pressing issues and concerns, and suggested ways that administrators can provide concrete support. Soliciting, instead of demanding, these reports can be an effective strategy in contributing to a collaborative mentoring environment. Figure 9.1 provides a sample covenant for religious education mentors and mentees.

Initiating the Covenant Roles

From a seminal, qualitative interview study on the phases of eighteen informal mentoring relationships, researcher Kathy Kram delineated four stages of the process of mentorship.[6]

Initiation: The first phase is initiation, namely, the time during which the mentoring pair familiarize themselves with one another and their respective roles. The initiation phase can involve one person, usually the mentee, seeking out the other person, often because of appreciation of abilities and competencies. For Shelly Rosenblum,

---

5. One of the recommendations resulting from educator Sandra Harris's review of a mentor program was that scheduled meeting times were rated as very important components by mentors and mentees. See "A Mentoring Program for New Teachers: Ensuring Success," *NASSP Bulletin* 79, no. 572 (1995): 102.

6. Though there are many descriptions of mentor-mentee stages/phases delineated in the professional educational literature (see note 3) I have chosen to highlight Kathy E. Kram's in the main text because they are based on a rigorous empirical study. While her phases represent informal mentorship in a corporation, the phases of formal mentoring relationships in a religious education context are likely to be much similar, once the initial mentor-mentee contact is made. See "Phases of the Mentor Relationship," *Academy of Management Journal* 26, no. 4 (1983): 608–25.

Figure 9. 1
Sample Covenant of Mentor, Mentee, and Administration

Name of mentor_____

Name of mentee _____

Time beginning_____

Time ending_____

Religious Education Mentee Only

I agree to the following number of meetings_____

My beliefs about mentorship are _____

_____

_____

Religious Education Mentor Only

Mentoring roles I promise to fulfill_____

Mentoring roles I cannot promise to fulfill_____

Administration Only

To support the mentor-mentee relationship, we will_____

Signatures

   Mentor_____

   Mentee_____

   Program administration_____

cantor and leader of a local Jewish yeshiva, the initiation phase was a time of unqualified admiration for her mentor, Deborah Barer, and her professional religious education achievements. For Deborah it was a time of respect and wonder at Shelly's abilities and a time of envisioning the possible contours of Shelly's future in the synagogue.

In a structured religious education mentoring situation, the mentor and mentee need to spend a great deal of time focusing on becoming acquainted with each other and on building up a communicative relationship. The mentor ought to be very conscious of the mentee's professional needs and begin to familiarize herself or himself with just how great these needs are and what approaches might work best with this mentee. In turn, the religious education mentee can spend time with the designated mentor, coming to know him or her and identifying how the mentor can be of most benefit during the initiation year.

Cultivation: In this second phase, the mentor and mentee develop a comfortable working relationship, and their interaction broadens from a focus on career issues to include psychosocial support. This phase is the time of greatest growth and development of the relationship, with the psychosocial functions being slowly introduced over time. For example, at first Deborah and Shelly focused on Shelly's work, with Deborah providing advice on her teaching and on communicating effectively with various members of the synagogue. As they came to know each other, they naturally broadened their conversation to more substantive topics. Deborah and Shelly's interactions gradually included intense discussions about Shelly's personal convictions and life direction. Shelly and Deborah became close colleagues and spent a great number of evenings drinking coffee and exploring serious issues in their life and work.

In the religious education situation, the cultivation phase also involves a deepening of relationship and a further refinement of the ways and means of addressing issues in the mentor's professional life. The religious education mentor can most productively use the time focusing on specific issues such as mentee skill development. Major educational problems such as instructional procedures might become the central concern for the mentor and mentee. The two participants can meet regularly, increasing their rapport and further refining the mentee's knowledge, skills, and lifestyle behaviors. In formal mentoring structures such as those recommended in this book, a deep level of personal sharing is optional (though informal mentoring relationships may contain stronger interpersonal interaction). Either way, the religious education mentor and mentee are responsible to share experiences of teaching and development.

Separation: In the third or separation phase, a gradual distancing occurs between religious education mentor and mentee. This distancing can be painful for both partners, since it generally involves a decrease in the supportive functions performed by the mentor. For Deborah and Shelly, this separation stage occurred when Deborah moved on to other responsibilities in the congregation and had less time available to meet with Shelley. As they continued to meet, at increasing intervals, it became obvious that Deborah was too busy to devote as much time as she previously had to her mentee's professional development. In turn, Shelly found that she needed less assistance and possessed increased confidence managing her own career.

In the formal mentoring relationship this separation may occur several months prior to the actual closure of the recommended first year. The religious education mentor needs to consciously ensure that the mentee is becoming increasingly independent and will be ready to operate on his or her own by the end of the year. Despite the temptations of having an often admiring dependent, the responsible mentor will encourage the mentee to make the vast majority of religious education decisions, without the benefit of a fallback.

Redefinition of Roles or Collegial Friendship: The mentor and mentee may or may not reach the last stage, redefinition, a phase that can include ongoing friendship and collegiality. Shelly and Deborah's affiliation lasted until Deborah left the congregation, three and a half years after they met. Their relationship had changed focus and was no longer centered on Shelly's career. But it still had a congenial flavor, based as it was on mutual respect and concern. The mentorship that Teresa of Avila (discussed in chapter 2) gave and received changed as the needs of the mentor and mentee changed.

In a structured religious education mentoring relationship a gradual redefinition of the mentor and mentee's relationship may begin to occur after the first year of initiation. At this point, both partners will have completed the requirements of their covenant and are no longer officially accountable to each other. Their relationship will likely begin to develop a collegial character whereby both are coworkers and have independent professional responsibilities. The challenge for the mentor is to relinquish the teaching role and allow the mentee to function separately. For the mentee the challenge is to act independently with the option of consulting peers when making major decisions. Finding a collegial balance is a continuing challenge for both religious education mentor and mentee.

Though Kram's four stages show a clear development from personal relationship building to an emphasis on career goals, other empirical researchers have not documented the same linear progression.[7] Rather, they have found that mentors showed interest in both the mentee as a person (psychosocial function) and in the mentee as a professional (career function) throughout the relationship. Such versatility is consistent with the example of Teresa of Avila. The mentorship she gave to mentees such as John of the Cross followed no predictable pattern other than call and response.[8] Mentoring relationships are usually not permanent and the specific emphasis that is given them depends on the religious educators involved.

The phases identified by Kram alert mentoring program designers and participants to the reality that mentorship is a complex process, and there may be variations of intensity and focus in the formalized relationship over time. Mentoring team members need to be aware of these subtleties in their religious education mentoring program and to share their awareness with participants. The professional preparation process will provide a unique opportunity for organizers to familiarize the mentor and mentee with the mentorship stages. Highlights on the phases can also be included during the ongoing education sessions throughout the year. Finally, when appropriate, mentoring program organizers can remind mentors that separation is approaching and that both mentor and mentee should prepare for it. The program designers also need to be aware of potential problems in the mentoring relationship.

POTENTIAL PROBLEMS AND
MAINTENANCE RESOLUTIONS

Mentoring relationships can become negative experiences. The educational literature rarely addresses this issue, although researchers have

---

7. See, for example, Robin Pollock, "A Test of Conceptual Models Depicting the Developmental Course of Informal Mentor-Protégé Relationships in the Work Place," *Journal of Vocational Behavior* 46, no. 2 (1995); especially Pollock's discussion of results on pp. 158–61.

8. For example, when John of the Cross was preparing to set out to establish his first reformed house of male Carmelites, he needed advice and direction. Teresa describes her tutoring of John in *Foundations* 13, especially paragraph 5, in *Complete Works of Saint Teresa of Jesus,* trans. E. Allison Peers, 3 vols. (London: Sheed & Ward, 1946).

highlighted the potential for problems to arise in otherwise positive re-lationships.[9] Difficulties in a relationship may occur because of per-sonality conflicts or even because of disinterest on the part of the men-tor or mentee. They may also occur because of negative societal perceptions of the level of intimacy that mentorship can foster. Lau-rent Daloz is one of the few educational writers who detail mentorship problems. He describes a somewhat interesting scenario with a mentee named Gladys who refused to grow from her educational and mentor-ing experiences, despite the best efforts of her mentor.[10] Gladys reached a point in her psychological development where she no longer wanted to learn or grow, causing her mentor great frustration. Some immediate questions suggest themselves: How can differences be reconciled? Which strategies work best? How can catastrophes be averted? In the following sections I look for answers to these questions.

Societal Perceptions

One of the most comprehensive summaries of potential complications in the mentoring relationship has been compiled by Kathleen Wright.[11] Wright identifies problems (such as the use of mentees to do menial jobs), mentor selection difficulties, and cross-gender matching issues (such as the potential for gossip). Despite these negative out-comes, however, Wright concludes that the results from mentoring ini-tiatives are promising for professionals in a wide variety of work-places. Though educational researchers have given considerable attention to the particular concerns women have about being mentors and in receiving mentorship,[12] these concerns can be mitigated if

---

9. Ann D. Carden, "Mentoring and Adult Career Development: The Evolution of a Theory," *The Counseling Psychologist* 18, no. 2 (1990): 293–94; Ruth E. Kling and Donna A. Brookhart, *Mentoring: A Review of Related Literature*, 1991, ERIC ED 346095, pp. 12–14.

10. Laurent A. Daloz, "The Story of Gladys Who Refused to Grow: A Morality Tale for Mentors," *Lifelong Learning: An Omnibus of Practice and Research* 11, no. 4 (1988): 4–7.

11. Kathleen S. Wright, "From the Odyssey to the University: What Is This Thing Called Mentoring?" *ACA Bulletin* 79 (1992): 45–53.

12. Bernice R. Sandler, "Women as Mentors: Myths and Commandments," *Chronicle of Higher Education,* 10 March 1993, sec. B, p. 3. For a discussion of Sandler's article, see chapter 5, note 36, of this book.

certain steps are taken. However, as in any human interaction, there is always the potential for interpersonal conflict.

Interpersonal Conflict

Significant educational change (such as the implementation of mentorship) frequently involves conflict and may cause major adjustments for religious educators. On the other hand, healthy tensions can invigorate the church environment because they force participants to examine what they are doing and why and prompts them to decide if they need to change. Mentorship likely represents a considerable change in ways of operating for religious education mentees, mentors, and administrators, so specific skills in negotiating conflict will be useful for program participants. Some of the strategies that mentor program participants can use in dealing with conflict situations are described below.[13]

Listen to Understand the Problem: When tensions rise in a mentoring relationship, the program participants need to control their emotions and try to listen to what the other person is saying. Though effective listening skills are difficult to put into practice, people caught up in conflict must be willing to work hard to hear all sides of the debate. Careful listening will assist religious education mentors and mentees in identifying the core issues and addressing them most effectively.

Give Feedback to the Participants: At times program participants will be required to give feedback to each other, whether positive or negative. In a nurturing environment that promotes learning, the feedback experience is less threatening to both the mentor and the mentee. Mentoring program organizers are challenged to provide concrete constructive feedback that promotes the positive growth and development of the mentor and the mentee.

Put the Conflict in Perspective: When conflict arises between the religious education mentor and the mentee, both of them should make an effort to step back, gain perspective, and focus on the issues involved. Becoming mired in trivia and insignificant details is not

---

13. These strategies are suggested in Rudi Grab, "Managing Tensions in Educational Organizations: Trying for a Win-Win Approach," *Education Canada* 36, no. 1 (1996): 36–38. Though Grab is writing for educational administrators, his wisdom about how to negotiate conflict is by no means exclusive to leaders. People at all levels of the organization can learn from Grab.

beneficial to either person. For instance, if mentoring pairs realize that they disagree on minor issues such as room temperature but have a significant degree of consensus on major elements of their professional work, such as philosophy of education and appropriate theological content, they likely can agree to disagree on the minor points.

Confront Other People When Required: Religious education mentors and mentees may have to confront one another if a specific circumstance requires up-front tactics. A mentor who constantly corrects a mentee's performance may demoralize the mentee. Gently bringing this pattern of behavior to the religious education mentor's attention likely will alleviate the situation.

Be Flexible: Religious education mentorship participants need to realize that there are multiple, equally valid, solutions to most predicaments. The ability to recognize the limitations of one's own perception and to see a problem from someone else's eyes is a necessary requirement for effective mentorship. Flexibility and the willingness to proceed in a way that you personally might not have thought of will create an educational environment that is respectful and open.

Discord was no stranger to Teresa of Avila and other Catholic reformers. Religious education mentors and mentees such as Teresa, John of the Cross, and Gratián negotiated the conflict among and between themselves wherever possible. Where a peaceful resolution was not forthcoming, Teresa formed new mentoring relationships with others.[14] Flexibility and openness to new and creative solutions are instructive in any day. Another important means of reducing potential complications is to advise religious education mentees of proactive behaviors to improve their mentoring relationship.

Proactive Mentee Behaviors

Religious education mentees must work as diligently as the mentors, perhaps more so, given their newness in the field and lack of

---

14. See chapter 2 of this book for a discussion of Teresa's description of the difficulties she encountered in mentoring Gratián. On one occasion she acknowledges they are having difficulties. Because their interpersonal problems pale in light of the larger reformational project, Teresa chooses to attempt to redirect him. See *The Letters of Saint Teresa of Jesus*, trans. E. Allison Peers, 2 vols. (London: Burns, Oates, & Washbourne, 1951), no. 79.

professional experience. Some proactive procedures for mentees to consider using during the mentoring relationship are sketched out below:[15]

Procedure 1. Working *with* mentors to determine which needs they can help the mentee meet. This strategy helps place realistic limits on what one person can do for another.

Procedure 2. Being respectful of the designated mentor's time. The mentee can set appointments for meetings with the mentor and limit their duration to the agreed upon amount of time.

Procedure 3. Respecting and appreciating the religious education mentor as a person and as a religious education professional. This behavior acknowledges the mentor's character and helps build a caring mentoring relationship.

Procedure 4. Maintaining a two-way conversation with the religious education mentor that will allow for mutual growth and insight. The mentee can inquire about the mentor's religious education interests or just listen carefully when meeting with the mentor.

Procedure 5. Promoting storytelling by the mentor. This procedure will give the mentor the opportunity to draw on past religious education experiences and share a variety of professional knowledge, skills, and lifestyle behaviors with the mentee. The mentee can initiate or solicit the stories and give affirming feedback to the mentor when appropriate.

Procedure 6. Acknowledging the use of religious education mentor support and advice. The mentee can give this feedback verbally to the mentor and share it with colleagues and mentoring team organizers as a way of indicating that the mentee is benefiting from the relationship.

Procedure 7. Giving direct positive feedback to the mentor. This affirmation will acknowledge the support and effort the mentee has received.

---

15. These procedures are identified in Susan Trimble, "A Protégé's Guide to Mentoring," *NASSP Bulletin* 78, no. 559 (1994): 46–48.

Joseph ben Gurion was mentored by the director of a Jewish after-school program. Joseph made a point of telling his director's supervisor what a fine job his mentor was doing, and he also told the director. Joseph's affirmation of the mentor's good work was greatly appreciated and contributed to a positive working relationship with his mentor.

Though there is no perfect way of maintaining a mentoring relationship, the religious education mentee can increase the chances of success by utilizing any of the seven procedures indicated above.[16] In the next section I discuss the specific strategies religious education administrators can employ to support the mentoring initiative.

SPECIFIC ADMINISTRATIVE SUPPORTS
FOR MENTORSHIP

Religious education administrators need to be directly involved in supporting and maintaining a formal mentoring program. They also can encourage ongoing attention to a mentoring environment by supporting attendance at the professional education sessions (discussed in chapter 7) offered for religious education mentors and mentees, promoting attention to spiritual growth, and adopting a flexible approach to mentorship.

Ongoing Attention to Spiritual Life Concerns

One of the primary ways that the religious education administrators can provide support for mentorship is to provide time for the spiritual side of mentorship.[17] A strong relational and spiritual emphasis may

---

16. Another way to increase support among new religious educators is to have them actively engage in computer conferencing, listserv participation, and e-mail exchanges with each other. Computer conferencing is recommended by Carol Rolheiser-Bennett, who suggests that new educators who utilize computer conferencing facilities experience ongoing professional support. "From Campus to Classroom: What Role for Faculties of Education?" *ORBIT* 22, no. 1 (1991): 23. Rolheiser-Bennett cites several studies supporting this contention, including L. Harasim, *Online Education: Perspectives on a New Environment* (New York: Praeger, 1990).

17. I use "spirituality" here in the same sense as religious educator Michael Warren. Warren sees spirituality as a concept broader than prayer. Warren contends that every person has a spirituality or a way of being in the world and that religious education has a role to play in encouraging individuals to identify their personal spirituality and to question their faith community's spirituality. See *Faith, Culture, and the Worshiping Community: Shaping the Practice of the Local Church* (Mahwah, N.J.: Paulist, 1989), pp. 88–106. See also chapter 4 of this book, note 30.

already be present in the religious education environment, but this can also be enhanced by regular invitations to prayer and reflection, such as characterized the historical situations. For example, a group of parish nurses find that their work is deepened by insights from education and spirituality as much as it is by health care principles. Specifically, their job challenges them to bring a different perspective on health and healing to their clients. Parish nurses have a particularly mobile ministry that brings them out into the faith community and requires them to combine their clinical skills with an understanding of the intricate connections between mind, body, and spirit. As proponents of a holistic approach to health, these parish nurses realize they are educating and healing patients simultaneously. As educators, they are especially in need of ongoing spiritual formation and nurturing.[18] In addition to attending to the spiritual concerns of those involved in religious education work, administrators need a flexible, open attitude to mentorship.

Flexibility in the Mentoring Program

One of the strongest supports for a mentoring program is an attitude of flexibility on the part of both church sponsors and participants. A mentoring program may start out well, but will probably have structural challenges and will require changes along the way. Though mentoring teams often establish well-defined program plans before initiating a project, the complexity and change implicit in almost every existential situation demands that their plans be viewed as guidelines only. Outreach program developer Lorilee Sandmann has drawn attention to the fact that most programs are not implemented as planned.[19] She cites several reasons for the discrepancy: changes in staff, inadequate budgets, lack of organizational support, and lack of participation.[20] As an alternative, Sandmann suggests a more fluid approach that allows for continuous evaluation and change in programing. The flexibility that she recommends is very much a

---

18. For a good introduction to the educational dimensions of parish nursing, see Sondra Matthaei and Lin Stern, "A Healing Ministry: The Educational Functions of Parish Nursing," *Religious Education* 89, no. 2 (1994): 232–46.

19. Lorilee Sandmann, "Why Programs Aren't Implemented as Planned," *Journal of Extension* 31, no. 4 (1993): 18–21.

20. Ibid., p. 18.

planned flexibility. In the case of a religious education mentoring program, team members would be required at the design stage to identify indicators for using flexibility, such as a lack of success in recruiting adequately prepared mentors. Certain steps are recommended when flexibility is required: (1) the change should be fully documented, (2) all mentoring team members and church contact staff should be notified, (3) the evaluation plan should be adjusted so that it matches the adjustment in plans, and (4) the new information regarding extensive recruitment of new mentors should be noted for designing future planning sessions, activities, and cycles.

Administering an interdenominational seminary can be challenging at the best of times because of the variety of interest groups involved in every decision. When the dean instituted a mentoring program for new faculty, he wondered if he had included sufficient members of representative denominations and graduate student caucus groups in the planning. Finally, when the mentoring team had met a number of times, built its own learning community, and reported to him with no major glitches in their plans, the dean felt comfortable with his initial choices. However, when the mentors and mentees were paired and their orientation session had been completed, the dean received a telephone call from a board member who was concerned that her interest group was not represented on the mentoring team. The dean anticipated that it would upset the team spirit to introduce a new member, but he knew that in the best interests of the program's public relations he should change the team composition. Even so, some of the mentoring team members experienced upheaval. After the new team members had been inducted, the dean was able to assess his decision to accommodate a new representative. Despite the initial team adjustment period of two meetings, he and the team concluded that his flexible approach was very effective.

Whatever choices the mentoring team organizers have to make, they face a continuing struggle in balancing the best interests of the religious education mentor, mentee, and the corresponding church community. Some decisions that may seem difficult are nevertheless necessary for the mentoring program to prosper.

SUMMARY

Mentoring programs require an influx of positive support from the organizers and participants if they are to remain viable. One concrete way of keeping the mentoring participants and the administration aware of their rights and responsibilities in the mentoring process is to keep drawing attention to the covenant they created and signed. The emphasis should be on the spiritual intent of the covenant—to nourish and foster the participants in every way possible. Mentoring organizers can provide invaluable assistance by advising mentors and mentees to anticipate challenging and rewarding developments in their relationship. Finally, religious education administrators can promote the spiritual growth of participants and can recommend flexibility in the implementation of the program.

10

Evaluating the Mentoring Program

> *The trick is to let*
> *a sense of simplicity inform our thinking,*
> *a sense of complexity inform our actions, and*
> *a sense of humility inform our judgments.*
> —Holcolm[1]

Young-Lee was determined that in the second year of the congregation's mentoring program he and his mentoring planning team members would learn from the successes and failures which participants experienced. In the program's initial year, Young-Lee and his team had not conducted a systemic evaluation and consequently they had insufficient data from which to begin planning another mentoring cycle for new participants. Young-Lee's research made him aware that educational evaluation of a religious education mentoring program draws attention to three major areas of concern:[2] (1) the

---

1. Holcolm, *Sermon under the Mount,* quoted in Michael Quinn Patton, *Creative Evaluation,* 2d ed. (Newbury Park, Calif.: Sage, 1987), p. 124. Holcolm seems to be a fictitious character created by Patton to dispense wisdom and to enliven this evaluation text. Holcolm's character is quite congruent with Patton's creative approach to evaluation.

2. A still valid definition of evaluation is provided by Daniel L. Stufflebeam: "Evaluation is the process of delineating, obtaining and providing useful information for judging decision alternatives." See "An Introduction to the PDK Book *Educational Evaluation and Decision-Making,*" in *Educational Evaluation: Theory and Practice,* ed. Blaine R. Worthen and James R. Sanders (Belmont, Calif.: Wadsworth, 1973), p. 129.

evaluation approaches to be used, which depend on the purpose for the evaluation and which help establish the evaluation's design; (2) the overall effectiveness of the professional education provided the mentor and mentee; and (3) the individual progress of both the mentor and the mentee during the religious education mentoring relationship.[3] In this chapter I will discuss these aspects of evaluation and offer concrete suggestions for conducting effective mentoring program evaluation.[4]

APPROACHES FOR EVALUATING MENTORING PROGRAMS

An important factor to keep in mind when deciding upon the evaluation approach is the purpose for which the evaluation is being carried out. Thus in the first section I will discuss the typical purposes for evaluation within religious education mentoring programs and then I will provide an overview of the regular steps in evaluation. Within all educational programs, evaluation approaches can be classified within the broad categories of formative and summative. In the second section I will review these two categories.

Purposes of Evaluation
With the exception of Sandra Odell's work, there is very little professional literature on the recommended purposes and approaches to

---

3. The mentoring literature is replete with attention to the issue of evaluation. See, for example, Mel P. Heller and Nancy W. Sindelar, *Developing an Effective Teacher Mentor Program* (Bloomington, Ind.: Phi Delta Kappa Educational Foundation, 1991), ERIC ED 332996, p. 15; Sandra J. Odell, "A Collaborative Approach to Teacher Induction That Works," *Journal of Staff Development* 11, no. 4 (1990): 14; Sandra J. Odell, "Evaluating Mentoring Programs," in *Mentoring: Contemporary Principles and Issues*, ed. Theresa M. Bey and C. Thomas Holmes (Reston, Va.: Association of Teacher Educators, 1992), pp. 95–101.

4. Unfortunately, evaluation has received short shrift in all areas of religious education, including facilitation and learning, program development, staff development, and administration. This lack of attention is due to a misguided belief that religious education is too intangible and otherworldly to be evaluated. James Michael Lee argues that evaluation of religious instruction, in particular, is crucial to determine if learning has occurred and, if so, what has been learned. See his "The Authentic Source of Religious Instruction," in *Religious Education and Theology*, ed. Norma H. Thompson (Birmingham, Ala.: Religious Education Press, 1982), pp. 139–42.

evaluation of mentoring initiatives.[5] Odell directs her attention to the four purposes for evaluating an educational mentoring program: accountability, understanding, knowledge, and improvement.[6] Whereas accountability has a distinct purpose of justification, the other three purposes for evaluation are associated with internal improvement of the mentoring program and consequently are more closely related to each other than they are to accountability.

Accountability: Accountability usually means demonstrating the overall worth of the mentoring program to external observers such as church boards and religious education authorities. Accountability is one of the most frequently cited reasons for conducting evaluation of a mentoring program. Accountability focuses on the measurable outcomes of mentorship, such as whether there is an improvement in the religious educator's instructional ability or in learners' academic performance. Accountability is most often connected with the end results of a mentoring initiative and is generally not focused on mentoring program improvement.

Evaluation for Improvement of the Program: Evaluation for improvement of the religious education mentoring program usually focuses on the activities and experiences of the mentoring program with a view to making them more effective. Evaluation for improvement might center on aspects of the professional preparation course so that the continuing education sessions can be adjusted to address unmet professional needs. It could also concentrate on determining the level of commitment required of the mentors so that changes can be made in the existing program to better accommodate available resources.

Evaluation for Increasing Knowledge: Evaluation for increasing knowledge of the mentoring process focuses on building the level of information available about mentorship. For instance, those who are planning their own mentoring programs can benefit from knowing more about the commitment of financial resources required for effective mentoring processes. They can also benefit from learning whether the myths about mentoring, such as whether cross-gender mentorship

---

5. Sandra J. Odell, "Evaluating Mentoring Programs," pp. 95–101.

6. Ibid., p. 95. Here, Odell is citing the work of Gary R. Galluzzo and James R. Craig, "Evaluation of Preservice Teacher Education Programs," in *Handbook of Research on Teacher Education*, ed. W. Robert Houston (New York: Macmillan, 1990), especially pp. 605–6.

is impossible, are true or false. Evaluation to increase knowledge can utilize perceptions obtained through questionnaires, attitudinal essays, or personal interviews with mentor program participants.

Evaluation for Increasing Understanding: Evaluation to increase understanding mainly has value for those internal to the program. It is used to inquire into the practice and dynamics of mentoring. For instance, knowing about the phases of a mentoring relationship can assist mentoring program planners in modifying their expectations for the participants. Such knowledge can also provide the local planners with a common vocabulary with which to discuss mentorship and consequently increase ownership of the program on the part of the participants. Evaluation to increase understanding can also advance mentoring program planners' understanding of the initiation process the new religious educators go through and how that experience can be facilitated more effectively.

All of these purposes can be part of an evaluation design; the challenge is to decide which focus the mentoring committee needs to take in a particular religious education situation.

Five-Step Approach to Religious Education Mentoring Evaluation

Religious educators need to be aware of the basic steps in planning educational evaluation. Before the steps are enacted, the basic question of who will conduct the evaluation must be asked. Will the local mentoring team conduct the program evaluation or will an external evaluator be employed? Financial and professional resources will help determine whether the mentor planning team starts this project on its own or enlists outside support. I assume in this chapter that most mentoring programs are too small to warrant an external examiner, so the mentoring team will take responsibility for evaluation. Once the planning team begins to focus on the requirements for evaluation, the actual process can begin. Because of the flexible approach I have taken to planning in this book, I recommend that the five steps cited below be treated as a guideline only and that they be modified to suit the needs of different church-related environments.[7]

---

7. These evaluation stages are delineated by Donald G. Emler in *Revisioning the DRE* (Birmingham, Ala.: Religious Education Press, 1989), pp. 201–4.

State Goals and Standards: The goals of a well-defined mentoring program constitute a necessary starting place for evaluation. For example, if one of the goals of a religious education mentoring program is to improve the overall quality of the adult religious education program in an urban congregation, an evaluation scheme that focuses solely on religious education mentor-mentee relationships is too narrowly defined to assess adequately the actual program goals. Contrariwise, if the primary mentoring program goal is to build up the mentor-mentee relationship but the mentoring evaluation focuses on church staff morale, the evaluation plan is too broadly defined. Careful attention should be given to fitting mentoring program goals to the evaluation design.

Formulate Evaluation Questions: In the process of planning and implementing evaluation, the mentoring team will have to begin by asking numerous questions about the type of data they need and how they will phrase their evaluation questions. What information about the mentoring program is needed? Who are the stakeholders, or people with a major concern or investment, in this mentoring program? Should the entire church community be consulted about the mentoring evaluation? How will the mentees be asked about their experiences?

Once the mentoring team has answered some foundational questions, they then need to decide on exactly what the evaluation questions are. The questions decided upon are often more important than the answers because they determine the type of data collected. Therefore, the questions asked should be tied to the purposes of the evaluation and to the stated goals of the mentoring program. For example, if a purpose of the evaluation is to measure the effectiveness of the existing program for the religious education mentee's professional growth, questions related to this specific intention should be asked. Asking the questions that solicit the type of information required will help increase the strength of the evaluation.

Gather Data: Information about the mentoring program can be gathered in a multitude of ways, including focus groups, interviews, questionnaires, observations, and rating forms. For instance, a religious education mentoring program evaluator can recommend that each mentee keep a learning journal during the year. With the individual mentee's permission, data from this journal can be examined to help determine if the mentee perceives the mentor's assistance to be beneficial. This data might be combined with on-site observations of such professional activities as the mentee's facilitation of a Scripture session. Likewise the designated mentors can be asked to keep a log of their interactions with the mentee during the course of the year. The data from these different sources can then be combined with structured questionnaires that require mentors and mentees to rate issues such as the usefulness of the mentor relationship. The type and quality of data collected determine the level of insight the evaluation can provide.

Analyze Data: Another step in the mentor program evaluation is analysis of the data that has been gathered. The technicalities of data analysis may present challenges to church personnel, so they should not be hesitant to call on competent parishioners with more expertise. Analysis of the data should be tied to the audience's needs and to the evaluation questions cited above, so that they receive the type and quality of information to make informed decisions about religious education mentoring programs. For example, if the congregation needs to make decisions about continuing the preservice education component of the mentoring program, a detailed statistical analysis of the quality of the mentee's relationship with parishioners may not be immediately beneficial.

Report Findings: Formal reports of the mentor program evaluation containing the findings of the evaluation need to be available in written format and circulated to all those influenced by the religious education mentoring program, such as financial supporters, program participants, parish directors of religious education, and congregational members. All reports should be compiled in such a way as to provide an overview of the program outcomes and not the specific findings in each case. If confidentiality of religious education mentors and mentees is impossible, such as when there is only one mentor-mentee relationship in a parish, then permission to release data should be obtained from the participants. Even if permission is obtained, all efforts should be made to respect the privacy of respondents. Moreover, the audience needs to be provided with an opportunity for discussion, clarification, and reaction to the mentor program report. Optimally, the report data such as educational performance ratings on the religious education mentors will form the basis of a responsive action such as further assistance for the program participants.[8]

These five steps provide a rudimentary guideline for religious educators who have not had extensive experience with educational evaluation. Those with a more advanced level of knowledge and skill may decide to follow another sequence. Another important consideration in designing mentoring evaluation is the balance desired between assessing the end results (summative evaluation) and assessing areas for improvement (formative evaluation).[9]

Formative and Summative Approaches

Formative evaluation occurs while a religious education mentoring program is ongoing and is centered on the continuous improvement of the program, specifically the performance of the the new religious educator. In formative evaluation, the focus is on evaluating mentoring

---

8. When one program planning cycle ends, another begins. Mentoring program planners need to consider all that has gone before, learn from previous mistakes, and ask questions of how specific procedures could be implemented differently another time. The effectiveness of the new cycle of educational planning depends on the willingness of the organizers to learn from evaluation data, whether it be positive or negative. Of course, the decision to use all or some of the evaluation data needs to be balanced with the reality that one group's wishes may not be representative of all cohorts. Planners then have to be attentive to the patterns that arise over a number of evaluation implementations, as opposed to one implementation. The caution of interpreting evaluation data correctly for planning is noted by Rita Johnston, "Evaluation: The Problem That Won't Go Away," *International Journal of University Adult Education* 31, no. 1 (1992): 71. Of course, the delayed effects of earlier mentoring programs can also yield useable data. See Alan Rogers, "Achievements and Outcomes: Evaluation, Adult Education and Development," *Adults Learning* 4, no. 3 (1992): 71. Rogers points out that there are many unforeseen outcomes in every program that should be attended to. Unexpected results, both negative and positive, are important to the future of mentorship and ought to be carefully noted. An example might be a sudden interest in providing continuous learning opportunities for all staff of the local church or school.

9. The distinction between summative and formative evaluation is attributed to researcher Michael Scriven. See "The Methodology of Evaluation," in *Perspectives on Curriculum Evaluation*, ed. Ralph Tyler, Robert Gagné, and Michael Scriven, AERA Monograph Series in Curriculum Evaluation, no. 1 (Chicago: Rand McNally, 1967), pp. 39–83. This monograph provides thorough foundational reading in program evaluation. See also the seminal evaluation work by Benjamin S. Bloom, J. Thomas Hastings, and George F. Madaus, *Handbook on Formative and Summative Evaluation of Student Learning* (New York: McGraw-Hill, 1971).

program activities as they take place. This approach helps the evaluator respond to the needs of the participants, in this case the religious education mentors, mentees, local mentoring committee members, and parishioners. Examples of formative evaluation activities are analyzing anecdotal teaching reports from religious education mentees and mentors and evaluating videotaped recordings of a mentee facilitating an adult spirituality session. Another means of conducting formative evaluation is to hold regularly scheduled meetings of mentoring pairs with the local mentoring committee in order to solicit informal progress reports. Formative evaluation has the potential to provide the religious education mentee and mentor with opportunities for constant growth because it deals with issues as they arise and it encourages the ongoing assessment of individual and collective progress. For example, Mary's mentor observes her while she chairs religious education committee seminars and meets with her afterward to discuss her progress. The points raised in their postseminar discussions helped Mary focus on her strengths and weaknesses so that when the time came for a year-end evaluation, Mary had already been working on refining her religious education skills.

Summative evaluation, in contrast, occurs at the end of a mentoring program and is designed to assess program goal achievement.[10] Decisions on the possibility for future religious education mentoring programs are made on the basis of summative data. Summative evaluation data can come from self-reported measurement of increased mentor instructional ability, mentee reports on mentee educational skills, final interviews with religious education mentees on the effectiveness of the mentoring program, direct observation of the mentee's year-end instructional ability, assessment of program operation records, on-site observations by external observers, or effectiveness ratings of mentees by religious education administrators.

---

10. The mentoring literature is replete with examples of summative evaluation. See, for example, Leonard J. Varah, Warren S. Theune, and Linda Parker, "Beginning Teachers: Sink or Swim?" *Journal of Teacher Education* 37, no. 1 (1986): 33. The researchers conducted structured interviews to evaluate mentee satisfaction with the completed mentoring program. For another illustrative example of a summative evaluation, see Nicholas G. Stupiansky and Michael P. Wolfe, "The North Country Mentor/Intern Teacher Program: A Rural Consortium," in *Teacher Induction and Mentoring: School Based Collaborative Programs*, ed. Gary P. DeBolt (Albany, N.Y. : State University of New York Press, 1992), pp. 87–91.

In the case of religious education mentorship, both formative and summative evaluation procedures can be used for program improvement and future planning. Formative evaluation data such as a mentor's ongoing observation log record the mentee's professional growth over the year. Because the difference between formative and summative evaluation is not always clear-cut, however, it may be important to focus less on *when* an evaluation is done and more on *why* it is done.[11] For instance, in one congregation a mentee is told that she will be formally evaluated at the end of the year because the church personnel committee needs to have an evaluation on file to meet the requirements of their policies and procedures manual. Though this particular procedure begs the question of usefulness of the evaluation, the reason is clear. Asking why of a mentoring process is important, given the typically limited financial resources of religious education.

Responsive Approach

The manner in which the evaluation is carried out is often as important as the type of evaluation (summative or formative). Consequently, some educational researchers recommend a responsive evaluation model because it provides useful information about the substantive issues raised in a program.[12] Responsive evaluation is concerned more with providing data useful to program participants than it is with providing quantifiable and precise measurements.[13] Responsive evaluation is sensitive to particular needs and can be used as part of formative and summative evaluations. It is consistent with the mentoring evaluation purposes of increasing understanding and knowledge and contributing to the improvement of the mentoring program. However, responsive evaluation is less consistent with the

---

11. See Robert E. Stake, *Evaluating Educational Programmes: The Need and the Response* (Paris: Center for Educational Research and Innovation, Organization for Economic Cooperation and Development, 1976).

12. Robert E. Stake distinguishes responsive evaluation from other traditional models that he labels "preordinate." He defines preordinate as "emphasizing the statement of goals, use of objective tests, standards held by program personnel, and research type reports." See his "Program Evaluation, Particularly Responsive Evaluation," in *Evaluation Models: Viewpoints on Educational and Human Services Evaluation*, ed. George F. Madaus, Michael S. Scriven, and Daniel L. Stufflebeam (Boston: Kluwer-Nijhoff, 1983), p. 292.

13. Ibid.

purpose of accountability because it is process oriented, whereas evaluation for accountability is more product oriented.

Responsive evaluation is more closely allied to assessment of activities than to goals in that it focuses more on what a mentoring program *does* than on what it is *intended to do*. An effective responsive evaluation emphasizes issues and describes events, reports on diverse opinions, and employs direct and indirect observation. A responsive evaluation might provide the reader of the evaluation report with a clear picture of what the religious education mentee experienced during the academic year and what professional issues arose for him or her. Responsive evaluation asks for the input of all mentorship participants in the design of the evaluation questions and the overall evaluation plan, as well as in the interpretation of the findings.[14] One caution about widespread involvement in the religious education mentor evaluation process, however, is respecting the limited amount of time volunteer participants may have available.[15] Another caution applies when using responsive evaluation. In the interests of giving thick, rich description, responsive evaluations sacrifice some dimensions of reliability and validity.[16] Researcher Robert Stake recommends, therefore, that program evaluators combine a responsive model with a preordinate, or

---

14. John Mayne and Joe Hudson discuss a collaborative type of evaluation that involves the evaluator as a service provider who does not stand in judgment of the program. In this collaborative capacity the evaluator's roles are to educate, help, and develop relationships with the program participants. "Program Evaluation: An Overview," in *Action-Oriented Evaluation in Organizations: Canadian Practices,* ed. Joe Hudson, John Mayne, and Ray Thomlinson (Toronto: Wall & Emerson, 1992), especially p. 12.

15. In documenting the effectiveness of an evaluation in which stakeholders had an integral evaluator role from beginning to end, researcher Jennifer Greene offers cautions about participant involvement. See "Stakeholder Participation and Utilization in Program Evaluation," *Evaluation Review* 12, no. 2 (1988): 114.

16. Validity refers to the ability of the evaluation to measure what it says it will measure. For instance, if the evaluation is intended to determine whether the religious education mentee's facilitating skills have improved because of being mentored, then the instrument used ought to measure teaching ability (presumably at the beginning of the mentoring program and then at intervals throughout the year). Reliability refers to the ability of the evaluation instrument to measure accurately and consistently. A reliable evaluation can be administered at different times and will consistently yield the same results. See Charles M. Judd, Eliot R. Smith and Louise H. Kidder, *Research Methods in Social Relations,* 6th ed. (Fort Worth, Tex.: Holt, Rinehart & Winston, 1991), pp. 51–58.

more traditional, model of evaluation where needed.[17] In practice this might mean assessing whether goals and objectives of the mentoring program were accomplished (preordinate evaluation), as well as providing an opportunity for religious education mentees to describe the process of being mentored and how mentoring affected their professional growth at various stages of the year (responsive evaluation).

An example of responsive evaluation is Sue M., who has been religious education director at her church for ten years. In that time neither she nor the educational programs she coordinates have been evaluated. That does not concern Sue unduly because she knows the congregation generally supports her educational programming for adults. But since she was assigned the additional responsibility of overseeing an existing mentoring program for new adult religious education volunteers, Sue has been forced to rethink her lackadaisical attitude toward evaluation. For instance, she knows that the church administrative board had a split vote when deciding to continue funding for mentoring programs because they were unclear as to what actually occurs during mentoring. Likewise, parishioners and the pastor seem to be very unaware of the mentoring program benefits and procedures. Consequently, there has been a steady decline of volunteers for mentorship, and the program itself has stagnated.

Sue realizes she will need to gather as much relevant data as possible to revive the ailing mentoring program. Sue decides to bring together everyone who is affected by mentorship—representatives from the religious education volunteer core, the pastor, a process facilitator, church board representatives, mentors, and mentees—to discuss ways of conducting a responsive evaluation. Sue begins by asking, Why do we need to evaluate? What information do we need to have? These initial questions are the beginning of many more.

In designing their responsive evaluation, Sue's team has a number of alternatives to choose from. As with all effective religious education evaluators, the team does not choose one specific means of evaluation. It looks for a wide variety of means in order to ensure that the

---

17. On this point, see Robert E. Stake, "Program Evaluation," in *Evaluation Models,* p. 303. Egon G. Guba and Yvonna S. Lincoln concur with Stake. See their "Emergence of Responsive Evaluation," in *Effective Evaluation: Improving the Usefulness of Evaluation Results through Responsive and Naturalistic Methods* (San Francisco: Jossey-Bass, 1991).

evaluation is comprehensive and fair and that it yields usable data.[18] Sue's team decides to begin with church records on retention of volunteers since the implementation of the mentorship program. They follow this with personal interviews with the religious education mentors and mentees to hear their experiences and their concerns about the mentoring they gave and received. They also talk to some of the church board members about their opinions and reservations. Sue's team knows that the ultimate test of the effectiveness of their responsive evaluation is whether it results in increased understanding of the mentoring program and the processes involved.[19] The team believes that its data collection and report will provide ample data for revising and reinvigorating the mentoring program. The collaborative stance of responsive evaluation carries over to the professional preparation offered to mentors and mentees.[20]

EVALUATION OF THE PROFESSIONAL PREPARATION PROGRAM

Thoroughness in evaluating a mentoring program for religious educators includes evaluation of the professional preparation program as well as the transfer of learning from the program to the actual mentoring relationship. The evaluation of the preparation program can be carried out during the program sessions and all through the year. Evaluating transfer of learning can occur by evaluating the actual transfer

---

18. A very useful program evaluation resource is a booklet written by human resource developer Hedley G. Dimock, *A Simplified Guide to Program Evaluation*, rev. ed. (Guelph, Canada: University of Guelph, 1987). Dimock includes a step-by-step guide for inexperienced program evaluators to follow.

19. For a brief, accessible discussion of the importance of responsive evaluation as a means of addressing the concerns and issues of stakeholders, see Egon G. Guba and Yvonna Lincoln, "Emergence of Responsive Evaluation," in *Effective Evaluation*, pp. 23–38.

20. An example of the type of responsive evaluation recommended here is educator Thomas Sergiovanni's suggestion that supervision should be a joint inquiry by educator and supervisor into these three questions: What *is* going on in this teaching site? What *ought* to be going on? What do the *is* and the *ought* mean to educators, learners, supervisors, and others? See Thomas J. Sergiovanni and Robert J. Starratt, *Supervision: A Redefinition*, 5th ed. (New York: McGraw-Hill, 1993), pp. 217–18. Sergiovanni's argument is that the educational partners ought to construct meaning together, not separately and antagonistically.

strategies as well as the implementation of them. Both types of evaluation are discussed below.

Levels of Educational Evaluation

Education evaluation designs are frequently based on the Kirkpatrick model, which has four distinct levels.[21] This model attempts to distinguish between the different ways of evaluating and to have program designers adjust to the diverse levels. The data from the program evaluations can be used to plan further religious educational activities. For instance, if the religious education mentors report on their program-end questionnaire that they need more information and skills on how to communicate more effectively with the mentees, then the mentoring program organizers will have to consider seriously supplementing their continuing education programs with communication information and exercises. I list each of the four levels here and provide examples from mentorship.

Level 1, Reaction: The question asked at this level is, Did religious education mentors and mentees like the sessions? Are they satisfied that attending the professional preparation sessions was a wise use of their time? Though seemingly useless data, these questions provide mentoring program organizers with valuable information on the level of interest and overall satisfaction of the participants.

Level 2, Learning: The question asked at this level is, What did the mentors and mentees actually learn from participating in the religious education program? The degree to which mentors and mentees learn and prepare for their respective roles ultimately influences their success in the mentoring relationship. Determining what participants have learned in terms of knowledge, skills, and attitudes, is useful information from which to develop further professional education and from which to assess transfer of learning. Though the learning that occurs is usually assessed during the professional preparation program, it also needs to be assessed midway through and at the end of the

---

21. This pattern in evaluation is noted by Anthony P. Carnevale and Eric R. Shulz, "Evaluation Framework, Design, and Reports," *Training and Development Journal* 44, no. 7, supplement (1990): S18. For a description of Donald L. Kirkpatrick's model, see "Techniques for Evaluating Training Programs," in *Evaluating Training Programs* (Alexandria, Va.: American Association for Training and Development, 1975); *Evaluating Training Programs: The Four Levels* (San Francisco: Berrett Koehler, 1994); "Great Ideas Revisited," *Training and Development* 50, no. 1 (1996): 54–59.

mentoring program to determine whether the education received continued to be beneficial.[22]

Level 3, Behavior: The question asked at this level is, Did religious education mentors and mentees have positive changes in subsequent mentoring behavior as a result of the preparation program? Were mentees better prepared for teaching than if they had not participated in the preservice education sessions? Different measures of this change in behavior will be required. For instance, a preprogram assessment will be needed to determine mentees' instructional level at the beginning of the professional education program.

Level 4, Results: The question asked at this level is, What were the benefits to the church, home, hospital, or educational environment? This question will have to be asked directly of these constituencies to determine if they are more supportive of new educators than in previous years and to evaluate whether this year's mentees are more effective instructors than mentees in previous years.

Though evaluation of a single program at all four levels is infrequent, it is helpful for mentoring program planners to determine what type of evaluation information they need and to design their data collection instruments around their decision. Careful planning will also ensure that the mentoring program evaluation is concerned with more than final results. Effective educational evaluation of professional preparation programs is also concerned with whether a planned education design will meet the needs of the religious education sponsors and whether ongoing education is effective.[23] These cautions are very important because they help local program planners focus more precisely on collecting the data that answers their need to know.

Informal Evaluation

Though there are many ways of evaluating the professional education program, some of the most effective evaluation takes place informally.

---

22. Human resource developers Jeanette and Leonard D. Goodstein describe seven methods of evaluating educational sessions: (1) individual interviews, (2) focus groups, (3) questionnaires, (4) rating forms, (5) pretests and posttests, (6) direct and indirect observations, and (7) staff analysis. "A Matrix for Evaluating Training," in *The 1991 Annual: Developing Human Resources*, ed. J. William Pfeiffer (San Diego, Calif.: Pfeiffer): 273–80.

23. Anthony P. Carnevale and Eric R. Shulz, "Evaluation Framework, Design, and Reports," p. S18.

Four possible scenarios through which informal data about effectiveness of the educational activities are collected include (1) the organizer of the professional education program instinctively knows about the inadequacy of one of the presenters, so he meets with her before the scheduled sessions to test out his intuition; (2) a facilitator feels tension in the workshop atmosphere, so she talks informally with several participating mentors over lunch about how they are experiencing the session; (3) the DRE who is organizing the mentoring program deliberately arrives at a professional preparation session during a coffee break in order to hear how participants are reacting; and (4) a mentoring program planner holds a casual meeting with the religious education mentor and mentee to assess their response to the session.[24] Though these informal techniques seem relatively unsophisticated, they highlight methods that experienced evaluators use to assess the effectiveness of their programs.

Formal Evaluation
Though the informal means of evaluating the professional evaluation are helpful, they can be balanced with more systematic, formal means in order to develop a more comprehensive profile. Consider the following three examples of formal data collection.

1. The facilitators of the professional preparation program distribute questionnaires at the beginning of their sessions asking questions about the participants' knowledge of mentoring and conclude the sessions by administering the same questionnaire.
2. During segments of the professional preparation program, which focus on practicing skills such as communication, a videotape is recorded. Afterward, the mentoring team uses a structured checklist of desirable characteristics to rate the participants' abilities.
3. The mentoring team holds one focus group session with program participants at the end of the professional preparation program, to determine their most significant learnings and holds another focus group session three months afterward to determine

---

24. These four examples are based on the suggestions for informal evaluation given in Rosemary Caffarella, *Planning Programs for Adult Learners: A Practical Guide for Educators, Trainers, and Staff Developers* (San Francisco: Jossey-Bass, 1994), pp. 124–25.

the usefulness of the preparatory program. Whether the evaluation is formal or informal, it ought to provide a learning experience for the mentoring participants.

Evaluation as a Learning Experience for Participants

Evaluation researcher Michael Patton discusses an especially useful way to make evaluation a learning experience for the participants.[25] He argues that evaluation can and should be integrated into the program that is being assessed (or portion of it, such as a professional preparation session). For example, a facilitator of a mentoring orientation session begins by administering a self-assessment inventory of knowledge, skills, and attitudes to the religious education mentors and mentees in attendance. She tells the participants exactly what she is doing, thereby increasing their level of involvement and their consequent satisfaction with the formal assessment process. The facilitator administers the same inventory at the end of the professional preparation course to measure any increase in mentor or mentee knowledge, skills, and attitudes. Her emphasis is on self-assessment to support individual learning. The usefulness of the actual professional preparation program can be assessed not only at the beginning and end of the sessions but also in subsequent weeks and months.

Usefulness of Preparation in the Subsequent Mentoring Relationships

The transfer of learning from the professional preparation sessions to the mentoring relationship also requires systematic evaluation. The mentor's and mentee's ability to transfer learning from these sessions is one test of the appropriateness and adequacy of the professional preparation received. Mentoring program evaluators can determine the degree to which transfer of learning strategies were incorporated into the mentoring education program design and religious education mentors and mentees actually transferred the learning to their mentoring relationships.

Evaluation of the ways in which transfer of learning are incorporated into a professional preparation design begins with knowing what

---

25. I model the illustration in this paragraph on Michael Quinn Patton's example in "Beyond Evaluation Myths," *Adult Learning* 3, no. 2 (1991): 10.

some of the actual transfer of learning procedures are.[26] Several of these procedures with particular relevance to the mentoring situation are described below.

Relevant Program Content: One key transfer of learning procedure is to provide mentoring program content that is relevant. Professional preparation program planners need to focus on information that will be specific to the mentoring experience, such as the rationale for a particular program and the ways in which religious education mentorship has been experienced in other church situations. A needs assessment of existing skills and competencies before the professional program commences can provide a useful benchmark for comparison, when it is complete.

Practical Program Content: Maximizing the practical content in the professional education sessions is very important for increasing transfer of learning. Practical content could include when and how to structure mentor-mentee meetings, how to deal with conflict, and other problem-centered procedures that can be transferred readily to the mentoring relationship.

Proximity of Preparation to Implementation: Mentor program planners should also conduct the professional preparation sessions close to the time when religious education mentorship begins, so mentors and mentees are more able to retain and use what they have learned. For instance, mentees and mentors are more likely to remember the details of their learning covenant, signed during the professional preparation course, if the mentorship begins shortly after the professional preparation program is finished.

Connections to Previous Knowledge: Yet another transfer of learning procedure is connecting new information to what mentors and mentees already know. If, for instance, self-evaluation is explained as an extension of regular educator evaluation, religious education mentees are more likely to be receptive to its introduction. In turn, they will be likely to practice self-evaluation during the year in which they are mentored.

---

26. On the practical application of transfer of learning to the field of religious education, see James Michael Lee, *The Flow of Religious Instruction* (Birmingham, Ala.: Religious Education Press, 1973), especially pp. 141–47. See also Caffarella, *Planning Programs for Adult Learners,* pp.108–15; and Mel Silberman, *Active Training* (San Diego, Calif.: University Associates, 1990), especially chapter 9, "Providing for Back-on-the-Job Application."

Utilizing Application Exercises: Finally, transfer of learning can be increased by utilizing application exercises such as practicing how to give religious education mentees effective feedback during the professional education program. Procedures such as this increase the likelihood that the mentor will know and will be able to give feedback to the mentee when required.

Evaluators can readily conduct an analysis of whether transfer of learning strategies is incorporated into the professional preparation program by studying the agenda for the component sessions; observing the preparatory sessions themselves, in person or on videotape; and by asking the facilitators and participants to highlight the specific procedures followed. For instance, a preparatory education design that does not include opportunities for the religious education mentors to practice specific mentoring behaviors such as giving effective performance feedback to mentees is not likely to be sensitive to transfer of learning strategies.

Once the mentoring relationships are established, mentoring program evaluators need to continue evaluating the transfer of learning. Evaluators in a mentoring program can observe religious education mentee instructional situations, mentor-mentee meetings, and mentee interactions with learners. For instance, one educational preparation design concentrates on assisting mentoring pairs to deal effectively with situations of conflict. Despite this focus, a program evaluator becomes aware midway through the year that religious education mentees and mentors generally do not seem able to negotiate even the smallest differences of opinion with any degree of success. The evaluator notes that conflict needs to be dealt with more thoroughly in subsequent education sessions.

Evaluators should be aware that transfer of learning cannot occur in workplace environments that do not welcome or agree with the professional preparation program for religious education mentorship. Barbara, for instance, learned during preparation that she was to meet with her assigned mentee once a week, but the personnel committee of the church refused her permission to take released time in the middle of the work day. A responsible evaluator will recognize the limits of professional preparation and will identify correctly the source of the problem in any feedback sessions. Connected to the transfer of learning is the individual assessment of the religious education mentor's and mentee's progress.

EVALUATION OF INDIVIDUAL PROGRESS

As identified earlier in this book, one of the principal reasons for initiating a mentoring program for religious educators is to enhance their professional growth. In fact, accountability for the mentoring program will likely be connected to the ability of mentoring program coordinators to demonstrate that participation in the program made a difference in the personal and professional growth of religious education mentors and mentees.

Evaluating the Personal and Professional Growth of the Mentor

The personal and professional growth of the religious education mentor is very important if mentoring is intended to accomplish more than adding to the personal growth of the mentee. Religious education mentor growth can be assessed in many ways. Logically, the amount of attention given to the assessment of this growth will depend on the degree to which mentor growth constituted a goal of the religious education mentoring program. One key way to assess professional growth is with standard rating scales of educator performance. Another method is to ask religious education mentors to report self-perceptions of their own educational performance. Self-assessment of mentors can be accomplished in the same way that self-reporting is established for mentees—journal entries and interviews with religious education administrators.[27] Mentor growth can be assessed

---

27. Adult educator Kathleen Taylor argues convincingly that self-assessment can be particularly beneficial for women in the developmental challenge to make sense of and find meaning in their lives. Given that self-assessment in the context of mentoring new religious educators involves considerable reflection on personal experiences of what and how one learns, there is ample opportunity for women to develop a strong sense of self. Taylor's thesis is based on the adult development frameworks of Robert Kegan (*The Evolving Self: Problem and Process in Human Development* [Cambridge: Harvard University Press, 1982]; *In Over Our Heads: The Mental Demands of Modern Life* [Cambridge: Harvard University Press, 1994] and on Belenky et al., *Women's Ways of Knowing: The Development of Self, Voice, and Mind* (New York: Basic, 1986). See Kathleen Taylor, "Sitting Beside Herself: Self Assessment and Women's Adult Development," in *Learning Environments for Women's Adult Development: Bridges toward Change,* ed. Kathleen Taylor and Catherine Marienau, New Directions for Adult and Continuing Education, no. 65 (San Francisco: Jossey-Bass, 1995), pp. 21–28.

periodically throughout the mentoring program, and also at the end. For instance, Barry's year as a religious education mentor seems to be proceeding well. He notices that he gets out of bed and goes off to the church office more quickly than he did a year ago. Barry's wife observes him reading more serious religious education books and becoming increasingly animated when discussing his professional beliefs with his mentee. As one component of the mentoring program evaluation, Barry is asked to submit a written self-reflection on his own growth during the year. Barry discusses his personal assessment with his wife who confirms his beliefs about his own growth. Additionally, Barry reviews the notes he made in the weekly journal he kept throughout the year.

A large religious education mentoring program (one that includes a number of mentoring pairs) has another means of collecting data on mentor growth: holding focus groups of seven to ten religious education mentors and asking them about their experiences in the mentoring program and the changes they can see in their professional skill as a result.[28] Researchers Alan Reiman and Lois Thies-Sprinthall advocate the use of guided reflection to promote mentor development. They also recommend the completion of psychological maturity assessment scales to determine if, in fact, the mentors experience personal and professional growth.[29] The ways and means of conducting the evaluation of mentor development are varied and depend on the actual intents of the religious education mentoring program to influence deliberately the professional life of the mentor. Evaluating the personal and professional effects on the religious education mentee presents just as many challenges and questions.

Evaluating the Religious Education Mentee's Progress

Evaluation of the religious education mentees' professional progress raises a number of issues, including who should conduct their formal

---

28. For an excellent practical guide to conducting focus group sessions, see Richard A. Krueger, *Focus Groups: A Practical Guide for Applied Research,* 2d ed. (Thousand Oaks, Calif.: Sage, 1994).

29. Alan J. Reiman and Lois Thies-Sprinthall, "Promoting the Development of Mentor Teachers: Theory and Research Programs Using Guided Reflection," *Journal of Research and Development in Education* 26, no. 3 (1993): 179–85.

job appraisals or performance evaluations.[30] Staff shortages and misinformation about the responsibilities of the religious education mentor may lead church administrators to ask designated mentors to complete the entire evaluation on their own. Having the mentor play such an administrative role causes concern because it jeopardizes the confidentiality and trust in a mentor-mentee relationship. A critical distinction must be made between assisting the new religious educator (mentorship) and assessing his or her educational performance (performance evaluation for employment purposes). Church administrators should not abdicate their responsibility to conduct supervision and assessment of the mentee for hiring purposes. However, they can legitimately require the religious education mentor to provide ongoing feedback and supervision for the mentee during the mentoring process, a role that is consistent with the mentor's teaching function.

Of all the roles assigned to a religious education mentor, formal job performance rating clearly should not be one of them. The formal evaluation of a mentee's performance by the religious education mentor runs counter to the goals and aims of religious education mentoring.[31] Moreover, confusing the roles of mentor and job evaluator may result in the religious education mentees' refusing the assistance they need to develop as professional religious educators.[32] The mentor's evaluation role is primarily in formative evaluation, and even this can cause problems because of the apprehensions about evaluation that some mentees may have. Yet religious education mentors are expected to conduct formative evaluation, that is, to

---

30. From his study of the successes and failures of mentor participants, Richard Dana Smith found that mentors want to limit their responsibility in a mentoring program to their own immediate mentoring activities. Mentors prefer that an independent coordinator be appointed to assume responsibility for administrative duties. "Mentoring New Teachers: Strategies, Structures, and Successes," *Teacher Education Quarterly* 20, no. 4 (1993): 16–17.

31. See Judith C. Neal, "Mentoring: A Teacher Development Activity That Avoids Formal Evaluation of the Protégé," in *Mentoring: Contemporary Principles and Issues*, ed. Theresa M. Bey and C. Thomas Holmes (Reston, Va.: Association of Teacher Educators, 1992), pp. 42–46.

32. See Sandra J. Odell in "Collaborative Approach to Teacher Induction," p. 14; Sandra J. Odell, "Teacher Induction: Rationale and Issues," in *Teacher Induction—A New Beginning*, ed. Douglas M. Brooks (Reston, Va.: Association of Teacher Educators, 1987), pp. 76–77.

provide ongoing feedback and constructive criticism to inductees to help them develop as religious education professionals.[33] Because mentors work so closely with the mentees, they probably will have some input into the summative evaluation of the mentee, but in no case should they assume all the official duties and responsibilities of the church administration.

An integral part of the religious education mentee's evaluation is self-evaluation,[34] which might include keeping a learning journal of educational initiatives and periodically assessing one's own facilitation skills through videotaping instructional sessions. Self-assessment data might also be supplemented by having mentees utilize scheduled reflection periods at the end of each day.[35] In a religious education environment, these self-reflective activities would be most appropriate because the personal and spiritual development of religious educators is positively correlated to effectiveness in their profession. However, self-reflection needs to be followed by personal interviews with mentoring evaluators to discuss the strengths and weaknesses identified in the mentee's self-appraisal. Religious educator Donald Emler suggests that this follow-up interview begin with nonthreatening questions about how religious education classes are proceeding, move to a discussion of problems and issues in the religious educator role, and finally, focus on concrete ways that the religious education mentee can constructively address any problems that arise.

Finally, the religious education mentee's progress can be assessed with independent observations by seasoned religious educators who can provide individual feedback to mentees. The observation method can be accomplished using a clinical supervision model, the dimensions of which are described below.[36]

Preobservation Conference: The religious education mentor and the mentee meet to discuss such issues as the upcoming observation of the mentee's instructional ability. During this time, the religious

---

33. Gail Huffman and Sarah Leak, "Beginning Teachers' Perceptions of Mentors," *Journal of Teacher Education* 37, no. 1 (1986): 23.

34. See Sandra J. Odell, "Evaluating Mentoring Programs," p. 100.

35. An informative discussion of means of conducting religious education staff evaluations is provided in Donald G. Emler, *Revisioning the DRE* (1989), pp. 207–8.

36. A similar five-step model was developed by James Michael Lee as a means of observing and assisting religious educators in improving their skills. See *The Flow of Religious Instruction,* especially pp. 282–84.

education mentee can describe what he or she is planning for the facilitation session and the mentor can outline and discuss the observation process he or she will follow (video-recording, rating schedules, etc.). They can discuss together which educational skills or competencies the mentee most requires feedback on.

Observation: The religious education mentor observes the mentee's implementation of the educational design discussed during the preobservation conference. The mentor should be prepared to observe closely and to record as much data as will be needed to analyze the educational experience with the mentee. Adequate observation demands that the mentor be very prepared, take good notes, and insofar as possible, help the mentee feel supported and affirmed.

Analysis and Strategy: The religious education mentor gathers the data that was collected in the previous phase and uses it to assess the actual educational experience. Once this data has been systematized, the mentor must develop a strategic plan for helping the mentee to improve. During such a process the mentor should prioritize the mentee's educational issues and decide how and where to discuss these with the mentee

Supervision Conference: During the supervision conference, the mentor meets with the mentee to give constructive feedback and to assist in instructional improvement. Ideally, the two of them discuss reasonable routes to take in addressing some of the educational issues that have been raised. For instance, the volunteer mentor may have observed that the mentee does not seem to have adequately prepared for the observation session. A reasonable plan is to investigate why this happened, if the mentee has adequate preparation time available, and how this problem can be remedied immediately. The mentor considers all the possible options and decides how to broach this issue without creating defensiveness in the mentee.

Postconference Analysis: This last step in clinical supervision involves a reconstruction of events from the supervisory conference with a view to making future conferences more effective. Here the religious education mentor evaluates the entire supervisory process to determine if it was effective, if the mentee benefited professionally, and if the mentor's supervisory skills can be improved.

This process model of supervision allows the religious education mentee to make mistakes and have successes throughout the year while being continuously involved in educational renewal and

improvement.[37] This approach is consistent with the process orientation described in chapter 4 of this book. Mathilda, for example, has
worked in the same church-sponsored school for fifteen years and is
known to take informal responsibility for initiating new faculty members. When a new religious educator, Julie, was hired, Mathilda decided that she would provide mentoring support for her. Julie seemed
to welcome the involvement. Coincidentally, they had the same class
preparation periods, so they were often in the faculty lounge together
during the second class period. In a few short weeks Mathilda knew
Julie was experiencing problems with class organization in religious
education. Mathilda decided to offer any professional advice she
could. Meanwhile, with Julie's agreement, the school's administrator
formally invited Mathilda to observe Julie's classes and to provide relevant professional assistance using the supervision model outlined
above. In contrast, Thomas was quite shocked when he received a
year-end review from his supervisor in Trinity United Church. The
performance rating scale indicated he was poor to mediocre in almost
every professional category. Thomas had not realized that his performance was inadequate because he was not involved in his own evaluation process and had not been formally evaluated during the year.
However, when he asked Pastor Frank about it, Frank admitted that
there was indeed a significant problem with Thomas's instructional
abilities. Thomas wondered about the kind of place in which he was
working, given that these professional issues had not been discussed
with him before.[38]

---

37. This is the best known educational models for supervising and evaluating educator performance. This clinical supervision model is described in Robert Goldham-
mer, Robert H. Anderson, and Robert Krajewski, *Clinical Supervision: Special Methods for the Supervision of Teachers,* 2d ed. (New York: Holt, Rinehart & Winston,
1980). For a concise version of their model, see the appendix, "The Clinical Supervision Cycle: An Overview," pp. 208–11. The clinical supervision model is supported
for year-long use by mentors in Theresa M. Bey, "A New Knowledge Base for an Old
Practice, in *Mentoring: Developing Successful New Teachers*, ed. Theresa M. Bey and
C. Thomas Holmes (Reston, Va.: Association of Teacher Educators, 1990), pp. 56–57.

38. An alternative to supervision as punishment is offered by M. McBride and K.
Skau, "Trust, Empowerment, and Reflection: Essentials of Supervision," *Journal of
Curriculum and Supervision* 10, no. 3 (1995): 262–77. McBride and Skau use the lan-
guage of *building trust* between educator and supervisor, *empowering* the educator,
and *encouraging* reflective problem solving. This collaborative model is supported by
J. Bradley Cousins, "Using Collaborative Performance Appraisal to Enhance

When mentor evaluators attempt to measure new religious educator competence they can begin with their own list of expectations and supplement it with insights from the existing research literature on new educators. The educational research suggests that at the end of the first year, the religious educator minimally should be able to[39] (1) plan religious education activities in which learners can connect the new concepts with previous knowledge; (2) facilitate learning activities in ways that facilitate learner connection and mental growth (including knowledge, affective and lifestyle goals); (3) develop effective interpersonal relationships with learners; (4) be fair and consistent with religious education rules and routines; (5) establish an educational environment (physical and social) that facilitates learning; (6) assess learning in a variety of ways and use the assessment information to refocus subsequent instruction; (7) reflect on his or her teaching and learning processes in order to improve educational practice.[40] This list of general expectations is only a starting place—different religious education circumstances will cause program evaluators to adjust their criteria for competence. For instance, educators who teach in distance diploma programs for religious education cannot be evaluated on the basis of many of these criteria because their professional tasks do not involve in-class sessions. These religious educators' jobs demand a different set of professional skills: a high degree of interpersonal skill to deal with distraught learners on the telephone; a keen ability to assess learner competence and needs from limited information such as written assignments and application files; and competence to direct religious education learners through written correspondence such as Email messages and assignment feedback. Consequently, the assigned mentors for these

Teachers' Professional Growth: A Review and Test of What We Know" (paper presented at the annual meeting of the Canadian Association for the Study of Educational Administration, Ottawa, Canada, June 1993).

39. These points are based on a list compiled by researcher Anne Reynolds. From her review of the existing educational literature Reynolds observes that there is little professional consensus on what constitutes new teacher competence. "What Is Competent Beginning Teaching? A Review of the Literature," *Review of Educational Research* 62, no. 1 (1992): 1–35.

40. Ibid., p. 26. Reynolds also includes a list of professional competencies that beginning educators should hold when *first* hired, such as the "disposition to reflect on their own actions and students' responses in order to improve on their teaching, and the strategies and tools for doing so."

distance religious educators need to be sensitive to a very unique professional situation.

A clinical supervision model can be used to guide the evaluation process throughout the year. Yet another way of measuring religious educator mentee growth is through the use of a self-reliance inventory which, if administered at the beginning and end of the year, can help mentees to assess their individual growth in professional self-reliance and promote the building up of a support network for themselves. Such assessment is important because both self-reliance and the ability to develop and maintain a support system are positive indicators of human growth.[41] In addition to assessing individual growth, attention can also be drawn to evaluating the usefulness of the religious education mentor's role.

Evaluating the Usefulness of the Mentor's Performance

Evaluating the effectiveness of a religious education mentor's performance can be a difficult proposition because of the highly sensitive nature of the task. Evaluation can be carried out most efficiently by having mentoring program team members conduct an evaluation and also by having the religious education mentors engage in a process of self-reflection. In the often understaffed work environment of the religious educator, this twofold solution may indeed be the most tenable. Thus, on way to assess the mentor's performance is to have a format available for mentor self-assessment. Though self-assessment has limits, specifically a tendency to subjectivity and subsequent distortion, it can be a useful form of evaluation. An example of a form for the self-assessment is provided in figure 10.1.

Another effective means of assessing the usefulness of the religious education mentor's performance is to have the mentee rate him or her on the five roles (befriending, sponsoring, counseling, teaching, encouraging). Once combined, these different evaluation measures provide useful data from which to plan a series of recommendations for future religious education mentoring programs. An example is the extensive evaluation of an East Harlem mentoring program in which

---

41. A sample of an inventory that measures self-reliance is James Campbell Quick, Debra L. Nelson, and Jonathon D. Quick, "Self-Reliance Inventory," in *The 1991 Annual: Developing Human Resources* (San Diego, Calif.: Pfeiffer, 1991), pp. 141–61.

Figure 10. 1
Example of Self-assessment Form for Use by the Mentor

Usefulness of My Performance as a Mentor
(*Please use an extra sheet for writing responses.*)

How useful have your religious education mentor roles been for the mentee?

Befriender

Approximately how often have you provided nonscheduled time to listen to your mentee?

How often have you made an effort to include the mentee in professional and social groups?

In one or two sentences describe an incident in which your friendship has been useful for the performance of the mentee.

Counselor

Have you listened to the mentee when he or she discusses problems?

Have you left your door open and is your presence welcoming for the mentee?

In one or two sentences describe an incident in which you offered advice judiciously and avoided overwhelming the mentee.

Teacher

Have you offered feedback to the mentee on his or her instructional ability?

Have you waited until the mentee was receptive to the educational advice?

In one or two sentences describe incidents in which you modeled effective facilitation skills for the mentee.

Sponsor

Have you spoken positive, true words about the mentee to your colleagues?

In one or two sentences describe an incident in which you affirmed what was positive in your mentee's work.

Encourager

Describe an incident wherein you helped the mentee through a crisis.

What types of encouragement have you provided the mentee when she needed it?

In one or two sentences describe an incident when you acted as a spiritual guide to the mentee.

mentee participants were asked to give their perceptions of the mentoring process and to rate the importance of various aspects of the mentoring relationship, such as the opportunity to experiment with different curriculum design ideas or practice different instructional styles.[42] The data from the mentee rating scales was analyzed with the data from similar scales completed by mentors and by administrators to give a complete evaluation of the mentoring program.

Evaluating individual progress in the religious education mentoring program is a challenging endeavor because it tests the limits of evaluator objectivity and accuracy. However, a well thought out evaluation can add a great deal to understanding how the religious education mentor and mentee grow professionally as a consequence of participation in the mentoring program.

SUMMARY

Effective evaluation is necessary for the development of a strong religious education mentoring program because it can yield helpful data for the local mentoring committee as it plans and implements the mentoring initiative. Evaluation data can also provide information for future planners of similar programs. This chapter addressed approaches for evaluating the religious education mentoring program, evaluation of professional preparation, and evaluation of individual participation progress. Though there are no precise means of carrying out a mentoring evaluation and evaluation itself is perplexing for program planners, the results it yields are important for present and future mentoring initiatives.

---

42. See Christina A. Taharally, Mae Gamble, and Susan Marsa, "Collaborative Relationships in a Mentoring Program in East Harlem Schools," in *Teacher Induction and Mentoring: School-Based Collaborative* Programs, ed. Gary DeBolt (Albany, N.Y.: State University of New York Press, 1992), especially pp. 127–36.

Index of Names

Index of Subjects

221